SAVING

AMERICAN CAPITALISM

SAVING

American Capitalism

A LIBERAL ECONOMIC PROGRAM

Edited with Introductions by

SEYMOUR E. HARRIS

Professor of Economics, Harvard University

568286

ALFRED · A · KNOPF · NEW YORK

1948

THIS IS A BORZOI BOOK,
PUBLISHED BY ALFRED A. KNOPF, INC.

FIRST EDITION

The Editor dedicates this volume

to

CHESTER BOWLES

Economic Statesman

Contributors

Charles Abrams, author of *The Future of Housing*

Wendell Berge, formerly Assistant Attorney General of the United States

A. A. Berle, Jr., Professor of Law, Columbia University; formerly Assistant Secretary of State

Chester Bowles, formerly Director, Office of Price Administration

Lester V. Chandler, Professor of Economics, Amherst College

Morris Llewellyn Cooke, formerly Chairman, Mississippi Valley Committee; Administrator, Rural Electrification Administration

John T. Dunlop, Associate Professor of Economics, Harvard University

Merle Fainsod, Chairman, Department of Political Science, Harvard University

Morris E. Garnsey, Professor of Economics, University of Colorado

RICHARD V. GILBERT, formerly Economic Advisor to Price Administrator, Office of Price Administration

GUY GREER, formerly of the Editorial Staff of *Fortune*

ALVIN H. HANSEN, Littauer Professor of Political Economy, Harvard University

SEYMOUR E. HARRIS, Professor of Economics, Harvard University

HOWARD MUMFORD JONES, Professor of English, Harvard University

LEON H. KEYSERLING, Vice-Chairman, President's Council of Economic Advisors

ABBA P. LERNER, Professor of Economics, Roosevelt College of Chicago

CHARLES E. MERRIAM, Distinguished Professor of Political Science, Emeritus, University of Chicago; formerly Member, National Resource Planning Board

CARLTON L. NAU, Executive Director, American Public Power Association; Editor, *Public Power Magazine*

JAMES R. NEWMAN, Editorial Staff, *New Republic*

ARTHUR M. SCHLESINGER, JR., Associate Professor of History, Harvard University

GEORGE SOULE, formerly of the Editorial Staff of *New Republic*

LORIE TARSHIS, Associate Professor of Economics, Stanford University

O. H. TAYLOR, Lecturer in Economics, Harvard University

EDWIN E. WITTE, Professor of Economics, University of Wisconsin; formerly Executive Director, President's Committee on Social Security

Preface

A book by many authors profits from allocation of tasks to the expert in each field, but it may lose in lack of integration, in gaps, in repetitions, and in disagreements. The editor, his research assistant, and finally Knopf's editor, have each tried in turn to deal with the problem of integration and *excessive* repetition. We hope that we have succeeded. Gaps have been the special responsibility of the editor who started on the assumption that he would merely write a brief introduction and conclusion, but soon found that he had to contribute about one-fourth to one-third of the volume; and the explanation was not merely the difficulty of finding qualified contributors. Yawning gaps which were not at all evident in the blueprint stage appeared as the manuscript took shape.

Disagreement is not a significant problem in this volume. When there has been substantial disagreement, the editor was disposed not to attempt coercion or even persuasion. Perhaps the most striking instance is Mr. Berge's plea for vigorous action on the monopoly front, in contrast with the views of several others who would accept bigness and attempt to control it in the public interest. Where facts seemed to be at variance, we made an attempt to reconcile them.

Apparently without exception, the authors in this volume have in common a disposition to save capitalism, or at least a large part of our system of private enterprise. They know only too well that the disappearance of our present system may well jeopardize our freedoms. They also know

that the way to save capitalism is not by refusing to compromise or by insisting upon the nineteenth-century variety.
Only by accepting a hybrid system which gives scope to adequate planning, to monetary and fiscal policy, to conservation
of resources, to public spending for the general welfare, and
to limited controls will we be able to preserve capitalism. The
difficulties increase as, with spreading economic chaos, the
rest of the world abandons private enterprise.

I am indebted to Mrs. Anna Thorpe for typing
much of the manuscript, to Miss Lillian Buller, my efficient
secretary and general assistant, to Mrs. Margarita Willfort
for research help, to Miss Winifred Carroll for her important
aid in editing and styling, and most of all to my fellow contributors who took time out of busy lives to write the essays
and adhere remarkably well to the time schedule. I hope
their sacrifices will prove worth while. My wife, as usual, has
kindly read the proofs.

Seymour E. Harris

Cambridge, Massachusetts
September 9, 1948

Contents

PART III

RESOURCES AND THEIR DEVELOPMENT

PART IV

PLANNING AND CONTROLS

Charts and Tables

TABLES

PART ONE

Introduction

CHAPTER I

The Issues

by Seymour E. Harris

The Task This country needs an economic plan, or at the very least an economic program for action. The President's Economic Council, hampered to some extent by limitations imposed by the Employment Act of 1946 and even more by an unfortunate political schism, has nevertheless done good work in assessing the current situation, in measuring the net effect of economic policies—frequently not integrated, and in suggesting what needs to be done to protect the country against distortions of the economy which bring instability and wasted resources. Even these achievements of the Council have been limited by the political milieu.

Our task is different. Ours is the responsibility to be bold; for we are not hamstrung by political pressures, or—with one exception—hampered by holding public office. Our assignment is to suggest a program, audacious but practical, not now acceptable to those in control and yet sound enough to appeal to the average citizen—in short, a design for our economy which can ultimately win the support necessary for it to become public policy.

Here is the explanation of the origin of this book. Many of us in the past three years have detected some backsliding from the Roosevelt economic program; liberalism is apparently in a Rip Van Winkle phase. Last year seemed to be an opportune time to ask a number of people who had been important officials and advisers in the Roosevelt Administration, and as many academicians in general agreement with them (most of

3

whom had also at one time or another been practitioners themselves), to express their views on what should be done.

Saving Capitalism   Like the National Association of Manufacturers and the United States Chamber of Commerce, we too are anxious to save capitalism. But unlike representatives of these groups, we believe that nineteenth-century capitalism, however well it served us in its time, will not do for another hundred or even the next twenty-five years. We have learned from experience since 1929 that the businessman, the human magneto of the capitalist system, cannot unaided keep the system steady—free from periods of exuberance and depression. We have learned that it is not his task to underwrite demand for the benefit of all of us and to his own detriment: we have only to recall President Hoover's policy in the early thirties of urging, with some success, this suicidal approach upon socially-minded businessmen. Unless we perform surgery on our economic system, it will not survive. Our prejudices are in favor of capitalism, but we believe that it must prove itself to be the most efficient economic system. That a system of free private enterprise also enhances the probability of the survival of individual freedom and of civil liberties is a strong reason for supporting capitalism.

The difficulties confronting capitalism seemed insuperable in the thirties; if possible, they seem even greater now: survival of a patched-up capitalist system against the encroachments of socialism is not by any means assured. Our phenomenal economic success in the forties is a tribute to the resiliency of the system; but even more it suggests the vital part played by government guarantees of markets and demand, and by government planning. Private enterprise should not be smug, for a good part of the credit goes to government and war demands. It is still up to us to prove that capitalism is not but a passing phase in the historical process from feudalism to socialism.

Progress and Disease   We start with economic history, a task entrusted to Bowles, Berle, Schlesinger, Keyserling, and the editor. The sweep of history shows us that our system of private enterprise has served us well. In 150 years the income of the country has grown from half a billion to more than

200 billion dollars, an increase of four hundred times or more. In the same period, population rose by 26 times and the supply of money by 1,150 times. It is a striking fact that this country now supports 27 times as many people at a standard of living [1] 10 or more times as high as in 1820. It is not difficult to understand why apologists for capitalism are impressed by its attainments, and in their satisfaction occasionally seem smug to advocates of other systems.

Closer examination reveals, however, that the rise in our standard of living has not been steady, that periods of exuberance and inflation have been followed by periods of depression and deflation, and that the most serious breakdown of all occurred in the thirties. Social diagnosticians have discovered other dangerous symptoms: the cancerous growth of large business units which consume the small unit cells; monopoly tendencies in labor and agriculture as well as in business; evidence of hardening of the arteries in the economy as a whole, revealed, for example, in an increased disposition to cut coupons and a reluctance to assume risks; growing dependence upon government in a world of intense nationalism and total war; gross inequities in distribution mirrored in part through vast amounts of unemployment. Many people therefore question the effectiveness of the present capitalist system and seek at the very least to reform it, or at the most to change or destroy it by revolution. Many more people face the future with misgivings and pessimism.

The New Deal and Beyond   Essentially the New Deal was an attempt to remove the excrescences from the present system and perform other bits of surgery, but within the framework of the capitalist or free-enterprise system. The liberalism of the nineteenth century had long been dead; free competition and nonintervention by government on behalf of special interests, the foundation stones of the old liberalism, were to be found in college textbooks, not in the real world. In the thirties, this government began to recognize a liberalism more consonant with the needs of the time, a liberalism which tolerated intervention by government to protect the many

[1] By "standard of living" we mean the flow of goods and services on a *per capita* basis.

against the few, and which was prepared to support public programs to assure stability and adequate living standards.[2] Later essays will deal more fully with the concept and evolution of liberalism. Here it suffices to emphasize that it no longer connotes a system of society with minimum restraints of government and complete freedom of the individual.

But however important the advances under the New Deal, few would insist that the Roosevelt Administration had the magic formula for providing stability, rising standards of living, and finally, the maximum approach to the egalitarian principle consistent with reasonable attainment of high standards. The use of incentives to attain maximum production will interfere with the movement toward equal income. There is a point beyond which even a socialist government will not advance on the path of equality, for the cost in output will prove excessive. Improvisation was the essence of the New Deal: never had an administration been bequeathed so many vexing problems with so modest a heritage of knowledge and tools to cope with them.

Moreover, Roosevelt and his co-workers in the New Deal epoch had to treat a depression economy. The psychology and techniques which were developed in the thirties will not prove effective in the world of the next generation where, in view of the changing institutional framework (for example, strong organization of workers and farmers), inflationary pressures are likely to be of increased importance. In war, the government learned much about an inflation economy; but we would be wrong to assume that the peacetime pressures on prices will be similar to those of the forties, or that the weapons forged under the banners of a patriotic war will suffice or be acceptable in peace. What this country needs are policies to deal with both excess and deficient demand, a willingness to experiment with new techniques, and a well-integrated policy which can quickly be adapted to the requirements of a protean economy.

Part II is largely devoted to the historical questions adumbrated here. The New Deal, as Schlesinger notes, went through two phases: first it sought economic recovery through

[2] Cf. below, Berle and Taylor.

co-operation with big business; then it sought to reform capitalism by fighting monopoly and by using public funds, including deficit spending, to offset fluctuations in the private sector of the economy. Like the others, Keyserling, a prominent official in government today, acknowledges the gains under Roosevelt, and like the others, he agrees it is time to solidify past gains and move on.

From this historical sketch we proceed to a preliminary cataloguing by Keyserling of important issues of policy and of suggestions for solutions. This is a preliminary treatment for the impatient reader and should be considered the broad sketching of a program, the colors and details of which are to be added later. Keyserling not only reveals weaknesses in the New Deal attack but suggests the contributions to be made in the future by government, labor, and private enterprise.

Importance of Conservation Economic conditions depend first and foremost upon the resources available. Irrespective of the intelligence and courage of the population, a country without rich resources is not likely to support a large *and* prosperous people. Great Britain, with a population per square mile 25 times that of the U.S.S.R. and 10 times that of our country, and with much barren soil, has advanced about as far as might be expected of a country limited in resources but favored by an unusually intelligent population and a head start in industry. India, with three to four hundred million people, a very large population in relation to resources, and a per capita income of about thirty dollars, suggests the importance of resources and the limited effects of the best possible policies (had they been applied). The spectre of Malthus stalks the country.

In Parts III and IV, we treat the problems of resources and the related problems of planning and controls. It is necessary to conserve and develop resources, and especially to develop regions. The potentialities of regional development have scarcely been tapped. In the New Deal period a beginning was made in conservation and development; and the country learned that by putting unemployed men and money to work, the nation's income and wealth would multiply. Now these techniques are known, and planners, architects, and engineers have explored the possibilities of applying them to a wide range of projects—for example, housing, urban redevelopment, hydroelectric power, and regional reclamation. No longer will the country tolerate extensive unemployment while resources ripe for development go to waste simply because fanatical budget-balancers have their way in Congress. The combination of unemployed money and unemployed men to reclaim many regions like the Tennessee Valley is, we hope, assured.

The development of natural resources raises questions concerning the allocation of economic resources, the timing of various programs, the choice between present and future consumption, the extent to which decisions about allocation will continue to be made by the consumer who, within limits, guides production by the preferences he expresses in spending his money. Planned combination of labor, raw materials, and capital may yield a pattern different from that expected in an unplanned economy. Divergence is most likely in the time pattern of consumption and in the distribution of consumption goods; for, under planning, resources may be diverted to producers' goods or to consumers' goods, to luxury products or to mass-produced items. But however they are used, development of resources offers an outlet for surplus labor and money, a needed outlet in advancing societies with large savings seeking investment. Wise planning in the development of resources may even work itself out of a job. It may provide the plenty that will make it possible to dispense with planning our economic life. It is scarcity that makes planning necessary. We should never forget that planning, particularly undemocratic planning, is the aftermath of crisis and destitution.

In short, the country wants to make the most of its resources, and to achieve this, resource development must be a continuous activity; but there is a special claim on the nation's dollars for this purpose in periods of unemployment. In periods of unemployment or full employment, the government will have to take a large responsibility for the most effective utilization of its rivers, its lands, and its mines. Under conditions of full employment, government projects can be reduced to the necessary minimum; in times of unemployment they can be expanded, according to a long-range plan, to take advantage of available labor. In both periods, the problem of optimum use of resources is germane. Resource development, therefore, not only offers a road to more goods but also is indispensable as part of a program to keep demand at an adequate level.

Importance of Government   In the modern economy, private enterprise may make most of the decisions and policies; but there is a residue which must fall to government. In the responsibility for total spending, for the effective use of resources that belong to the nation, for stability, for assuring production when private agreements bog down, government takes a hand. The more successful private enterprise is in attaining and maintaining high levels of employment and fair distribution, the less responsibility government has to assume. But even under the most favorable conditions, government has to be responsible for some planning, for spending, and, under special conditions, for controls.

Under the liberal economic system, a million or two producers determine what is to be produced, guided to some extent by the expressions of demand by 140 million consumers. Actually in gauging demand, and, as a result of the long production period, in forecasting demand, producers make substantial errors. Operating independently or in collusion among themselves and subject to all kinds of errors resulting from optimism and pessimism and from inadequate knowledge, producers and sellers alternately offer too much and too little in general, and overestimate and then underestimate the needs in particular markets. The miracle is not that errors are made but that supply and demand are equated at all without continuous serious disturbances. Each businessman, presumably operating independently, has to guess not only what consumers want today and what they will want a year or two from today, but also what other producers will contribute to meet this need and, therefore, what he is to make available. Whatever the present intentions of consumers, their actual purchases at the end of the production period will deviate from the amounts suggested by rational considerations at the beginning of the production period. These deviations will in part be responses to the errors made by the businessman, for consumption depends on employment and income.

All of this suggests the need of some planning, of at least making available the facts concerning intended consumption and output. But it suggests even more: if government stands ready to subsidize demand when demand proves inadequate to move the goods off the market at profitable prices, and to take away the purchasing power when demand is excessive, the peaks and troughs can be flattened out. Obviously, with operations based on knowledge and some planning, the excesses and deficiencies will be whittled down. But as long as they are not quickly counteracted there is danger that partial planning will prove inadequate and will be supplanted by complete planning and regimentation. It is therefore necessary for the government to be prepared to introduce measures which will influence private spending and also public spending in a manner to offset the excesses and deficiencies of demand which inevitably occur even in an economy subject to some central planning. Hence the importance of the policies discussed in Part V and, to some extent, in Parts VI and VII. The most important task of monetary, fiscal, and cycle policy and, in large part, of international, wage, and social-security policy is to assure stability of demand. This is the keynote of economic policy today.

Demand, Productivity, and Distribution   That does not mean that we should not be concerned with productivity and distribution. Resource development and planning and controls are in part concerned with both these problems. One objective of agricultural policy is to raise output per man-hour; of trade policy to raise output by increasing the amount of trade and thus achieving a more efficient distribution of output; of social security to enhance productivity through relieving men and women of a feeling of insecurity, and through raising educational standards; of labor policy by relating contribution and reward; of science policy (Part VIII) by improving scientific standards.

Similarly one of the objectives of modern economic policy is an improved distribution of income. Surely our tax, trade, agricultural, labor, social security, and resource policies are concerned with the problem of distribution. Survival of our system of government and enterprise requires a more effective application of the egalitarian principle than we have so far achieved; and yet a delicate line must be drawn at the point where further moves in the direction of equality and security will seriously jeopardize progress and standards of living. We still are moving in the direction of security: just as the nineteenth was the century of progress, so the twentieth is the century of security. The masses want freedom from want and from fear even if the pace of progress must be slowed down.

The Central Theme Despite the importance of productivity and improved distribution, the core of modern economic policy is stabilization of demand. In part the explanation of this emphasis is the remarkable gain in productivity over the last 150 years, reflected in higher standards all along the line; achievement, in itself, causes a loss of interest in further effort in the same direction. The explanation also lies in the breakdown of our system, especially the spectacular collapse of the thirties with its large and long spells of unemployment; and failure quickened interest in stabilization. In addition, the influence of Lord Keynes with his concentration on demand as the barometer and target of economic policy, and of the New Deal and war economies, showed what stimulation of demand can do.

If this book has any central theme, it is that adequacy, not saturation, of demand is the goal of economic policy; and it is not a goal that can be reached without government aid. Adequacy of demand will, moreover, assure high levels of productivity, for it yields capacity output at low unit costs, and it can provide surplus funds to further the advancement of science. Moreover, high levels of employment, the accompaniment of adequate demand, will solve many of the problems of insecurity; for it is well to recall the results of Lord Beveridge's study—80 per cent of the incidence of economic insecurity is accounted for by interruptions to work.

Because we realize the importance of demand, we devote much space to monetary and especially fiscal policy. By the proper use of monetary policy, we make money the servant of industry, adjusting supplies to the needs of the economy.

Monetary policy alone, however, will not get us far. The lesson of the Keynesian revolution, widely accepted now even in nonprofessional circles, is that it is necessary to influence demand directly through increased public expenditures and reduced public revenues in depressions, and reduced public expenditures and increased revenues in prosperity. In this manner, government laces its policies with those of the private economy.

In the next chapter, Chester Bowles presents the keynote essay. Its coverage is wide, for he looks back as well as forward; and he is both critical and constructive. In his essay, the reader will find pride in past accomplishments, faith in the essentials of our system, candid admission of its flaws, and the courage to support experimentation and unorthodox measures to assure the continuance of our system.

CHAPTER II

Blueprints for a Second New Deal

by Chester Bowles

World War II has left a legacy of destruction almost beyond human comprehension. It has destroyed cities, factories, dams, power plants, and railroads. Worse still, it has sapped the vitality, hopes, and capacities of hundreds of millions of human beings upon whom world recovery must depend.

Against this background of world devastation, America appears as an economic dream world—physically untouched by war, her resources undamaged, her people largely prosperous and united. We own 70 per cent of the world's automobiles and trucks, 50 per cent of the world's telephones. We listen to 45 per cent of the world's radios. We operate 35 per cent of the world's railroads. We consume 59 per cent of the world's petroleum, and 50 per cent of its rubber.

Our great natural resources, our abundant skills, our cars and telephones and railroads, our radios, movie houses, public libraries and public schools, our hundreds of thousands of miles of good highways, all add up to the highest standard of living in the world, infinitely beyond that of any other major country.

And yet, today throughout America there is a growing uneasiness about our economic future. As we look abroad at the chaos of Europe and Asia, we wonder if we can continue to prosper on an island of plenty in the midst of a world of want.

We are proud that our private-enterprise system has demonstrated itself over a period of many years to be the most dynamic and most productive that the world has ever known, but we also know that this demonstration has been intermittent. We know that for every period of boom, our system has suffered a period of depression, and that as our economic system has grown more complicated the severity of these depressions has sharply increased.

In the 1800's, our economic difficulties were, for the most part, crises of our banking and monetary system. While they caused grave hardship among special groups, most of our people living in small towns and on farms came through relatively unscathed. But gradually the centers of population shifted to the larger cities and towns. Even country families produced less and made less for their own use. As individuals, we became more dependent on the ebb and flow of trade in the market places.

When our more complicated modern economy got out of balance, investment dried up on a vast scale, millions of families postponed all but their essential purchases, and production and employment levels dropped sharply in every part of the country. The great depression, following the collapse of 1929, taught us that any new economic collapse must be felt in every home in the land, that there will be few indeed among our workers, farmers, and businessmen who will remain unaffected.

A serious economic upset has followed every major war. World War II, because of its magnitude and intensity, engendered inflationary pressures far greater than any we had known in the past. And yet, from 1942 until June 1946, through price, production, and credit controls, rationing, increased taxation and savings, we managed to keep inflation in check and our price level remarkably stable.

For once, it began to look as though inflationary history would not repeat itself. But in June 1946, several business groups, such as the National Association of Manufacturers, convinced a wobbly Congress that "If price controls are discontinued, production will step up fast . . . prices will soon drop to reasonable levels." As a result, controls were eliminated prematurely, and by July 1948 wholesale prices had risen 53 per cent above the levels of June 1946.

Most of us know that such excesses must eventually be paid

for. As we see our economy distorted by inflation, we remember the dismal period from 1929 to 1933 when collapse followed the shaky good times of the 1920's. Our farmers know that corn once sold for 12 cents a bushel, cotton for 4½ cents a pound, wheat for 32 cents a bushel, and cattle for $3.28 a hundredweight. Our workers have not forgotten the days when fifteen million of them tramped the streets hopelessly looking for jobs. Our businessmen remember that in a single year thirty thousand firms went bankrupt, while 75 per cent of all American corporations operated in the red with a net total loss of 6 billion dollars.

Our uneasiness over the future of private enterprise in America has been increased by the gradual weakening of capitalism in many countries overseas before the war and at an increasing tempo in the postwar period. In the 1930's, we watched Hitler and Mussolini grow to power on the wreckage of capitalistic systems which had failed to protect the people against the increasingly violent swings of the business cycle.

In the United Kingdom and France and other democratic European countries, we saw during this same period the gradual decay of the capitalistic framework. Capitalists in the United Kingdom and France were clearly losing their old willingness to take risks, their traditional drive to increase sales and profits through improved products and lower prices. Increasingly, they were turning to economic bomb shelters in the shape of cartels and monopolies, designed to control production and prices and protect them from the rigors of the free market. As a result, we saw industrial production in these countries level out and labor productivity diminish for lack of plant modernization. These were not the only reasons, of course. Rigidities of other kinds were also harmful.

The decay of free capitalism in Europe during this critical period cannot properly be charged to the interference of unfriendly governments. The deterioration of risk-taking and enterprise took place, for the most part, under conservative governments. For sixteen of the nineteen years between 1919 and 1939, the United Kingdom was governed by the Conservative party.

In our own country before the war, we saw signs of the same

ominous influences which had seriously weakened capitalism in France, England, and other countries across the seas. Monopoly was growing. Many business groups, with little understanding of the workings of our economy—and even less understanding of the political temper of our people—were stubbornly resistant to even modest reforms. In our more exclusive clubs, it was freely stated that if our society was to remain "free," we must become accustomed to the presence of from five to eight million permanently unemployed.

The Stimulus of War   When war broke out in 1941, our economic development had been seriously hampered by this philosophy of economic despair. In January 1942, when President Roosevelt called for the annual production of 50,-000 planes, many of the "practical" men were certain that he was asking the impossible. When he called for 5,000,000 tons of shipping, they said that only an economic novice could make such a demand, even though its purpose was a worthy one—namely, to fool the Nazis and the Japanese.

But the timid thinkers of prewar America were soon proven wrong. As the months wore on, our country hummed again with all the full power of its huge industrial capacity. We met the President's goal of 50,000 planes and went on to double it. We quadrupled his estimate of 5,000,000 tons of shipping annually. Our farmers, with 10 per cent fewer workers, produced 30 per cent more farm products. In 1942, 1943, and 1944, the records show that we produced more *civilian* goods than in any period of our history. And, on top of that, at the peak of the war effort, we achieved an annual production rate of 100 billion dollars worth of military equipment and services.

Our wartime production record re-established our faith in what our industrial machine could provide for our people. As he saw our war factories working day and night, the man in the street visualized the torrent of consumer goods which these factories could produce for all of us in peace time.

Gradually, the conviction developed that depressions in the future must not be accepted as inevitable; that we must put outworn economic theories behind us; that somehow, and without loss of our individual freedom, we must keep our factories and our farms fully at work turning out the goods

and services which our people—and indeed the whole world—
so badly needed.

The Choice before Us The conviction that we cannot
again accept a major depression is not a mere theory. It is a
fact which will have a profound effect on our economic future.
I have been face to face with it in every section of America.
Today, our people are determined that we must not and cannot accept the economic waste and heartbreak that go hand
in hand with depression; and with this new conviction, for
better or for worse, goes the knowledge that if our private-
enterprise system fails, other alternatives are possible.

Today, throughout the world, there are four more or less
clearly defined economic systems. One is Fascism. In the
Fascist state, corporate ownership has been left largely intact
under rigid government direction, labor has been regimented,
and hours, wages, prices, and profits closely controlled. Workers in Germany and Italy before the war were induced to accept this system through the promise of greater job security,
welfare benefits, and full employment. It exists today in
Spain, Portugal, Turkey, and other countries.

A second approach is that of Communism. Here private
ownership is eliminated and the state owns as well as directs all
production facilities as part of a national economic plan. It
differs from Fascism in that the industrialists and the landowners are wholly removed from positions of power.

The economic and social planning of the Communist state
offers industrially backward countries the promise of increasing living standards and greater economic security. But Communism insists on the complete responsibility of the individual
to the state, regardless of his personal beliefs and preferences.
It imposes its will through a small group who are responsible,
not to the people but to the party.

Both Communism and Fascism are characterized by the
ruthless regimentation of the lives and activities of all private
citizens. Political democracy ceases to exist. The leaders of
the government, in order to protect their authority inevitably
resort to secret police, concentration camps, and increasing
brutality.

But if we are to maintain the strength of our own system we

must not underestimate the appeal of totalitarianism to people who have known nothing but hunger, squalor, and insecurity. To them the sacrifice of a political freedom which in their countries has often been corrupt or non-existent, is a small price to pay for bread and the tangible promise of economic security.

The third and fourth economic systems—private capitalism and democratic socialism—are both vigorously anti-totalitarian. Neither system exists anywhere in a pure form. We find private capitalism in its purest state in the United States and Canada. In the Scandinavian countries, in England, France, Holland, Belgium, New Zealand, and Australia, private ownership has been sharply modified by government ownership of some basic industries, the development of strong co-operatives, and an increased dose of central planning. In all of these countries, while they are dominantly capitalistic or socialistic, political democracy and individual freedom are strongly rooted.

Among peoples who have experienced the advantages of democratic government, faith in freedom of choice and opinion are strong bulwarks against the forces of totalitarianism. People who have lived under democratic governments for any length of time are not easily pushed around. They value deeply the rights of the individual to work where he pleases, to think as he pleases, and, within reasonable limits, to act as he pleases.

Czechoslovakia is the only country with a long record of democratic government that has accepted a dictatorship of either the Right or the Left, and this was under duress. In the countries where dictatorships have flourished—in parts of South America, in Russia, in Germany, Italy, and Spain— democracy had had little or no time to grow its roots.

Although the great majority of our people are vigorously opposed to the tyranny of either Right or Left, we in America cannot afford to be complacent. If we attempt the impossible economic and political feat of standing still, we may find ourselves pushed unwittingly towards one of the two extremes which violate all our traditional principles of free democratic government. If this occurs, the chances are overwhelming that we will move to the Right.

During the last year, the campaign against the Communist party in America has taken on hysterical proportions. This campaign and the witch hunts which accompany it are diverting progressive-minded Americans from the real threat to our democratic future.

Communism, although an evil thing, has a positive appeal to desperate, underprivileged people. It cannot be met successfully by negation and name calling. The most effective means of opposing Communism is a bold, dynamic program of economic, social, and political reform. If we proceed vigorously to rebuild our cities, to improve the health of all of our people, to provide modern education for all of our children, to eliminate depressions, to increase security, opportunity, and freedom for all people in all parts of our country, the Communist party in America will remain an ineffective minority.

The most dangerous long range threat to our democratic institutions in America comes not from the inept Communists to the Left but from the reactionaries at the extreme Right. Our relationships with Soviet Russia are strained, and likely to be strained for some time to come. The average American citizen is rightly fearful and distrustful of the "Communist menace." If the present inflation ends in an economic blow-up, with widespread unemployment and disillusionment, some groups which are bent on blocking economic evolution will surely use the tense international situation and our fears of Communism to divert our people from our basic economic problems.

Our unemployed could be put back to work through armament programs as readily as in building new TVA's and in eliminating our slums. The danger of war, either real or simulated, could be used as a means to bring divergent groups together and to quiet the clamor of the masses of our people for economic and social reform.

A political development of this kind in America is by no means impossible in the "right economic climate," that is, a period of prolonged depression. There are powerful influences in our country which are quite capable of directing it. A "solution" of this kind to an economic depression would make inevitable a world conflict of catastrophic proportions.

The millions who value human freedom cannot accept the dismal choice which the totalitarians of the Left and the Right seek to impose upon us. We must insist that our economic problems shall be solved constructively, peacefully, and above all under democratic institutions which respect individual rights.

Our task will not be an easy one. If we are to achieve a future in line with our American tradition, we must develop a clear understanding of how our economy works and why on occasion it has failed us in the past. We must reject the economic and political influences of the Hayeks, Hazlitts, and Robeys, who seem to argue that the best means to improve the economic welfare of the many is to increase still further the economic power of the few.

The Problem of Spending and Demand   The basic economic principle on which a full-employment, full-production economy must be built, can be stated simply. *For every dollar's worth of production of goods or services, there is created one dollar of potential purchasing power.* If we produce 200 billion dollars worth of houses, vacuum cleaners, canned goods, industrial machinery, farm equipment, wheat, cotton, public schools, permanent waves, plumbing repairs, or highways, we create 200 billion dollars worth of purchasing power in the hands of all of us.

If the level of production is to be maintained and increased, all of this money must be spent currently by individuals, groups, and institutions. Otherwise, our economy will slip into a depression. If, for instance, 10 billion dollars of the 200 billion dollars in purchasing power created by 200 billion dollars in production remains unspent, then 10 billion dollars worth of goods and services will remain unpurchased and our production will be decreased by a similar amount.

This, in turn, will lead to the cancelling of orders for new equipment and new plants, to increasing lay-offs and unemployment. Purchasing power will shrink and we will begin to go downhill towards a depression, with each reduction of employment and each drop in purchasing power feeding on itself.

There are three groups in our economy which together are in a position to spend all the money represented by our total purchasing power. One of these groups is business. Each year, this group spends a varying amount of money on industrial expansion, inventories, new equipment, and on buildings.

The second of our three groups of spenders is government—federal, state, and local. Each year, and in varying amounts, our governmental institutions spend money on schools, hospitals, roads, bridges, irrigation projects, police and fire departments, and on military and naval establishments.

The third of our three groups of spenders is the American people themselves. Each year, and again in varying amounts, we as consumers spend our wages, salaries, and dividends for food, clothing, travel, movies, washing machines, haircuts, vacuum cleaners, books, and houses.

Although each of these three groups will change its pattern of expenditures from year to year, the total spent by all three must add up to the total income earned by everyone in the production of goods and services. The problem, therefore, becomes clear. In some way, a balance must be maintained between these three groups so that there will be a market for all the goods and services which we produce; so that production and employment can be maintained at a high level, a level which increases as our productive power increases.

Role of Government   The government's role in maintaining our total purchasing power is of vital importance, because of the impact of our present governmental budgets on our economy as a whole. It is doubly important because the percentage of our total purchasing power which is supported by government expenditures can be varied within reasonable limits each year in line with our total needs.

As we examine what government must and can accomplish, we are faced with many deep-seated inhibitions and prejudices. Americans over forty years of age came to manhood in an age when government's primary responsibilities were largely to keep down crime, to see to it that we had the nucleus of an army and navy, to keep up the roads, and to levy a minimum of taxes. We were told that any expansion of government represented an encroachment upon individual liberties to be resisted to one's utmost, and that even the necessary minimum of government was to be condoned rather than admired. The cartoons of our childhood presented public servants as fat politicians with chewed cigars, derby hats, and thousand-dollar bills labeled "graft" dropping from their pockets.

In this tradition, the leaders of the National Association of Manufacturers and their conservative forebearers have resisted each development of governmental responsibility. One hundred and twenty years ago, the question was whether or not our entire banking and currency system should be run exclusively by private individuals without responsibility to the people. Later came the questions of anti-monopoly laws, public education, the income tax, child-labor legislation, laws calling for minimum safety requirements in factories, pure food laws.

In the 1930's, it was social security, home owners' loans, the Securities and Exchange Commission, minimum wages, unemployment insurance, the Tennessee Valley Authority, slum clearance, school lunches. During the war, it was excess-profits taxes, price and rent controls. Today, it is public housing, slum clearance, medical insurance, increased social security, and public power developments.

Throughout our economic history, the people have been forced to fight their way forward step by step against narrow vested interests. Each new effort to insure greater economic security, opportunity, and freedom for the average citizen has been resisted as bureaucratic, unsound, socialistic, communistic, or just plain foolish.

To the man in the street, this shop-worn view has been harder and harder to take. With the development of the country it has become increasingly clear that our government must grow up to larger responsibilities. As our economic and social system evolved and took on new complications, a revision of the older attitude toward government was inescapable. Without such a revision, how could we expect government, forced by implacable events into new responsibilities, to discharge them efficiently, adequately, and without destroying our liberties?

If we are unprepared to accept *enough* government, we will end up with *too much*. It may be paradoxical but it is true. If we are reluctant to grant our government enough power to meet its essential tasks, the unsolved tasks will overtake us, and in the ensuing crisis we will be obliged to go far beyond what would have been necessary in government control had we taken adequate steps sooner.

The government, as I see it, has five fundamental roles. Its first responsibility is a traditional one—the maintenance of an adequate army and navy, the collection of taxes, the building of roads, schools, hospitals, the maintenance of an efficient post-office system, and other fundamental government services. On this, there can be but little disagreement.

The second role of government is to act as an umpire between the four major groups which make up our economy—business, labor, the farmer, and all of us as consumers. In the early days of our economic history, this role was relatively unimportant. But the growth of Big Business led to Big Farming and Big Labor. This, in turn, has led us towards Big Government, government strong enough to protect the interests and rights of 140 million citizens, who otherwise would be at the mercy of the highly organized groups representing business, labor, and the farmer.

One of the major responsibilities of government in this field is the curbing of monopoly. In the last twenty-five years, the march of American business towards monopoly has been rapid. Giant corporations have gained control of large segments of our economic life. Opportunities for the little fellow have gradually diminished as tens of thousands of G.I.'s anxious to go into business for themselves are beginning to realize.

In many industries, this tendency towards bigness has led to increased efficiency. But in most areas it has driven us further and further from the capitalistic ideal of a free market and free competitive enterprise. There are three million businesses today in America. And yet, 455 corporations, totaling one-eighth of 1 per cent of all corporations, now control 51 per cent of American business assets.

We have already witnessed the destructive effect of monopoly on the prewar capitalism of Britain, France, and other countries. In this testimony to the development of monopoly in America, we see the same cancerous growth at work in our own economy.

If the decline of competition proceeds during the next few years at its present rate, and if the economic (and, therefore, political) power of the United States continues to be concentrated in fewer hands, then we shall find ourselves face to face to an increasing degree with monopoly fixed prices, directed markups, inferior products, wholesale destruction of small business, and eventually a regimented economy.

We cannot fight monopoly with outworn slogans and concepts. We need, first of all, a clearer concept of what monopoly is and how it works. This concept should be based on the realities of our modern economy and the economic need for mass-production techniques, and not on an emotional prejudice against "bigness" as such.

We should then start by tightening our present anti-monopoly legislation and providing funds for its vigorous enforcement. In industries where the law is skirted rather than broken, government studies of economic malpractices, well publicized where necessary, may serve to develop an increased degree of competition. If, as many respected economists suspect, this effort should prove at least a partial failure, a more direct approach will become necessary.

Government could, for instance, establish production goals for basic industries where production restraints are holding down output. These goals would be based on the needs of our economy operating on a basis of full production and full employment. If these goals cannot be met by existing privately owned industries within a reasonable period, government would fill in the production gap by establishing its own plants. If, at any time, private owners wished to take over these government-built plants, they could do so by paying the current replacement cost.

Such direct action would be a long step short of government ownership. If a tightening of our anti-trust legislation fails to achieve its objective, the fact that government itself had the legal power to fill in the production gap might be sufficient in itself to increase production and bring down prices in monopolistic areas in our economy. By moderate means, if possible, but by more far-reaching methods if moderate means fail, we must free our economy of monopolistic road blocks.

As part of our campaign against monopoly, we should carefully re-examine our patent legislation. No individual or firm should be allowed to hold back a new product or an improvement in an old product through a patent monopoly. Today, many inventions remain on the shelf because their owners are unwilling to undertake the necessary capital investment to put them to good use. In the meantime, others are deprived of an opportunity to move ahead in the spirit of risk-taking and enterprise, which will always be the life-blood of our private enterprise system.

Restricted industrial production has its counterpart in the labor movement in featherbedding and other make-work practices. Both of these evils grow out of the concept that we dare not use all our resources, both industrial and human, because there is not enough work to go around.

A third responsibility of government is to provide those services which we cannot reasonably expect to be created by individuals operating on a profit and loss basis. We could not reasonably expect, for instance, that the Tennessee Valley Authority, calling for an investment of more than one billion dollars, could be created by private capital. Nor can we expect to control the waters of the Missouri, Arkansas, Columbia, St. Lawrence, and other major river waterways with private funds.

For the same reason, we cannot expect private investors to finance the elimination of our slums, the building of modern parks and hospitals and recreation areas. There are many services in this broad field to which the American people are entitled and which are not yet fully available to them. It is the responsibility of our modern democratic government to proceed aggressively to provide them.

Equality of Opportunity   The fourth responsibility of government under our private-enterprise system must be to assure reasonable equality of opportunity to every citizen, regardless of race, creed, or color. Throughout our history, we have pointed with pride to those among us who have risen from poverty to positions of responsibility in government, business, and the law.

And yet, any objective observer must admit that we are a long way removed from our ideal. The son or daughter of wealthy parents has opportunities in education, health, recreation, and general development which are denied to the children of the lower-income groups. In competition for top-paying jobs and positions of responsibility, the dice are loaded from birth against the sons of the sharecroppers, the garment workers, and the stevedores. The fact that some exceptional men and women, born in poverty, have risen to the top does not change the basic situation.

Our greatest single need, if we are successfully to meet the responsibilities of our modern world, is a higher standard of public education. Two million boys were rejected by the army and navy because they were illiterate. Even in the richest states, our school system is inadequate. In our poorest states, it is a national disgrace. Poorly educated boys and girls in Louisiana, Mississippi, and Alabama are a liability not only to the states in which they live, but also to our entire democracy.

It is the responsibility of the federal government to see that a high standard of education is available to every boy and girl in the United States, regardless of the income of their parents. This must include a selection of students for college according to ability, not economic status. What has been so clearly right for young men and women of the armed services through the Veterans' Bill of Rights is equally right for his younger brothers and sisters.

We must also establish a minimum standard of public health and this minimum should be a high one. The American Medical Association has been quick to label any such proposal "socialized medicine." This is a clear falsification of the program which has been proposed in such legislation as the Wagner-Murray-Dingell bill. The best available medical care should not be denied to any citizen simply because his income or his savings do not enable him to pay for it.

The medical data gathered by the Selective Service Boards gives us a drab picture of public health in America. It has been estimated that twelve times as much productive time is lost each year through illness as through labor-management disagreements which end in strikes. Much of this loss is avoidable. A comprehensive medical insurance program will call for the building of many thousands of hospitals and the training of tens of thousands of doctors, dentists, and nurses. But we are a rich nation, and our government, which belongs to all of us, cannot afford to shrink from this responsibility.

Closely coupled with the establishment of minimum basic standards of health is the need for a minimum standard of food consumption. As long as people are hungry or lack the proper balanced diets, it is shocking to talk about restricting agricultural production. The program proposed in November 1947 by the Department of Agriculture calls for an all-out farm production program and the guarantee that all the food which our farmers produce will be made available to the people who need it. The Aiken-LaFollette bill, which was proposed in the Seventy-Ninth Congress and which is a variation of the food stamp plan of the 1930's, provides a rational approach to this problem of a guaranteed minimum level of nutrition for every family in the country.

Our government must also act as the spearhead in the fight to provide decent housing for all of our people. It was estimated before the war that more than one-third of all American families were living in dwellings which were grossly inadequate. The number today is far greater. The monopoly-ridden housing industry, with its featherbedding and politically instigated building codes, has fallen down miserably on its public responsibilities.

We are capable of building 1,400,000 homes a year. If we build fewer than that, we will have failed in one of our basic obligations to our people. Nothing short of a flat government guarantee that these homes will be built is likely to achieve our objective. A half million of these homes built each year will need to be directly subsidized by the government. The majority of the people who are most desperately in need of homes can afford only from $20 to $55 a month rental. Even if prices come down somewhat, it is impossible for a builder to build a decent home at a profit for less than a $75 to $80 monthly rental. As long as this is so, the government should not shrink from its obligations to pay the difference. The cost will be modest indeed compared with the gains which we will make in improved health, happier children, and more closely integrated families.

Everything possible should be done to see that the remaining 900 million homes are built by private enterprise. Quotas should be established for all communities where housing is needed. Only where private enterprise has failed to meet these quotas should government itself step in. But if private builders fail to move ahead, it should be government's responsibility to buy the land, let the contracts, buy the materials, and see that the houses are built. Single-unit dwellings should be sold by the government to individual home owners; multiple dwellings to insurance companies or to co-operative owners. Only a direct approach of this kind is likely to stir the slumbering housing industry from its lethargy.

As part of its program to provide a high minimum standard of living for all of our people, the government should broaden the coverage of the social-security program and increase its benefits, many of which are sadly out of date, particularly in view of present high prices.

It is also essential that minimum wage rates be raised to a level no lower than 75 cents an hour. Even this minimum wage level will provide only a minimum standard of living to those who receive it. In a country as rich as ours, we certainly cannot ask people to accept less.

The fifth responsibility of our government is so to integrate our export and import program that the work of relief and rehabilitation throughout the world will be pushed steadily forward.

Ours is the only major nation in the world untouched by war. We are rich in natural resources, in human skills, and in productive capacity. The world in which we live keeps growing smaller.

There are some among us who still say that we have no responsibilities to the rest of the world, and that our efforts should be concentrated solely on increasing the wealth of our own people. It is essential to our own welfare and that of the world that this viewpoint should be rejected. We cannot successfully build a palace for Americans in the midst of a world of slums. Unless the standard of living is raised steadily for all peoples, there can be no peace or security for ourselves or for our children.

The investment of from 8 to 10 per cent of our productive wealth every year in rehabilitation overseas would have a profound effect on world living standards within the next generation. It would be the soundest peace insurance that we could buy in a world that is tense and desperate and disillusioned.

If we are to raise the world's productive power and with it the security of the world's people, we must first modernize world agriculture. This is a fundamental challenge for the next generation. We must also help to build modern transportation systems, power developments, and basic industrial plants. The opportunity for American management skills is unlimited.

The European Recovery Plan is an imaginative start. But this should not be the limit of our efforts. It should be the beginning of a long-range program which can lead the way toward greater understanding, security, and democracy in all parts of the world.

The Soviet Union and the Communist parties offer hungry people the hope for higher living standards and increased economic security. If we are successfully to meet this challenge it will not be sufficient simply to argue, however rightly, that Communism means the end of political democracy. We must promote on a world-wide scale not only political freedom but economic democracy as well.

Such an effort calls for boldness of concept, for confidence, and for economic skill. Clearly, its conception and planning must rank among the major responsibilities of our federal government.

Guaranteeing a Ready Market   The sixth and final responsibility of our government is to co-ordinate all of its policies in such a way that a market will be provided for all that we are capable of producing.

What I am urging is a flat government guarantee that the purchasing power will always be present to buy all the goods which our workers, farmers, and businessmen can produce each year. This is a basic responsibility of government if we are to maintain full production and full employment. Clearly, the more effective this government guarantee, and the more widely it is accepted, the less will be the positive action which the government will be called upon to take to make good its commitments. The more effective the guarantee, the greater will be the confidence in the economic outlook, and the more certainly will pent-up demand be translated into orders.

In so-called normal times, every businessman is forced to take two risks. The first is the normal risk of competition; the test of his ability to compete with other businessmen in his industry in producing quality goods at reasonable prices. This is a proper risk which every businessman who sincerely believes in our system of private enterprise must accept.

The second risk is the possibility that depression lurks just around the corner. A depression drives the efficient into bankruptcy along with the inefficient. The constant fear of depression leads businessmen to restrict their production, to curb their plans for expansion, to pile up huge reserves on which they may hope to survive during a period of hard times. This second risk, in view of all that we know today about the workings of a modern economy, is an unnecessary risk. It can and must be eliminated by intelligent, democratic action.

If government aggressively fulfills the first four roles which I have outlined, it will go a long way toward guaranteeing that a market will exist for all that we produce. But the steps I have proposed are not in themselves sufficient.

We will need, first of all, to co-ordinate and to time the

construction of public works. Every year, of course, there is considerable public building which cannot be delayed. But there are thousands of long-range projects which can be held up temporarily until the business indices suggest a need for larger government expenditures to make up for diminished spending on the part of either our business groups or all of us as consumers.

We shall also need to review carefully our tax and fiscal policies. The tax legislation under which we have operated for the past few years has grown like an old country house, with a wing added here, a barn there, and a tool shed somewhere else. It needs a thorough overhauling if our tax program is to contribute to full production and full employment.

The corporation tax, for instance, represents double taxation. Profits are first taxed as they are earned by the corporation. That part of the remaining profits which is paid out in dividends is then taxed all over again through the personal income tax. Over a period of time this double tax should gradually be eliminated. A major part of the resulting addition to net profit would normally be paid out in dividends. Much of this addition would be taxed in the higher personal income-tax brackets.

Profits held back in reserve should be scrutinized by the Treasury Department. All profits not clearly set aside for planned expansion for dividends or as working capital necessary to finance a growing business, should be subjected to a tax rate well in excess of the present corporation-tax level. Our modern tax program should also provide a high incentive for the development of new enterprise. New businesses should be allowed to balance losses in their early years against the profits they may make after they have turned the corner.

A tax program of this kind would force additional funds into the spending stream. It would serve as a powerful lever to induce businessmen to expand and modernize their facilities. It would penalize the hoarding of idle corporate funds.

We should also work towards the elimination of excise and sales taxes on all items, except those in the luxury class. These hidden taxes are, in reality, a tax on consumption.

If the government is to accept its proper role as the guarantor of the market for all that we can produce, we will need to modernize our political approach to the economic needs of our society. Most economists agree that the basic tax rates in any given period should reflect current economic conditions. In a period of rising prices, taxes should be high. In a period in which under-production is threatened, taxes should be reduced so that purchasing power and incentives will be increased.

I would like to see the functions of the President's Economic Council expanded to give them authority, within specific limits, to move taxes up and down to meet the current needs of our economy. The council should, of course, operate on clearly established legislative authority and under sharply defined standards. This legislative authority might also include the right to expand or contract certain social-security payments—such as unemployment payroll taxes—to meet changing economic conditions. In normal times, when jobs are plentiful, these payments might be reduced. When jobs become more scarce, they could be increased.

A further possibility in this approach lies in the field of farm support prices. Theodore W. Schultz's proposal for stabilizing farm income deserves particular study. Under this proposal, we would eliminate all farm support prices in periods of full production and allow farm prices to seek their own level in a free market. When a reduction in purchasing power seemed imminent, the Economic Council would be authorized to put into effect a program of direct payments to farmers, which would serve as a guarantee that the total income which they would receive from their annual production would not be allowed to fall below a specified level.

What I am suggesting is an "economic brain" responsible to Congress, with the authority to increase or decrease the total flow of purchasing power as our economy tends towards inflation or deflation. I believe that we have sufficient economic knowledge to enable an agency of this kind to fill an important role in leveling out the business cycle.

If we are to avoid periodic breakdowns in our economy, the responsibility of all of us, acting through our government, is a heavy one. It will call for wise administration and improved governmental efficiency. Our government must be streamlined, and overlapping functions eliminated. It must be staffed by competent men and women who look upon their positions in government not as political plums but as a chance for a lifetime of service to a democratic people.

The proposals which I have so briefly outlined will call for more activity on the part of our federal government than we have had up to the present time. But the *increase* in functions which I have proposed adds up to far less than the increase in government responsibilities during the 1930's. With few exceptions, each of these separate proposals is an expansion of an already accepted function of our government minimum-wage legislation, farm support programs, food-stamp plan, river-valley developments, aid to schools, the use of taxation to encourage production and employment, a guarantee of minimum health benefits, subsidized slum clearance, and subsidized housing programs. In other words, these proposals are not new. For the most part, they are an amplification of programs which have already been accepted and developed in the political platforms of our two major parties.

It would be a mistake, however, to assume that government by itself can solve all our economic problems under a private-enterprise economic system. Even greatly expanded government programs would amount to only a relatively small proportion of our total economic effort. The TVA cost only a billion dollars. For 12 billion dollars we could establish similar projects on every major waterway in the country. This expenditure would necessarily be spread over several years.

Two thousand schools can be built for a billion dollars, two thousand hospitals for an additional billion. On an annual basis, health insurance might cost a billion or two over current expenditures; a slum clearance program 500 million; a guaranteed college education for all those able to meet reasonable standards, one or two billion dollars. The total of all such expenditures in any given year would have a far more modest impact on our economy than the money which we now set aside for military and naval defenses.

Role of Private Enterprise   Clearly, then, government expenditures, even though carefully co-ordinated, cannot make up for sweeping failures on the part of business, labor, and farm leaders to carry out their proper economic functions in a private-enterprise system. As long as we maintain our private-enterprise system—and surely we would be foolish to abandon it—the biggest impact on our economy will come from the decisions of individual businessmen, workers, and farmers, in establishing wages, prices, and profits, and planning the expansion of our industrial facilities.

If we are to arrive at a rational solution to our economic future, we shall need responsible labor leadership. We shall need an end to featherbedding practices and a determination on the part of the individual workers that a full day's work will be provided in return for a full day's pay.

Our farmers will carry a heavy responsibility in providing increased food production at reasonable prices, not only for ourselves but at least for the next few years for many millions across the seas. Agriculture must be constantly made more efficient. Labor-saving equipment must be used to the limit. The family-sized farm, fortified with co-operatives, must be encouraged.

But our businessmen will carry the heaviest responsibility of all. This is so because a private-enterprise economy is a business economy. It would be unfair to expect businessmen to follow business practices which are clearly unprofitable. Profits are the lifeblood of business. It is the hope of increased profit that creates the urge towards expansion and the modernization of equipment. It is the prospect of building a business for themselves that induces able and talented young men to risk their savings and to branch out for themselves.

But if our businessmen are to carry out their responsibilities, not only to themselves but to our economy as a whole, their approach to profit-making must be a long-range approach. Let us examine the key areas in which the tens of thousands of decisions which they make each year will sharply affect the health of our economy. Among the most important is the establishment of wages through collective bargaining.

There are only three ways in which wages can be raised. A business which is making a more than adequate profit can pay a higher wage, maintain its present price level, and still maintain a reasonable profit. A business which is paying sub-standard wages and making no more than a normal profit can and should raise its wages by raising its price. Where wages are sub-standard, there is every reason why this step should be taken. If employers cannot meet a minimum wage standard, they should not be in business. None of us as consumers have a right to be subsidized by sub-standard wages.

Finally, wages can be increased, prices either kept stable or reduced, and profits either maintained or increased, through an increase in labor productivity. It is this latter approach on which we must largely depend for an increase in our standard of living. During the twenty years before the war, labor output per man-hour increased 4 per cent annually. In the three years beginning in 1920, the increase was 10 per cent per year. In the early postwar period, labor output per man-hour seems to have been reduced. But although accurate statistics are still unavailable, the indications are that a sharp upward trend is now in progress. This trend should continue upward. Far more comprehensive government studies should be made to determine, industry by industry, the changes which may take place from year to year in labor output per man-hour. These figures should become a basis for collective bargaining.

The increase in labor output per man-hour will result largely from improved machinery and facilities. To some degree, it will be the result of improved efficiency on the part of management and improved skill on the part of our workers. If management is to have the incentive to invest its profits to improve the efficiency of its plants, it has a right to expect part of the proceeds from increased labor productivity as an increase in its profit. But just as clearly, a substantial proportion of the increase in labor output per man-hour should be set aside for increased wages. If management fails to accept this view or if labor fails to present it forcefully, we will lack the increased purchasing power necessary to buy the increased output of goods. This is exactly what happened in the 1920's.

For awhile, these profits were siphoned off into increased plant capacity, the building of hotels and resorts, casual loans to foreign governments, and speculation in Florida real estate and the stock market. But in the absence of wage increases, the purchasing power of the great masses of our people remained nearly stagnant. There was less and less ability to buy the extra supply of goods which our increased productivity had made possible. The collapse that followed was inevitable.

Business is entitled in a full-production economy to generous profits. Unless generous profits are forthcoming, let me emphasize there will be but little incentive for business to push forward. Labor and the public must accept this as one of the economic facts of life.

But just as clearly, exorbitant profits are a threat to the health of our economy. Beyond a certain point, the opportunities for constructive investment in any given year are limited. Funds which remain stagnant in idle reserves represent just that much lost purchasing power which must be made up by either increased consumer spending or increased government spending, if we are to avoid a depression. Such potentially idle funds, passed on to the people through lower prices or higher wages, will help keep our economy healthy, and government activity at a minimum.

A third and all-important area in which businessmen under a private-enterprise system must make the key decisions is in the establishment of prices. Sometimes prices are set too high because of monopolistic influences. According to the theory of the monopolists, a high price set and maintained by a single monopolist or agreed upon by a group of producers will enable the demand for a given product to be spread out over a period of years. Clearly, this is not what even conservative economists mean by "free enterprise."

Some prices are also set too high because of haphazard factual knowledge. In many businesses, cost figures are arrived at by guess-work, with a few cents added here and there for safety's sake. In the war period, it was evident that even some of our best run industries had only a meager knowledge of what it cost to produce and distribute their goods. We need better accounting practices and a more realistic evaluation of business costs.

Another reason why prices are often set too high is because of the traditional worship of margins which has developed in many industries. Percentage margins have been established from raw-material producer to manufacturer to retailer over many years with much haggling. Once these margins have been accepted, businessmen are reluctant to change them, in spite of the fact that it is unit cost in relation to total volume that determines over-all profits rather than an arbitrary markup percentage.

As a corollary, some prices are also set too high because many businessmen, in all honesty, fail to appreciate the opportunities for increased volume and increased profits which may result from lower prices.

In every section of American business, we have seen instances where a lower price has resulted in such an increase in volume that a generous increase in profits has been forthcoming. But without adequate research, it is difficult for a businessman to estimate how much additional volume he will get from a reduced price, or what will happen to his over-all profit figure. Under these circumstances, it is easy to understand his caution. There is urgent need here for imaginative business research which will enable businessmen more clearly to evaluate the profit opportunities which lower prices and greater volume may bring.

What I am urging in this essential field of private decisions is more enterprise, more imagination in labor-management relations, improved business methods, and a clearer understanding of the long-range profit opportunities based on increased volume.

Government has an important responsibility if we are to maintain the markets and the purchasing power on which full production must depend. But the responsibility of our businessmen, our workers, and our farmers in setting wages, prices, and profits adds up to an even greater responsibility.

If Private Enterprise Fails?   If, for any reason, we fail in this area of private decisions, the government's role in our economy will surely increase. If monopolistic price-fixing continues to flourish, there will be an increased demand for government control and ownership. If labor-management disputes continue to develop into widespread disruptions in our economic life, there will be a demand for government control of wages, prices, and profits. And once government in peacetime is forced to invade the territory which should be set aside for private decisions, then government controls will spread. One control will lead to another. This we must make every effort to avoid. But if there is no other way to eliminate monopolistic control of prices and production, our people will properly demand increased government authority over the day-to-day functioning of our economy.

If our system of free private enterprise fails to enable us to maintain reasonably full production and full employment, the best hope for the maintenance of our political democracy would be the development of a "combination" economy, such as that of Sweden, Norway, and Denmark. Certain economic areas would be marked out for government enterprise, others for co-operative enterprise, and still others for private enterprise. The people of Scandinavia, through this approach, have developed a high standard of living and widespread opportunities for the individual citizen under vigorously democratic governments.

But together with many millions of American citizens who earnestly believe in the private-enterprise system, and who are distrustful of too much government, I hope it will be unnecessary for us to take the steps which they have taken. If we are forced into even limited government action in the field of production, prices, wages, and profits, we may succeed as the Swedish people and the Norwegians have succeeded; or, because our economy is so complex, our resources so much vaster, our effort may prove a failure. In that event, there is little likelihood that we would retrace our steps toward greater freedom of enterprise. Without question, we would move further and still further toward all-out government regimentation, with grave implication for our democratic traditions.

The task for those of us who believe that our best hope lies in the modernization and not the emasculation of our private-enterprise system, is clear. What stands in the way of accomplishment? Selfishness, bad economic habits, shortsightedness, greed, and economic ignorance. And time is short.

In the nineteenth century, we were able to fumble along from generation to generation accepting thankfully whatever progress we might make. Those who ran into economic troubles at home could always move to a homestead in the West and a new chance to regain their bearings.

In the year 1948, we have lost the priceless asset of time. Ours is a dynamic world. Other systems and other ideologies are competing with our own for the confidence of the world.

Karl Marx wrote that inevitably the capitalistic economies would break themselves to bits through periodic booms and busts. The leaders of the Soviet Union are Marxists. A basic assumption of Soviet foreign policy is that the American economic system is soon destined to come apart at the seams. Unless we throw off our smugness and put our economic house in order, this assumption may be proven correct within the next ten years.

Dominant leaders in each period of history have stubbornly refused to accept change. They have fought bitterly to hold back economic evolution, and for awhile they have succeeded. In each instance, however, their success has been shortlived. Eventually the pent-up forces—forces which a few years earlier might have been co-ordinated into constructive action —have broken loose. This was true in Greece. It was true in Rome. It was true in the France of Louis XVI. It was true in Czarist Russia.

The dominant groups in America, and particularly our businessmen, have a golden opportunity now to change this historical pattern. If they succeed, they will have furthered the cause of human freedom in every part of the world. They will have furnished the basis for better understanding with the Soviet Union and with other foreign powers—a basic understanding on which mutual respect may grow and through which a lasting peace may still be secured.

In any event, the fight for economic, social, and political democracy must go on. In the tradition of Jefferson, Jackson, Lincoln, Wilson, and Roosevelt, we must continue to strive toward the ideal of human freedom and opportunity in behalf of all of our people.

Our responsibilities are great. But so are the opportunities. Let us hope that we will live up to the future.

CHAPTER III

A Liberal Program and Its Philosophy *

by A. A. Berle, Jr.

The Challenge to Liberalism Liberalism was the great result of two centuries of European revolution. Its values were asserted, denied, struggled for, and gradually obtained. Liberalism became a dominant world ideal more than a century ago.

Only in our generation have liberal values been challenged anew. Hitler and Mussolini proclaimed as part of their world aims the wiping out of liberalism, root and branch; and they meant it literally. They intended, where they could accomplish it, to exterminate liberalism as thoroughly as Genghis Khan massacred his political opponents.

And liberalism was challenged from another quarter, the extremist wing of the Communist movement. Probably Lenin was the author of the attack from the extreme left. Certainly he gave major impetus to it. "We," he said, referring to his particular group, "are thinking of things which you, my little liberal, could never understand"; and the diatribes against liberalism in the *Handbook of Communist Revolutionary Tactics* are equalled only by the diatribes against liberals in Hitler's *Mein Kampf*. It remains only to add that the assumption that liberals could not understand is naive. For liberals have been meeting, and fighting, and conquering just this sort of attitude since the days of the Reformation.

The challenge to liberalism is not ill-timed. Actually, it is very welcome. Challenge compels restatement of values, and

* Part of this article was previously published in the *Survey Graphic*.

renewed effort to apply those values to daily living, to politics, to measures, and to men. It forces liberalism from the position of easily accepted dogma to become once more the active, dynamic doctrine which has in the past two centuries given the world most of its progress—scientific, material, and political. Without challenge, liberals might easily have degenerated into easy phrase-mongers. Now they are compelled to act from knowledge, from conviction, and from faith; to abandon the comfortable position of safety and to bear again the oriflamme bequeathed to them by the great warriors for humanitarian progress.

The Basic Truths of Liberal Thought For liberals, life has both significance and design; there is no anarchy in the universe. Men, in their view, are most creative and freest, most useful and happiest, as they realize some unity with the great moral pattern of things. At bottom, liberalism springs from a deep faith in the moral order of the universe.

This is abstract, but it is important. Without it neither the nature of liberalism nor its unconquerable quality can be understood.

From this proceeds the second great liberal premise: the object of life—political, intellectual, technical—is to develop people to their highest creative ability. By "people," the liberal means all people, excluding none. The measures he must develop and put through, the men he must follow or assist or support, must be the measures and men contributing toward this end. The true liberal can say with Eugene Debs: "While there is a lower class, I am in it. . . . While there is a soul in prison, I am not free." A liberal's idea of hell might easily be imprisonment before a table of luxurious plenty, while the procession of unfortunate or weak or unhappy pass by, with whom he is forbidden to share. In the fulfillment of anyone else, a liberal mind is itself fulfilled. To deny creation or opportunity or hope to any group means denying, to a liberal mind, a part of itself; to giving up of a part of the universal heritage.

The third great premise is unflinching acceptance of the duty to get the facts. A liberal lives in a real world. Problems are not abstractions; they are realities. It is not accident that the scientific reawakening of the world (which began, roughly, with Galileo, who discovered the solar system by observing phenomena) was a typical liberal product; nor that the totalitarians of the time tortured Galileo to make him recant his scientific conclusion. The nineteenth and early twentieth centuries, the age of world-wide liberalism, produced the greatest galaxy of scientific discovery in recorded history; and the end is not yet.

Believing, as he does, in a universal design; believing that the mind and heart of man can comprehend some part, however small, of that design; believing (it is all too obvious) that only through such comprehension can there be real sharing of knowledge and opportunity which make man free, the liberal is bound to look at facts and to attempt to meet reality in the light of these facts. Louis Brandeis, perhaps the greatest of twentieth-century liberals, used to initiate his disciples in just this way. "Get the facts," was his constant advice. "There is no substitute for arithmetic. To act without regard to the facts is to act from blindness or prejudice, or worse." The liberal in politics was here applying quite simply the rules which liberals have applied for three centuries in physics, medicine, and the arts. Liberals have had to fight, and not infrequently they have died, for the right to apply this method in all of these fields. Out of facts, measures can be outlined which, in greater or less degree, can contribute to the development of all human beings toward their greatest attainment of creative possibilities.

Values and Means   It is an obvious but often forgotten point that liberalism, by its nature, is not mortgaged to any particular system or method.

Left-wing totalitarians identify liberalism with capitalism because eighteenth-century liberalism conceived (and most liberals still agree) that men are freer if they possess a reasonable amount of private property. At the same time, reactionary conservatives steadily attack liberals because liberals have been the foremost and most successful opponents of unbridled and unlimited capitalism which enables a very few to rule over, bind, and exploit masses through ownership or control of property. To the liberal, socialism is a method of obtaining an objective, useful in certain regards; private property and enterprise are likewise desirable, also capable of obtaining certain results; neither is, by hypothesis, good or bad in itself. One must judge whether the method of socialization will produce greater development of men—as it does and has in certain fields; or whether it will produce a bureaucratic tyranny, indistinguishable from the feudal tyrannies from which we escaped after three centuries of warfare. A liberal will accept the capitalist method as able to produce certain kinds of goods and services, and will foster it for certain purposes, as Jefferson did; but he will be coolly judicial in determining on the basis of the facts whether capitalism in some fields may not tend to produce greedy and ruthless oligarchies as callous to human development as were the nineteenth-century mill owners whose cruelty inspired the flaming eloquence of Karl Marx.

Where liberalism ceases to be flexible and becomes rigid is in its choice of values. The end result—freedom and development of individuals—is the great criterion; the methods adopted must be developed out of the fact situations. The truly free mind—which must include the mind of the humblest agricultural worker as well as that of the greatest professor or officer of state—must be freer and better able to develop as a result. In consequence, the liberal is equally appreciative of the positive opportunities which are offered in some cases by socialism and in others by free enterprise; and he is equally at war with those qualities in both systems which enslave men mentally, oppress them economically, or deny their right to equal opportunity in the heritage of ideas or in the heritage of the potential material welfare which the world's resources and their scientific development make possible.

Based on his study of historical and sociological facts, the liberal has a steady and ingrained scepticism of concentrated power, whether political, economic, or ecclesiastical. His observations have led him to the conclusion that Lord Acton was right: "Power corrupts, and absolute power corrupts absolutely." He has seen the revolutionary commissar become first a tyrant and then a despotic emperor with or without a title. He has seen the successful property manipulator become the cartel director or trust organizer or profiteer. He has seen men in power lose their sensitiveness to human beings, and become callous to all kinds of human problems including (as a selection) intolerable working conditions, child labor, race prejudice, large-scale profiteering and, as in the case of the financial community in 1929, sheer dishonesty. He knows, as Lincoln did, that no man is good enough to be another man's master; or, to add to that aphorism, the man who is another man's master stops being "good" in a very short time. Consequently, he believes in the steady liberation of new individuals and enterprises and forces and currents of ideas which will lever against the old, so that no group shall be immune from challenge and from competition. His passionate belief in free speech and free education is one phase of this conviction. For it is precisely through free speech and free education that the young and new and struggling may challenge the old and established and self-satisfied, that concentration of power may be attacked, and that the order of things may be subjected to perpetual judgment, thus enabling perpetual development.

Liberalism should not be confused either with capitalism or with doctrinaire socialism. In the true sense of the word, liberalism is democratic in politics, economics, and philosophy. Indeed, no use of the word "democracy" except as a political expression of liberalism has any validity—despite the violent attempts of certain totalitarians to appropriate the word for their own, less legitimate use.

It may be added that, of all political systems, liberalism has been the most successful method yet devised. A South American looking at the United States exclaims that we are a nation of nations, and wonders how a country not mortgaged to a philosophy, nor pledged to an empire, can have absorbed millions upon millions of men and women of diverse racial and philosophical backgrounds. Yet the answer is plain. Democratic liberalism made demands on all, provided a task for all, gave to all a reason for being. And in that ideal, the immigrant Italian, the immigrant Pole, the immigrant Irishman, the immigrant Jew, all met with the immigrant Englishman or Scotchman and found common creation and a common happiness.

Politicians since the days of Julius Caesar, and undoubtedly before, have commonly promised immediate and material rewards to their followers for supporting their doctrine, their men, and their measures. Liberal politicians do this too, and probably will go on doing so. But to stress this phase unduly is a mistake. It is true that liberal doctrine has advanced and will continue to advance the material welfare of people and the national welfare of the countries which follow its precepts. This is a by-product of the overshadowing philosophical values; one remembers the Quakers who certainly did not profess the Quaker creed because that would make them prosperous. Yet the world learned that the Quaker was an eminently satisfactory person to have as neighbor, business associate, representative, or political leader, and thus as a by-product Quakers acquired influence, prosperity, and not inconsiderable power. With liberalism as a political philosophy, as with its older religious forms, strength lies not in what the liberal hopes to get out of it but in what he puts into it. Men are loyal to what they give far more than to what they are given. The liberals in this generation are men seeking to take their part in the creative process. They, like everyone else, benefit from the creation; but they take more joy in the creation than in the benefit.

What the Average Citizen Knows   The year 1946 ended, temporarily, liberal development in the national economy of the United States. Liberals disappeared from the national government. The word "planning" was banned. "Controls" were anathema, and "private initiative" and "normalcy" were the watchwords.

As a political development this was not wholly bad, because it gave liberals a chance to get back to their own affairs and do some serious thinking. Also, universities, regional developments, and local organizations had been drained of the men who did the studying and the scientific work which underlay such progress as had been made. Time to overhaul ideas was needed. Every period of progress in the United

States has been rooted in a previous period of study and thought.

Looking ahead, most liberals agree that the public has definitely learned certain facts about itself, and has pretty definitely indicated the areas in which the next big job will have to be done. The public certainly does not want the United States to look forward to a centralized, statist economy, but it will accept statism for emergency work. The evils of private enterprise on the loose are beginning to be understood; but it is equally clear that a wholly statist economy can unloose abuses as great or greater.

For liberal politicians, the conclusion, based on interpretation of public opinion, has been both philosophical and practical. Philosophical: the country wants responsibility thrown as far back as possible—upon individuals, communities, regions—on the ground that this kind of organization develops and educates individuals to higher capacity, happiness, and responsibility. Practical: the government, federal in certain matters and in other respects regional and local, must supply a central core of regulation and organization, and a kit of tools, and must be ready with stand-by machinery so that the economic system will at all times provide for the jobs, needs, and wants of 140 million Americans through intelligent use of their natural resources and their human ability.

In reactionary circles, as also on the extreme left, theoretical debates go on as to the role of the state in the national economy. The average citizen seems equally unimpressed by both groups. Where the government can do a better job than private capital and enterprise, there he wants the government. Where private enterprise can handle the situation, in general, he prefers that. On principle, he does not care in the least whether his water supply is provided by New York State or by the American Water Works, or his electric light by Pacific Gas and Electric or by a government-owned dam— provided the service is good, the product moderately priced, and the organization courteous. But he is afraid of concentrated power, either in the hands of a centralized bureaucracy or in the hands of a centralized corporate monopoly.

Most of all, he wants an economy that works continuously.

"Depressions" are not, to him, valleys in a statistical chart. Unemployment, misery, and fear are very real. Whatever Congressmen may say against planning, and economists about the glory of free capitalism, the citizen does not want alternations of "boom" and "bust" if he can help it.

He has a pretty clear idea that these evil times are somehow connected with the phenomenon of badly distributed national income; and he has learned that, in proportion as the standard of living of the lower income groups is raised, the violence of "boom" and "bust" is relieved. This is the result the average citizen wants and he turns to political and economic liberals to work out ways and means.

That is about the state of the political discussion at date of writing.

What the Liberal Program Offers   Liberal thinkers have accepted these general premises and have attempted to get down to practical measures. The more thoughtful have done a solid job in getting facts. Aside from the mass of data collected by various agencies (among which special mention should be made of the data of the Committee for Economic Development gathered under the supervision of Gardiner C. Means, and the President's Economic Reports from his Council of Economic Advisers), the greatest piece of research was done by Frederick Dewhurst and his associates for the Twentieth Century Fund.

The resulting volume, *America's Needs and Resources*, not only brought the statistical picture up to date, but undertook to prophesy the probable course of events through the year 1960, contributing an almost encyclopedic review of what America consumes now and what it would consume *if a modestly respectable standard of living were assured to everyone*. This goal has never yet been achieved in any large country, though the United States more nearly approaches it than any other. With these, and a large number of other studies, the factual data for solutions are reasonably blocked out. American liberals, in consequence, are now able to look at social and economic problems not from the point of view of doctrinaire politics as Europeans do but from the point of view of reasonably well-equipped social engineers.

This alone is an almost revolutionary result. It will be remembered that social problems in the past have been met with "guess" solutions, as the panic of 1873 was met with greenbacks, the depression of the 1890's by Bryan's free silver, and the panic of 1907 by a justifiable but clearly inadequate reliance on breaking up trusts and monopolies. In none of these cases was there any scientific evidence demonstrating that the cure really adequately fitted the disease.

Out of the mass of data, a few main-line solutions are beginning to gain general acceptance. They start from the demonstrated fact that the United States has the resources and capacity not only for present consumption but for an increase of production and consumption capable of providing an adequate standard of living and opportunity for every man, woman, and child in the country. One has but to consider the doubling of the nation's income every fifteen to twenty years despite long spells of unemployment and the resources wasted on war, to conceive the possibilities of the future. That fact appears to be proved beyond reasonable doubt; and the problem resolves itself into finding methods for social and economic organizations to do the job. Where a European wonders how he can get the necessary material, the American progressive is figuring out how capacity and resources can be organized to work continuously, and how distribution can best be effected.

In this search, one of the first preoccupations of progressives is to assure a continuing and more or less even flow of capital into necessary requirements. They know that the national income, and with it a level of employment ("sixty million jobs"), is directly dependent on steady reinvestment of savings in actual capital goods. This, plus the spending for normal consumption, keeps the economic plant running at or near capacity, and at or near full employment. When the flow of capital into productive enterprise falls off, unemployment begins, and is followed by contraction of consumption, and the downward spiral of recession. Actually the business cycle, so far, has been a series: a greatly stimulated capital flow, followed by a drying up; and for both employers and workers, industrial life has been a series of alternations of prosperity and distress.

Assuring continued expenditures of capital is thus the first line of attack on eliminating depression. It is here that the cleavage begins between the liberal and the conservative. The conservative says that if conditions are made attractive enough to capital, it will go on flowing and no one need worry. This, of course, is an illusion; conditions were entirely satisfactory to private capital in President Hoover's time, but it stopped flowing nevertheless.

The liberal says that when its supply stops, or begins to stop, the government must assure a flow in any event, spending itself, if need be. Capital can go into cold storage for a time without serious loss, but human beings cannot remain unemployed without terrible consequences. Liberals, therefore, have been giving a great deal of thought to outlets for capital investment when and as private capital is unable or unwilling to move out. High on the list for the liberal's program is this: *the supply of capital must never be closed.*

Several main methods have been suggested to achieve this and each has ramifications. All are worth looking at.

The first, and least controversial, is for the government to provide capital to private enterprise which needs, wants, and can use it in those times when private banking does not fill the need at a reasonable rate and on reasonable terms. Though begun under Hoover, this was one of the first and most successful developments of the Roosevelt administration. Riders on the Pennsylvania Railroad between New York and Washington may not know it, but the electrification of that line was the fruit of the first public-works loan made by the Reconstruction Finance Corporation. This sort of thing could be done on a large scale. Thus, it is calculated that the electric-power industry alone could actually use about five billion dollars of additional capital to develop services which are urgently needed now. At the moment there is a ready flow of capital for that purpose. But if private capital should dry up, the Reconstruction Finance Corporation or some similar agency must be there to provide the funds. The country needs the additional electric power. Labor needs the jobs. The suppliers of material need the markets. And there is a great unfilled need for consumption.

Public credit for private operation is the easiest hurdle to cross. But it is not adequate by itself, for private organisms may not wish to develop. The second main-line solution, however, though well demonstrated, is more controversial. Through governmental action, certain great resources can be developed on a regional basis as a combined means to achieve greater employment, production, and consumption.

The typical project of this type is the development of river-valley systems. Such projects combine protection against floods and soil erosion with additional development of power, and consequent growth of industries. A number of such developments have been surveyed; one—the Tennessee Valley Authority—already has a well-established record of successful operation.

The ten projects most commonly named are, respectively: the TVA (partly developed at a net expense of $718 million dollars); the Great Lakes–St. Lawrence project; the Connecticut and Merrimac Valley development in New England; the Ohio Valley development; the lower Mississippi project; the Arkansas Valley project (one of the most promising from many points of view); the Missouri Valley development (which would cost less than the flood damage in the spring of 1947 alone); the Pacific Northwest plan, begun but not filled in by the Grand Coulee and Bonneville dams (which are the completed uppermost and lowermost of a proposed system of eleven major dams with some seventy-five additional projects on the Columbia tributaries); the central valley of California project for developing the Sacramento and San Joaquin rivers (both already begun); and the added development of the Colorado Basin.

Over a period of fifteen to sixty years, between 40 and 50 billion dollars could be profitably spent on these projects. Capital assets fully equal to the expenditure would be the result. These ten do not exhaust the list; they are merely major proposals which are more or less worked out. Of these, the Missouri Valley Authority seems to be the most pressing from

the standpoint of need. At date of writing there is clearly no
need for additional capital development to maintain a stable
economy; but the need is there that the work be done, as
many a washed-out Missouri-Valley farmer can testify.

Most liberals have studied the famous controversy between
David Lilienthal and Harold Ickes about organization. That
controversy, it will be remembered, was whether projects of
this kind should be centralized, as Ickes wished, in a Washington administration (say in the Department of Interior), or,
following Lilienthal's ideas, decentralized as separate regional
developments based on the active participation of local
interest.

That debate was won hands down by Lilienthal. Again the
principle: throw the responsibility as far back as possible.
Regional development is more comprehensible to the average
citizen if it is run from the region itself. More men are developed by it; the work done more nearly conforms to the
needs and capacities of the community it serves.

This line of operation is controversial. Private utility companies have as yet been unable to find a way of doing the kind
of job done by these great regional developments; they do bitterly resent, however, and finance violent propaganda against,
having these jobs done by public or semipublic authority.
Liberals believe, I think with reason, that the voters will support them when the need for action comes.

A second great group of projects which can be uncorked to
maintain an even flow of capital concerns urban development.[1] Here no end of expert work has been done, a good deal
of it by Alvin Hansen and Guy Greer under the auspices of
the Federal Reserve Board. This has been supplemented by
the work of a good many planning commissions: the New York
City Planning Commission has made a very respectable beginning on the problem of metropolitan New York.

But clear agreement on methods still remains to be attained. Redevelopment acts have been passed in New York,
Illinois, Michigan, Kentucky, Maryland, Wisconsin, Missouri, Indiana, and New Jersey. It is plain that these acts
need further revision. Nevertheless, an area of capital ex-

[1] Cf. Chapter 15.

penditure that will yield results well worth the money lies already at hand.

A demonstration program would be carried out if the Taft-Ellender-Wagner bill became law; the experience under that, or a similar act, could be drawn on for unnumbered uses in the event of a national depression. This class of project, as in the case of the river-valley developments, will kill two birds with one stone. It will maintain capital flow, and with it employment and commercial activities, when private capital goes to cover. And we will get the houses that we sorely need and better cities to live in.

Still another set of projects is found in the conservation field—one of the desperately neglected fields of American endeavor. This subject is technical and it is connected with an allied problem which is humanly pressing: the tenant farmer. This problem, a dangerous development in American agriculture, is a preoccupation of all liberals. Actually, tenants now operate nearly 40 per cent of American farms, and they till nearly 30 per cent of the farm land. The combination of land rehabilitation and a tenant purchase program is very nearly a "must." It can be combined with the problem of preventing or curing depression.

This does not exhaust the kinds of projects which liberals have been studying. Enough has been said to show that there are ample ways in which American productivity can be put to work through capital expenditures, when and as the purely private operations do not fill the bill. None of this is boondoggling. All is worth doing for its own sake, and doubly worth doing as part of a program to keep the economy working at all times.

Many liberals resent the fact that modest expenditures have not been made to draw accurate plans and specifications for a considerable number of these projects. Were a depression to be threatened tomorrow and were the public to demand action (as it would), six months or a year would be needed to do the blueprint engineering and to draw specifications so that work could actually start. The cost of doing this elementary work now is small; but the cost of doing it and keeping several million men on unemployment relief or dole, while the plans are being drawn or finished, would run into staggering figures.

Few will forget those Congressmen who, in 1944, voted down an appropriation to draw such plans on the ground that this meant "planning"; and "planning" meant socialism. That memory is not pleasant. We may have to pay a heavy bill for their shortsightedness.

The Implications of Government Spending   Liberals have had to face and think out the problem: "What are we going to use for money?" In this field the theorists and academic students have given precious little help. Experience, on the other hand, has given a plain demonstration (1) that money can be obtained whenever there is need; and (2) that the oft-raised cry of "inflation" is unfounded *so long as men are idle and productive facilities are unused.*

If academic studies have been lacking, the public has learned that inflation comes only after money has outrun production. In short, you do not get inflation in time of depression. Government credit can safely be used when production slackens off. The time to worry about inflationary use of government credit is when production is at its peak and cannot readily be increased. In general, experience shows that Americans, though optimists in most respects, underestimate their own ability to produce. Our data (I rely again on the Twentieth Century Fund study) indicate that even today we have still untapped productive resources—though there is at the moment no pressure of unemployment requiring unusual measures.

Further, the New Deal experiments of the 1930's (which today seem small compared with the possibilities we now know to exist) suggest that expenditures of the kind proposed are anything but losses. In point of fact, the operations of the Reconstruction Finance Corporation have shown a profit. Even a purely protective organization like the Home Owners Loan Corporation, which did not construct homes but merely took over mortgages from frightened owners and worked out the situation with time instead of foreclosure, likewise is winding up better than even.

It can be shown, I think, that the United States is making, and not losing, money on the Tennessee Valley Authority, the Grand Coulee, Bonneville, and Boulder (now Hoover) dams.

Clearly, when government debt is as high as it is now, liberals—who, contrary to the usual impression, are rather canny in money matters—prefer to find ways of using private accumulations wherever possible; but they will not abandon a project rather than use government credit. Liberal thinking and studies have demonstrated that money and credit ought to be considered as means of transportation, organization, and exchange, not as a private hoard. There is simply no use in facing modern civilization and social engineering with the primitive ideas of an Indian hill Rajah who thinks of money as a hoard of gold and jewels in a palace hiding place.

Therefore, liberals who think about these things have been generally in favor of keeping available for future use organizations like the Reconstruction Finance Corporation, the Home Owners Loan Corporation (and possibly extending it to take care of a collapse in consumer credit—for instance, household furniture bought by veterans on the installment plan), and the War Plants Corporation, which financed the building of the country's additional war-production equipment. Still more, we must know where to find informed and capable staffs for these and like institutions, which can be called together when the time arrives to begin operations.

Most liberals who have studied our currency and credit system are shocked to find that it took World War II to educate even technicians in its possibilities. The greatest peacetime economic program ever dreamed of was microscopic by comparison with the draft on the productive system and its companion, the money and credit system, involved in the war. A peacetime economic program produces values for expenditures made, whereas wartime expenditures are mainly destroyed or wasted.

The problem, "What are we going to use for money?" has ceased to be a question of whether it can be done. *We now know by experience that it can be done.* The problem is how can it *best be done*, done with least danger, least waste, greatest conservation of values—financial, economic, and social—for all concerned.

    Social Security and the Right to Work   There remain three other fields not strictly connected with economic stability and certainly different from control of depressions and unemployment, though the third of them lies closely in that range. Of these, the most pressing is that of medical care. A great public servant, Surgeon General Thomas Parran, has taught the country that a far higher level of health can be had if and when the country wants it badly enough to pay for it. Various experiments, like the New York City experiment in group health insurance, demonstrate that ways can be found to assure that illness does not mean bankruptcy to a family which though not rich, is not so poor as to claim pauper's care. No single measure has yet been worked out which meets the general need. Partial measures do exist; and at least one is ready for introduction in the Congress.

    Here, liberal thinking is unequivocal. If health is worth having, it is worth having now. There is no point in waiting. There is, for example, no solid reason for permitting the continuance of venereal disease at the present rate; or for failure to make available throughout the whole country the methods by which the common diseases are controlled; and no reason for permitting malnutrition in childhood to exact a terrible toll in later weakness.

    This is not a "self-liquidating" expenditure, but a human obligation. You do not get your money back. You want health. You want it at least as badly as, say, you want a movie. Of the national expenditures, less is spent on medical care (4 billion dollars in 1940, including everything) than on tobacco (almost 8 billion dollars). Here is a straight case where each man must decide what he wants. The liberal has a job of education as well as of technical planning.

    Speaking of education: here also the liberal is unequivocal. He knows that the greatest single reason why the United States has been successful is the fact that Jefferson gave it a system of universal education. American human resources have thereby been developed more widely than those of any other great country. He knows, too, that in certain areas education is not keeping pace with the needs of the country. Probably the local and regional governments ought to be doing this job, but they are not. Education is one of the matters in which we cannot take a chance. For this reason, the liberal wants federal aid to education. He wants the inequalities of opportunity which prevail in various regions wiped out, because he knows no part of the United States can begin to degenerate without affecting the entire nation.

To permit the continued lack of educational opportunity for Negroes, for instance, is not only a crime against the Negro; it is a danger to the nation. A noble state like Virginia violates the tradition of Jefferson by being close to the bottom in education for everybody, and it rejoices in an average salary of $987 for a white teacher and $605 for a Negro teacher. Virginia certainly ought to do better; if she cannot by her own means the rest of us must help her.

The third measure liberals want is still in process of formation. Though liberals chiefly rely on sound handling of national economy to avoid depressions and to level off booms, unemployment will still exist to some extent. In part, we can meet this by widening the system of social security (a standard liberal measure), but more is needed. You cannot satisfy a man who wants a job either by a dole or by a discussion of national economic policy. He wants to be put to work. This was Fiorello LaGuardia's idea when he dealt with the problem of unemployment relief in New York City.

In other words, any man who really wants a job ought to have a place where he can go and get it; and certain public works ought always to be available for that purpose. In the case of rural development, reforestation, and certain kinds of soil conservation, this was roughly the principle of the Civilian Conservation Corps, though that was limited to youth. Charles W. Taussig adapted the principle to the large and successful operations of the National Youth Administration. In good times, the necessity of ready employment for particular groups would not be great; in bad times, it may be essential as a bridge between jobs. Consequently, the liberal wants this sort of machinery worked out and ready.

He has another reason for wanting this. Being of a ranging

turn of mind, he follows scientific developments. He knows
that we have had a run of technological development whose
proportions are hardly suspected. On top of that, atomic
power for civilian use is undeniably coming up. This will
mean both a great increase in productivity and a great shift
in employment. But even admitting that in the end there will
be more and not less employment, most people are not interested in statistical results; they are, and must be, thinking
about their jobs and their families, not someone else's. So
provision for ready funds for immediate employment, with
training for youth, or retraining for new types of employment,
must be very much on the minds of liberal thinkers.

Conclusion   We began with the philosophical conception that a liberal program is concerned with people.
Everything from there out has been a mechanism for developing individuals. The liberal does not want to make a
dictatorship of the proletariat. He wants to abolish the concept of the "proletariat." The United States has a fair chance
of doing this. The liberal is preoccupied with practical methods of getting this result.

He would begin by trying to stabilize, educate, and
strengthen the private economic machinery, though he gets
little help from the conservatives who fundamentally do not
like to be bothered until they are in trouble, and then want to
be saved at public expense. He is prepared to work with
private enterprise if it liberates and develops individuals, or
with semi-governmental or wholly governmental operation if
need be.

If a depression were to begin tomorrow, the measures outlined above, and others besides (for this article cannot be
complete), would become the active program of the country
in just the time it takes for the country to register its desire in
effective political action. There is no question about this.
Never again will the country wait in dumb misery as it did
from 1929 to 1933, praying for a change of economic weather.

The point has been made: the job of meeting economic and
social misery can be done, whenever the United States really
wants to do it.

PART TWO

*Liberalism and Economic
History*

Introduction

Seymour E. Harris

In Parts I and II, we present the views of an important liberal in the Democratic Administration (Bowles), one of the few outstanding New Dealers retained by the Truman Administration (Keyserling), and Arthur Schlesinger, Jr., now at work on a history of the Roosevelt era. All these writers are aware that New Deal policies, evolved in a depression milieu, will not do for the late forties and fifties. They are all, however, committed to the philosophy that liberalism in the modern world charges the government with the responsibility to intervene in a positive manner to aid the many. New Dealism was an interpretation of the liberal creed, and in turn contributed to the evolution of the new liberal philosophy.

With varying emphasis, these writers uphold the view that substantial unemployment of resources is a threat to the maintenance of the present system, and, therefore, that treatment of unemployment through monetary expansion and fiscal policy will not only help sustain activity but will also correct specific maladjustments. In the next ten or twenty years, there undoubtedly will be periods of under-employment and maldistribution; but if the managers of our economy learn from the lessons of the thirties, they will be able to mitigate depression more effectively than the New Dealers who had to improvise. With inflationary pressures increasing as agriculture, labor, and capital tend to become more monopolistic, and with demand sustained by destruction wrought

61

by war and preparation for war, new techniques will have to be developed for attacking inflationary forces. New Deal experience will give little help on this score, although the war experience should prove helpful.

CHAPTER IV

The Sweep of Economic History, 1800 to 1947

by Seymour E. Harris

Growth over 130 Years　　Over a period of 130 years preceding the collapse of 1929–30, this country had experienced a rate of growth unparalleled in world history. Despite a rise in population of 23 times, income per capita had grown from 131 to 685 dollars; and the *net* upward movement in prices had been but 5 per cent. The nation's income had increased from less than 700 million dollars to 83 billion dollars, or about 120 times, and the monetary stock from 38 million dollars to over 55 billion dollars, or about 1,440 times. By 1948, even greater advances had been made: the country was supporting 27 times as many people as in 1800 at a standard of living about 10 times as high as that of the early 19th Century.

This phenomenal rate of growth can be attributed to the opening up of vast resources in the West, to an intelligent population enriched in numbers and skills by European immigration and strengthened by universal free education, to a vast free trade area, to the incentives offered under a system of free private enterprise and the accompanying technical advances. All these factors contributed to the denial of the Malthusian theory which holds that population growth will press upon the means of subsistence and bring distress.

The monetary history of the period underlines a point succinctly phrased by Berle, namely, that expansion of money in a growing or expanding society is not necessarily inflationary.[1] The explanation may be, as he points out, that the increase in money is offset by an increase in employment; or it may be (a long-run explanation) that with rising standards of living people seek larger hoards of money, and in greater proportion than the rise of income. In the period 1800–1929, the rise of money was twelve times that of income.

The Break in 1929   After 1929, something happened to the American system. There followed a decade in which unemployment averaged ten million and in which about three hundred billion dollars worth of resources was wasted on account of idleness; unemployment and unsatisfactory distribution of wealth persistently confounded the government. In contrast with the hundred years preceding 1929, when national income (real) doubled every fifteen to twenty years, it took ten years of heroic measures, which shook the capitalist structure at its very foundation, to re-establish a national income equal to that of 1929. And even then it was an income badly distributed in a world of unemployment.

By 1933, money national income had fallen by 55 per cent, and when corrected for the decline in prices, output had fallen by 40 per cent. The twenties had been a period of unsurpassed optimism, of unprecedented gains in technology and business management, of the ascendency of big business, of increased availability of bank and private credit. Despite the vast growth of bank deposits, the ordinary price indices showed little net change; but the rise in prices relative to unit costs, and the 300 per cent rise in stock-market prices, reflected an unhealthy situation. As in 1948, the American people had forgotten about depressions and turning points, about the decline that always follows a rise; they had lost their sense of history. Both the decline in 1929–33 and the later recovery are revealed in Chart 1. National income in recent years was as follows: [2]

IN BILLIONS OF DOLLARS

1929—87	1944—182
1933—40	1946—178
1939—79	1947—203

[1] See above, Chapter 3, pp. 53–55.
[2] *The Economic Report of the President* (January 1948), p. 102.

GROSS NATIONAL PRODUCT, 1929-1946

BILLIONS OF DOLLARS

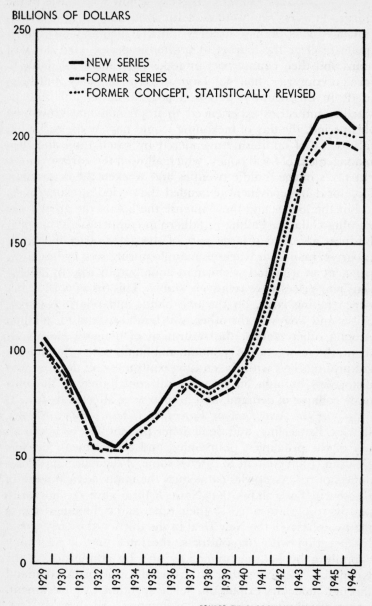

NEW SERIES
FORMER SERIES
FORMER CONCEPT, STATISTICALLY REVISED

SOURCE: *SURVEY OF CURRENT BUSINESS*, JULY 1947.

CHART I

Mistaken Policies   It is easier now than it was in the thirties to assess the twenties. Ultimately, the outflow of consumers' goods became excessive in that demand was inadequate to clear the market at profitable prices. Had not vast loans and their counterpart in goods been made available to foreign countries, had not large investments of capital been made in this country, and had not the automobile and its satellite industries experienced their phenomenal growth in this period, the day of reckoning would have come earlier. A false sense of optimism engendered by speculation and mismanagement of fiscal policy, which allowed the government to cut taxes in the middle twenties and weaken the contractive force of debt repayment, extended the period of exuberance.

But the longer and more intense the boom, the greater the ensuing collapse. Failing to adhere to competitive principles, business absorbed a large part of the gains of technological progress: man-hour wages in manufacturing rose by but a few per cent in a period when man-hour output rose by 40 per cent and prices were relatively stable. This disproportion between falling costs, on the one hand, and relatively stable prices and wages on the other, was bound to lead to collapse. Among other factors, the saturation of demand for investment, the resurgence of economic nationalism, the glut in agricultural markets with the ensuing contraction of demand, the distortions brought on by war—all contributed to the ultimate collapse of demand, and in turn were affected by it.

The New Deal as Viewed by Others   Since Messrs. Bowles, Keyserling, and Schlesinger present an excellent survey of the principles, philosophy, and achievements of New Dealism, I am content to discuss some of the more important details of policy. Bowles catalogues the many advances under Roosevelt, Berle shows that New Dealism gave the liberals a positive program suited to their time, and Schlesinger traces the two phases of the New Deal in the thirties, the early one of co-operation with big business, the later one of reforming capitalism by fighting monopoly and by administering the Keynesian medicine, that is, artificially supporting demand through monetary expansion, deficit spending by government, and redistribution of income by taxation. All three, in fact, emphasize the importance of subsidizing demand under government aegis. Keyserling, on the other hand, stresses the qualitative weaknesses of New Deal policy as well as its achievements.

History determined the course which Roosevelt had to take in economic matters; for the twenties and early thirties had underlined the excesses of big business, the abuses of financial capitalism, the deficiency of demand and the accompanying maldistribution, the weakened bargaining position of farmers and labor, the distress brought on by unemployment and perverse fiscal policy. Gradually, and after much fumbling, the Administration stumbled upon appropriate policies.

Advances on the Financial Front   Attacks by New Dealers on monopoly, restriction of output, and inflexible and high price policies were slow in coming and meagre in results (as Berge has well shown). In financial reform, they made their earliest advances. The closing of the banks, the rigging of speculative markets and speculative excesses in general, and the failure of banks to check the boom made a great impression on the public. The Democratic Administration had a mandate to correct these evils. By the middle thirties, the Administration had provided for restraints on speculative use of banking funds, for meticulous examination of new issues of securities, for insurance of bank deposits, for the provision of cheap credit for borrowers not adequately served by the existing institutions, and for insurance on various types of loans. These are important achievements and clearly they have contributed to financial soundness, integrity, and adequacy, and to restraining speculative forces.

Lifting Demand   A more difficult task was that of assuring adequacy of demand. Unfortunately, this problem was but dimly seen. Yet the Wagner Act, which strengthened labor's position, the various agricultural acts which improved the income of farmers, the programs for relief and public investment, the Social Security Act—all of these contributed to a strengthening of demand or a better time distribution of demand and to a redistribution of income in favor of spenders against savers, a counteraction required in an over-saving economy.

Untutored in the potentialities of fiscal policy, Roosevelt used fiscal policy as an instrument for supporting demand, but with timidity: deficits were an aftermath of spending to relieve distress rather than a weapon for sustaining demand directly. The Administration was inclined to rely on monetary expansion and on direct aid to business and other groups in distress, and to accept budgetary deficits as the unfortunate outcome of these measures rather than to use fiscal policy as a powerful weapon for combatting depression, unemployment, and insufficiency of demand.

Keynes and the New Deal   An interesting point for speculation is the influence upon New Dealism by Keynes, the outstanding figure in economics in the last fifty or possibly one hundred years; for Keynes produced a mosaic of monetary expansion, falling rates of interest, government subsidization of demand, taxation favoring consumption, which attracted the attention of thinkers and men of action. Elsewhere I have written as follows.[3]

> In this country, the view is widely held that Keynes contributed greatly to the evolution of New Deal economic policies; and the mere mention of his name will bring forth the most vituperative remarks by conservative American businessmen. Indeed, American economic policies in the thirties conformed to the Keynesian pattern much more than did the British. . . .
>
> In the acceptance of deficit financing and loan expenditures, the United States authorities put into practice the theories of Keynes. Whereas the British nullified the gains of exchange depreciation to some extent by imposing measures of economy, the United States embraced deficit financing. In the years 1931–1938, for example, the public debt of *all governments* in this country rose by $24.8 billion, and federal net capital investments accounted for $11.6 billion.
>
> In other respects also, the American economy seemed to have become a testing laboratory for Keynes' ideas. The National Recovery Administration (NRA), the Agricultural Adjustment Administration (AAA), various relief programs, the Social Security Act were interpreted in part as programs which would transfer purchasing power from non-spenders to spenders. As

[3] *The New Economics: Keynes' Influence on Theory and Public Policy* (New York, 1947), pp. 15–19.

General Johnson, the querulous head of the NRA, said, since the millionaire cannot buy forty dollars' worth of ham and eggs daily, the way out of a depression is to enable each American to buy fifty cents' worth of ham and eggs. . . .

Yet Keynes did not fully approve of early New Dealism. He was not pleased with the gyrations of the dollar; nor with the attempts to raise prices by restrictions of output or by increasing wages and farm incomes; nor with the failure (1) to raise prices through monetary policies, and (2) to expand demand through loan expenditure. All of this was made evident in his letter to *The New York Times* of December 31, 1933. Even while he was criticizing, however, the Administration, disturbed by the setback in the latter part of 1933, began to accelerate its spending program. . . . In 1934, Keynes visited the White House. According to the report of Mrs. Perkins (*The Roosevelt I Knew*, 1946), the President reported that Keynes had visited him, and apparently the President was not pleased with Keynes' "rigmarole" of figures. Keynes, on his part, expressed surprise that the President was not more literate in economic matters.

American economic policy was indeed full of inconsistencies and paradoxes. The Administration supported concomitantly a program to assure monetary expansion (revaluation of the dollar, the gold clause, and the Thomas Amendments), and the Banking Act of 1933, which in many respects was deflationary. . . . In the platforms of both 1932 and 1936, the Democrats stressed their intention to balance the budget. Close advisers to President Roosevelt are well aware that he had never really accepted unorthodox theories of public finance: he would not, however, balance the budget at the expense of human lives. In his budget message of January, 1940, the President came close to accepting the Keynesian thesis: the experience of 1938–39 should remove any doubt as to the effectiveness of fiscal policy related to economic need; with government intervention, the decline of income from 1937 to 1938 had been kept down to $8 billion—compare the drop of $42 billion from 1929 to 1932; and whereas in 1937–1938 productive activity had turned upwards in 9 months, in the earlier episode the country had experienced four years of liquidation and depression.

Yet the general pattern, especially as New Dealism evolved, checked well with Keynes' strategy and tactics. More money, lower rates of interest, loan expenditure, measures to raise the propensity to consume, some freedom from dictation from abroad—all of these were the ingredients out of which the New Deal cocktail was made. The severely restrictive measures, the excesses of economic nationalism, the over-emphasis on raising money incomes as the means to rising output—all of these were ultimately largely repudiated. . . . Keynes' theories and programs undoubtedly had a substantial effect, even if it is difficult to trace. By 1933, the supporters of the new policies and even the man in the street, though unaware of the sources, were using arguments that Keynes had made commonplace.

Accomplishments of the New Deal   As is evident by now, the New Deal had accomplished much: income had risen from 40 billion dollars in 1933 to 73 billion dollars in 1939; unemployment had fallen from 13 million in 1933 to 7 million in 1937 and 9 million in 1939, and employment had risen by 7 million from 1933 to 1939; and, as has been indicated, the authorities had provided large additions to monetary supplies, and despite a marked increase in the public debt had brought the rate of interest down from 4.5 to 2.5 per cent. Contrary to what might be expected from the law of supply and demand, a rise of the public debt outstanding by two to three times was accompanied by a rise in the price of federal securities.

—And Errors   Indeed, the Administration had made many errors: the early alliance with industry and labor for the purpose of reducing output and exploiting consumers (cf. Schlesinger); the torpedoing of the London Conference with a policy of competitive debasement of the currency not clearly thought out and introduced to appease the farm groups; the failure to deal with agricultural problems through expansion rather than contraction; the surrender to farmers on the rights of the submerged tenants and farm laborers (cf. Berle); the concomitant pushing of contradictory policies (for example, reduction of government pay, restrictions on banking activities, on the one hand, and spending programs and the Thomas Amendments to inflate the currency, on the other).

The Net Result   Yet, despite these blemishes, the record was a brilliant one. At last a government was in power which was ready to support the interests of the many against the privileged few; to implement the professions of egalitarianism with legislation in favor of the masses; to turn its back on fetishes like the gold standard and 'the balanced budget, which had put the interests of finance against those of man; to put the vast revenue potential of the federal government behind local and state governments to relieve distress; with new reservoirs of money and with spending and tax reform to buttress a capitalism groggy from the collapse of the early thirties.

Depression Policy in Prosperity? We are aware of the limitations of the New Deal. We are apprised of the mistakes made. We agree that the policies which were appropriate after three years of a record depression are not likely to be appropriate after seven or eight years of unprecedented prosperity and strong inflationary pressure. We know now that we must steer a course between the Scylla of depression and unemployment and the Charybdis of full employment and inflation. Having attained full employment, we now are impressed by the difficult problems raised in a society with more jobs than applicants.

Fortunately, in depression we could afford to collect facts and analyze them, as we were unwilling to do in the prosperous twenties or the exuberant forties. One of the great contributions of the New Deal was to call to Washington objective scientists, collectors and analyzers of facts, arbiters on behalf of the public's interest between vested interests. That we know much more about how our economic Frankenstein works and what can be done to make it serve us, should make our future task easier.

CHAPTER V

The Broad Accomplishments
of the New Deal*

by Arthur M. Schlesinger, Jr.

The Crisis   Sullen men lived miserably in Hoover-villes, huddled against icy blasts, waited in grim lines for bread and soup, pondered a desperate march on Washington to collect bonus payments. Farmers, fighting bitterly against dispossession, moved toward open violence. Businessmen, stricken with panic, pleaded for government aid. Labor was disorganized and impotent. Intellectuals were clutching at Communism or at Fascism. And our national leadership? Clinging with frightened obstinacy to the theory that the forces which brought the depression would bring the revival, Herbert Hoover resisted the demand that the government act. It was the winter before the New Deal.

The election of 1932 presented America with one more chance to solve its problems democratically. Few considered Franklin Roosevelt a very strong or a very profound man; but the warmth and energy of his personality inspired confidence, and close observers could detect a new and bolder philosophy of government lurking behind the innocent generalities of his speech at the Commonwealth Club in San Francisco and behind such phrases as "the forgotten man" and "the New Deal." With his victory there began the resurgence of hope.

His debut—the bank holiday, the strong, ringing tones of the President, and the evaporation of fear—serves almost as a

* This chapter is a revision of an article published in the *New Republic*.

symbol of the Roosevelt policy. The cycle was to be repeated many times: stagnation and despair; a bold presidential stroke restoring hope; quick and spectacular action; and a conclusion which represented a substantial improvement but not a permanent solution. When Roosevelt finished with the banking crisis, the banks were established on a sounder basis than ever before in our history. Whether he might have taken the opportunity to nationalize the banking system is a question which used to exercise radicals in the middle thirties but which is perhaps based on a misunderstanding of Roosevelt's purposes.

First Phase of the New Deal   The hundred days thus began, with their brilliant, resourceful, and somewhat chaotic moves to prop up a crippled system—the start of a career of prolonged and ingenious improvisation. What else could there be but improvisation? Roosevelt, with his enlarged conception of governmental responsibility, had to face problems without administrative precedent and without trained personnel, and he had to act fast. No one knew better than he the tentative character of his program. "The country demands bold, persistent experimentation," he had said in the campaign. "It is common sense to take a method and try it. If it fails, admit it frankly and try another." This was to be his rule (except for the part about admitting failure frankly).

The Agricultural Adjustment Administration tried to solve the eternal farm problem by curtailing crop production. The Public Works Administration was set up to expand purchasing power through public works; under Harold Ickes's cautious management it remained free from suspicion of graft at the price of a slow start in its job of stimulating recovery. The Works Progress Administration, providing work relief, became the great challenge to New Deal ingenuity. Though some of its projects were correctly denounced as boondoggling, the total WPA achievement was substantial, and its contribution to cultural life rich and varied.

In certain respects the National Recovery Administration was most significant for the future development of the New Deal. In this experiment in business self-regulation, the government undertook to enforce codes of fair competition set up more or less by business itself. In exchange, business accepted minimum working hours, minimum wages, and the abolition of child labor, and, above all, Section 7A, with its guarantees for collective bargaining.

In operation it soon became clear that the big companies were running away with the show. Exemption from anti-trust prosecution led to happy public indulgence in such formerly secret vices as price fixing and production quotas. While Section 7A encouraged considerable honest labor organization, it was also diluted in many cases to permit the formation of company unions; and labor's bitterness found expression in an outburst of strikes. Moreover, though there was an upswing in business, it did not look as if the NRA was going to deliver the goods on employment and production. When the Supreme Court bailed out the President by calling the whole thing off in 1935, Roosevelt wisely abandoned the experiment.

The failure of the NRA was accompanied by a growing bitterness toward business and a basic redirection of the New Deal. The change, which took place late in 1934 and early in 1935, was signalized by the fall of the first brain trust and the rise of a new set of presidential advisers. When he first went to Washington, Roosevelt had surrounded himself with men— Raymond Moley, Hugh Johnson, Donald Richberg—who shared the belief that bigness was here to stay. These men were convinced of the futility both of trust-busting and of nationalization and were seeking some means of stabilizing the economy through (in Moley's phrase) "cooperative business-government planning." Roosevelt had remarked on signing the National Industrial Recovery Act, "It is a challenge to industry, which has long insisted that, given the right to act in unison, it could do much for the general good which has hitherto been unlawful. From today it has that right."

And the result of business self-government? Restrictions on production, chiseling of labor and of 7A, squeezing out of small business, savage personal criticism of the President, and the general tendency to trample down every one in the rush for profits. Experience was teaching Roosevelt what instinct and doctrine had taught Jefferson and Jackson: that, to reform capitalism, you must fight the capitalists tooth and nail.

Roosevelt's new advisers—Ben Cohen, Tom Corcoran, Harry Hopkins, Harold Ickes—encouraged his natural tendencies to fight it out on a more liberal line. At the same time, the raucous activities of Huey Long and other pseudo-radical prophets (Father Coughlin and Dr. Townsend), as well as the labor militancy stirred by John L. Lewis, showed the political necessity for a tack to the left. The result was the New Deal as we chiefly remember it—that determined, stalwart, eloquent fight against business domination, conducted by F. D. R. at his fighting best, backed by the loyal and alert intelligence of the New Dealers and by that weird coalition of city bosses, Southern Bourbons, trade unionists, liberal Republicans, Progressives and Farmer-Laborites, writers and intellectuals.

The attack on the Supreme Court, following Roosevelt's smashing victory in the 1936 elections, marked the high point of confident liberalism. The proposal to enlarge the court was itself disingenuous, cooked up in private jocularity and sprung without adequate preparation. Nevertheless the New Deal instinct to back the measure was probably correct, given the concrete situation. Recurrent attacks on the Supreme Court are an essential part of the physiology of our system; they constitute the natural and wholesome process by which the tissues of the court are restored before they are fatally overstrained.

One result was the court's change of heart and a constitutional green light for the New Deal. But the political price of even this partial victory was the alliance between the conservative Democrats and the Republicans. What Burt Wheeler joined together, Roosevelt could never quite put asunder. The so-called purge of 1938 snapped further bonds of party loyalty; and the President's growing concern with the South as "the nation's No. 1 economic problem" warned the Southern Bourbons that new popular forces might be unleashed against them. Thus began that long and destructive guerrilla warfare which was to reduce the New Deal to practical impotence by the early forties.

This breaking up of the Democratic party was all the more unfortunate since it coincided with the gradual clarification of the New Deal economic program. The proscription of NRA enabled the New Dealers to clear the decks and begin anew on the problems of the American economy. This enterprise concentrated on two questions: recovery, and post-recovery economic organization.

Second Phase   During Roosevelt's first term, problems rained on the White House so furiously that the President could only improvise for short-term relief, not plan for long-term solutions. But, somewhere out of the welter of legislation, economic recovery received stimulus, and the curve of business activity began to go up. About this time Keynesian views of public spending were domesticated by Marriner Eccles and Alvin Hansen.

The President himself probably remained a balanced-budget man to the end, and Henry Morgenthau, Jr., his loyal Secretary of the Treasury, conducted a vigorous battle against the Keynesians—Ben Cohen, Leon Henderson and others—in 1937–38. But the recession of that winter, following the drastic cutbacks on spending in 1937, supplied the advocates of spending with a kind of circumstantial support; and the massive success of war spending in solving problems of production and employment appeared to demonstrate beyond reasonable doubt that you can stop the downward swing of the business cycle.

In its first formulation, the Keynesian program aimed at treating the problem of economic maturity; but it was later adapted to an attack upon the business cycle. Prosperity, it argued, depends on the maintenance of a high level of national income; and this high level, in turn, depends on the maintenance of capital formation and of purchasing power. Over-saving will cause a sag in both real investment and consumption and thus a sag in the national income. When such a decline begins, the government must offset the decrease in private spending by subsidizing capital formation and by subsidizing purchasing power.

The development of the anti-depression program was accompanied by a pretty thorough-going revision of NRA notions about American economic life. This process involved a restudy of the role of the concentration of economic power in restricting production. It was marked by the rise to dominance of people more or less in the Brandeis "anti-bigness" tradition (many of them brought to Washington by Felix Frankfurter): the lawyers Corcoran, Cohen, Landis, Douglas, Arnold, and the economists Henderson, Currie, and Lubin. It culminated in the appointment in 1938 of the Temporary National Economic Committee, whose conclusions are embodied in the TNEC monographs of 1940–41.

Roosevelt's terms of reference for the TNEC showed the great change from the days of the NRA. The NRA, he had said in 1933, "represents a supreme effort to stabilize for all time the many factors which make for the prosperity of the nation." But in 1938 he denounced interlocking financial controls for having taken away from American business "much of its traditional virility, independence, adaptability and daring." The basic TNEC thesis was "not that the system of free private enterprise for profit had failed in this generation, but that it has not been tried." The new effort aimed, not at stability, but at giving business incentives to take risks, expand production, and assume the main burden of maintaining the rate of real investment, all within an economy bounded by social security and by guaranteed rights for labor.

Achievements of the New Deal   By the time the TNEC conclusions were fully formulated, however, Roosevelt's attention had turned to a new and more urgent problem—the problem of the Axis war. For the rest of his life questions of strategy and diplomacy absorbed his attention; and, lacking his direct leadership, the New Deal itself transformed its character. All domestic issues were inevitably subordinated to the single goal of increasing war production. Toward the end, Roosevelt turned briefly to the domestic scene and indicated the directions in which he thought the New Deal should expand: government-guaranteed full employment, public housing, health insurance, enlarged social-security coverage, valley development, and a renewed anti-monopoly drive.

The New Deal had performed its necessary tasks well. It kept vital options open in American life. It faced up to an economic crisis that was widening rapidly into a moral and spiritual crisis, and it brought the country through, morally renewed and economically on a far sounder basis. Its ac-

complishments are so much a part of the landscape today that
the twenties have acquired in retrospect the character of
fantasy. Perhaps the best evidence of the extent to which the
New Deal reshaped American ideas about society is to be
found in the evolution of Republican platforms from 1932 to
1948. Perhaps the best evidence of the extent to which it
healed the depression failure of nerve is to be found in the
swift recuperation of the stricken American productive machine: a net national income which had fallen below 40 billion dollars in 1933 reached 74 billion in 1937 and 203 billion
in 1947.

The immense expansion in productivity was accompanied
by a far more equitable distribution of the national income,
though marred by maldistribution induced by unemployment. An increasingly progressive tax structure served national economic policy by putting money into the hands of
those who would spend it. The social-security system, and
minimum-wage laws, the federal expenditures for welfare and
relief, in addition to their obvious social functions, assisted the
necessary economic task of maintaining purchasing power.
Through the Wagner Act and related policies, moreover, the
New Deal gave the labor movement power to fight for an increasing share in the national income.

The implications of the New Deal for the structure of the
American economy are less clear cut. "The power of a few to
manage the economic life of the nation," Roosevelt said in his
instructions to the TNEC, "must be diffused among the many
or be transferred to the public and its democratically responsible government." But the TNEC solution of anti-
monopolism combined with social security and compensatory
spending is not so simple as it sounds. The record certainly
shows that existing anti-trust laws are inadequate to cope with
the growing concentration of economic power; and, even if
someone could devise an effective anti-monopoly program,
the formula of free competition among small units in a social-
security state would not by itself produce prosperity. The New
Dealers made no fundamental attempt to grapple with the
problem of the economies of concentration or of the decline in
outlets for real investment.

The fact is that public spending, to be effective, will require a volume of capital formation which will rapidly bring government into new areas of economic activity. The question of the type of government activity then becomes acute. The European experience has corroded our faith (if, as followers of Jefferson, we ever had any) in the virtues of total state ownership; but the New Deal contribution to the exploration of other possibilities has been limited. In this light the TVA may be in the long run its most fruitful innovation. As a form of public ownership which does not conduce to economic or political centralization, the TVA provides a model to which officials seeking investment outlets for government funds will pay close attention. The U. S. A. is a vast country, and expenditures in valley development, public power, and conservation of natural resources can go far without having any effect on private capitalism except to invigorate it. There are other such non-competitive outlets. Even Senator Taft has admitted that the free-enterprise system cannot provide adequate housing. The expansion of the social-security system, federal aid to education and for health, effective anti-inflation measures, and, above all, federal aid overseas under the European Recovery Program and its extension—all these provide means of keeping up demand which poach negligibly on the area of private enterprise.

Liberals must face the problem, however, that in another depression these outlets for government investment will not be enough. Can we then discover means of public spending which will not tend toward the establishment of oppressive public institutions or which will not rigidify and choke up the economy? Experience would suggest that we can go further than we have yet gone before the extension of government will mean the loss of essential liberties. The next generation will surely do a good deal of thinking about the problem of nationalizing basic industries—perhaps employing the device of the independent public corporation under a system of decentralization which would affect market incentives as little as possible. The experiments of Western Europe in democratic socialism may throw important light on the extent to which political freedom and state economic planning are compatible.

The great achievement of the New Deal was to introduce the United States to the twentieth century. Roosevelt redressed the defects of the Jeffersonian tradition by equipping the liberal party with a philosophy of government intervention—a belief, as he put it, that "the government has the definite duty to use all its power and resources to meet new social problems with new social controls." Much of the New Deal was imperfect, abortive, or ambiguous. Roosevelt's own administrative methods were insouciant, disorderly, and often demoralizing. But the shortcomings of the New Deal vanish in the general perspective of its supreme success: that is, in the restoration of America as a fighting faith, and in the restoration of democracy as a workable way of life.

The New Deal took a broken and despairing land and gave it new confidence in itself. Not perhaps new confidence; but rather a revival of the ancient faith in the free people which, speaking through Jefferson and Jackson and Lincoln, has been our great source of national strength. Roosevelt had a vision of democratic America and the strength to realize a good part of that vision. All his solutions were incomplete. But then all great problems are insoluble. The New Deal left us the fighting spirit and the broad democratic faith in which we may strive to advance the solutions a few steps further.

CHAPTER VI

Deficiencies of Past Programs and Nature of New Needs*

by Leon H. Keyserling

Appraising the Immediate Future   If a group of economists and other observers of current affairs gathered to appraise America's economic future, opinions would be about as follows: Some of the group would regard a recession as inevitable in less than a year; others would believe that it still might be averted by prompt action. (The average definition of a recession would be a drop in production ranging from 5 to 10 per cent and unemployment running up toward five to six million.)

A majority would agree that, if a recession should come, it

* This essay reflects some revision of a 1947 article first printed in the *New York Times Magazine*. In view of the author's official position (Vice Chairman, Council of Economic Advisers), it should be understood that the inclusion of this essay does not necessarily involve classification within any "school of thought" or endorsement of any "general theme" or "purpose" which this collection may be deemed by some to represent. The essay reflects only the author's personal views and he would permit its inclusion in any collection of essays by experts dealing dispassionately with problems of the American economy, no matter how varied their economic or political viewpoints might be or how divergent from his own.

The fact that about half of the other contributors previously held government posts has led the author to feel that someone now in the government service should join in their symposium. Too much of the spirit of the "ins" versus the "outs" is in the air. The country needs a joinder of efforts among all who may add to our common store of knowledge or opinion bearing upon the national and world economic problems we all face.

would be shorter and milder than the one which started in the second year after World War I and that there would then be a few years of high prosperity. Most significant, a large majority would think this: Unless substantial changes in popular attitudes and economic practices occur, the new prosperity era will be followed within three to ten years by a depression which might be as much larger than the one commencing in 1929 as the second World War was larger than the first.

This concern about a major depression in the fifties does not spring from unwarranted pessimism or from a superstitious belief that history must repeat itself. It has a more solid basis. While all economists do not agree as to all the causes of the last depression, a listing of the causal factors generally agreed upon indicates that many of these factors are again present now or will be present within a few years.

Some of these are the tendency of our productive capacity to outrun our mass buying power, the chronic weakness of such bellwether industries as residential construction, the seeming reluctance of capital investment to expand as dynamically as it once did, the uncertain elements in foreign trade, the enormous disparities in the price-and-wage structure, and huge differentials in the enjoyment of national income whether measured by regions or by individuals. Above all, the country as a whole has not yet adopted and put into action a fully rounded anti-depression program.

The majority opinion that this depression threat is several years off rather than imminent rests largely upon the backlog of demand resulting from the war. This pent-up demand is regarded as sufficiently powerful to forestall a depression for some years. But it may not be powerful enough to avert a recession in the shorter run, for the war boom and the postwar restocking boom have resulted in many maladjustments, the most serious being price inflation. Yet even the recession which may be just around the corner can be avoided or reduced to minimum proportions if remedial action is taken in time.

A short-range program to avert this recession was contained in the eight points which President Truman submitted to the

Congress at the opening of the Special Session on July 27, 1948.[1] At that time the President said:

> First, I recommend that an excess profits tax be re-established in order to provide a Treasury surplus and provide a brake on inflation.
>
> Second, I recommend that consumer credit controls be restored in order to hold down inflationary credit.
>
> Third, I recommend that the Federal Reserve Board be given greater authority to regulate inflationary bank credit.
>
> Fourth, I recommend that authority be granted to regulate speculation on the commodity exchanges.
>
> Fifth, I recommend that authority be granted for allocation and inventory control of scarce commodities which basically affect essential industrial production or the cost of living.
>
> Sixth, I recommend that rent controls be strengthened, and that adequate appropriations be provided for enforcement, in order to prevent further unwarranted rent increases.
>
> Seventh, I recommend that standby authority be granted to ration those few products in short supply which vitally affect the health and welfare of our people. . . .
>
> Eighth, I recommend that price control be authorized for scarce commodities which basically affect essential industrial production or the cost of living. . . . The Government should have the authority . . . to limit wage adjustments which would force a break in the price ceiling, except [those] essential to remedy hardship, to correct inequities, or to prevent an actual lowering of living standards.

Whether or not these immediate anti-recession efforts receive the co-operation necessary for their complete success, the current situation provides us with a laboratory in which we may learn a lot about preventing the depression which looms a few years off.

America has the power and the time to prevent another 1929 or worse. This preventive effort, however, cannot begin with prescriptions. It must begin with wider popular agreements on general principles, for only on the firm foundation of common consents can we proceed harmoniously and

[1] Cf. the President's similar Recommendations of November 17, 1947.

swiftly to the development of specific measures. What broad principles, then, can we now evolve from experience? In what direction should this experience propel us to act?

Lessons of 1929 Future historians alone will be able to measure the full costs of the depression which started in 1929. Even they may fail to allow adequately for the happier course world events might have taken if America had remained prosperous throughout the third decade of this century.

But we can make some evaluation even now. Over the ten-year period beginning with 1930 our national income fell far short of what it would have been if prosperity had been maintained; the amount exceeded 300 billion dollars (adjusted)—approximately the dollar cost to us of the recent war. This takes no account of the lingering effects of human deprivation and social discontent.

Another major depression could mean a drop of nearly 100 billion dollars in our annual national income, and unemployment which could possibly reach 20 million. And just as the last depression here impeded world revival and thus paved the way for war-makers, another American economic collapse would undermine world reconstruction and thus blast away the foundations of enduring peace.

But while the record of the last depression alerts us to the danger, it does not provide us with a complete remedy. The most significant lesson we can learn from the past is that we have not yet learned enough. Without underestimating the far-reaching social legislation (for example, old age insurance) and permanent economic programs (for example, securities regulation) that were initiated during the thirties, we must recognize that the recovery, strictly speaking, was not complete until the advent of the defense program in 1939–40. In fact, by the middle of 1937, we were again on the economic down grade for a spell.

True, there are some who maintain that the imperfections in the recovery program were mainly quantitative. They say, for example, that the public-works program did not succeed fully because it was too small and too slow and because it was tapered off too sharply after 1936. But it seems far more likely that the insufficiencies in our former approaches have been qualitative as well as quantitative.

The first of these insufficiencies arose from circumstances beyond the control of those making the effort. They were empowered to act only after the depression was upon us in full force. They checked the economic fire, but they did not put it out entirely. Nor did they develop an apparatus which can be used without modification in the future. It is hard to build an adequate fire-prevention system in the middle of a big fire.

Another insufficiency in our previous efforts cannot be extenuated so easily. Too much trust was put in the idea that direct government programs can be used to enlarge employment regardless of their effect upon the whole business system. To illustrate: The employment of three million people on public works does not necessarily add three million to the net number of employed. It may add four million if its indirect consequence is to stimulate private employment by one million; or it may add only two million if its indirect consequence is to retard private employment by one million. When such hypodermics are given, the most important thing to watch is their effect upon the whole economy—in the long as well as in the short run.

The most serious insufficiency in our previous anti-depression efforts, however, was that they did not place enough emphasis upon restoring balance within the enterprise system itself. It is easy to illustrate this in terms of a more recent situation. In 1947, our gross national product was 232 billion dollars. Of this, personal consumption expenditures amounted to about 165 billion dollars, gross private domestic investment to about 30 billion, net foreign investment to about 9 billion, and government purchases of goods and services to about 28 billion. Without entering into detailed description or economic analysis, it is clear from these compounds of expenditure that the price-wage-profit policies pursued within the enterprise system in peacetime must continue to exert a far larger direct impact upon the nation's economic health than any programs the government may undertake, unless the government should undertake to run practically the whole economy.

Responsible, vigorous enterprise and responsible, vigorous government are both essential to the maintenance of prosperity within the framework of our democratic freedoms, and neither can do its full share unless there is a precise delineation of the role of each and of the working relationship between the two.

The Role of Enterprise   We may begin this delineation by stating briefly, at the risk of some over-simplification, the core requirement for maintaining maximum employment, production, and prosperity. As our already fabulous capacity to produce increases, the flow of income to producers must be kept in equilibrium with the flow of income to consumers, and while certain government devices may help, prime stabilizing or unstabilizing factors are the wage-price-profit relationships in the enterprise system.

Concerning these relationships, there will never be complete agreement between management and labor. Some disagreements will continue to be settled by the relative strength of the parties. But mere tests of strength will no more add up to economic equilibrium than the impersonal competitive forces conjured up by Adam Smith. Both industrial leadership and labor leadership will be tested by their capacity for foresight, forbearance, and appreciation of the national interest, which is also their own.

Their common aim should be to answer this question: What kind of profits, prices, and wages will keep supply and demand in balance at the highest levels which our resources and individual freedoms permit? When management and labor, in conjunction, get a better answer to this question than they have at present they will both be better off than ever before. And so shall we all.

In this context, the recommendations by President Truman that selective price and other controls be invoked for a time to deal with a critical inflationary situation were not inconsistent with the President's earlier and repeated advice that labor on its own volition should be moderate in its wage demands, and that businessmen should undertake voluntarily to reduce prices where profit margins permit. Those who deprecate or sneer at the value of "a moral suasion campaign" would seem either to be maintaining that the government should show no leadership or even concern about the national economy, or to be maintaining that the over-all compulsory regulation of prices and wages in peacetime on a permanent basis represents the blend of private and public action best suited to our American traditions and needs.

President Truman's approach has been in accord with the evolution of American experience. But while this experience shows the need for a wise admixture of private and public action, it has not yet forged all of the instrumentalities required for the blend. Only strong action, comprehending the needs of the whole economy and sensitively adjusted to these needs, can stabilize a system as complex and interdependent as ours. The economic system, like nature, abhors a vacuum; and if the price-wage-profit relationship is not to be fixed permanently by government fiat, this question thrusts itself inescapably forward: What other devices within the enterprise system itself will accomplish workable results? This requires a fresh look at the whole problem of business size and practices.

While we should work steadfastly to keep the doors of opportunity open to small, individualistic enterprise and to prosecute monopolistic misdoing, we cannot re-create the pre-Civil War pattern or achieve economic stability by applying standards of size alone. Today some industries which are organized on a large, integrated basis are charging prices under the limit of what the traffic will bear.

In contrast, the home-building function, which can hardly be called an industry at all because it is mostly in the hands of very small operators, has been notoriously inefficient, highly resistant to technological change, and periodically prices its product out of the market.[2] And one reason for the erratic price movements of farm products is the lack of organization in farming which makes a wise price policy hard to adopt even were it defined.

This suggests that the older and simpler concept of trust-busting needs to be modernized by attention to problems such as these: Where certain industries have already acquired a degree of concentration which makes monopolistic abuse pos-

[2] Cf. Chapter 14, pp. 185–189.

sible, how can this concentrated power be used to stabilize rather than to exploit the economy? [3] In those industries where competition still exists or is attainable, how can this competition serve as a stimulus to efficiency without preventing the co-ordination of effort which healthful price policies may require? Where prices of a particular item should be lowered, and no one businessman can afford to take the first step alone, how can many businessmen similarly situated take the step together? Where the retailer and the wholesaler must synchronize their price policies, how can this be accomplished? Where industrial prices, agricultural prices, and wages are interrelated, how can the businessman, the farmer, and the laborer work things out instead of calling each other names?

While both the National Recovery Administration and the Office of Price Administration had their defects, and while there is scant desire to resuscitate either in full bloom, the fact that the country turned to the first to fight deflation and to the second to fight inflation indicates that some co-ordination becomes essential when economic stability is seriously endangered. The government should not discourage such stabilizing efforts by enterprise as show fair promise of an adequate and preferable alternative to intensive government control and regulation. And avoiding the evils of the corporative state does not mean industrial self-regulation free from government vigilance in the public interest.

Similar considerations are applicable to labor organizations. The true purpose of large-scale labor organization is not to enable ever more powerful labor leaders to fight on equal terms with ever more powerful employers. Large-scale labor organization, at its best, can help to reduce the glaring disparities in the wage structure and standards of living, can aid in the development of a self-disciplined labor movement, can put a powerful shoulder to the wheel of social progress, and can join with industry and government in the formulation and application of stabilization policies on a scale large enough to be significant.

Sound competition, directed toward increased efficiency, should be encouraged. But there is also need to evolve instru-

[3] Cf., however, Chapter 8.

mentalities through which industry and labor can work together and with government to master the gigantic problems of twentieth-century industrialism instead of succumbing to them. Otherwise economic collapse could lead to super-government and not to the preservation of enterprise. The recognized primacy of government should be used not solely to prohibit bad practices but also to encourage good practices. Both price making and wage negotiation will require flexible and realistic experimentation with new modes adjusted to new needs.

The Role of Government While determination of wage-price-profit relationships should rest mainly with enterprise for the long pull, the government can help in developing some useful economic guides. It can provide nation-wide facts and analyses beyond the capacity of individual employers, trade associations, workers, or labor unions to ferret out by themselves. The government may set up forums for study and exchange of information. It may enlarge the understanding of safe and dangerous policies, and promote wider areas of agreement as bases for action.

All parties concerned are only in the initial stages of this economic fact-finding and analysis. Frequently conclusions are drawn that profits are too high because the return on net worth is greater than in 1929, or that wages are too low because since early 1946 their percentage increase has been less than that of profits, or that agricultural prices are in greatest need of reduction because they have gone up more than industrial prices. These conclusions may be true or false in whole or in part. But at best such facile comparisons with the past are inadequate. The patterns of the past may have been undesirable; presumably they could not have been entirely desirable in view of the instabilities which ensued. Moreover, a healthy level of profits or wages cannot be measured solely by national totals. It depends also and even more upon their distribution.

The moral is this: While currently available economic guides have considerable utility when not misused, there is imperative need to refine and classify these guides into more precise categories for practical application.

This entails a better portrayal of production goals and national requirements. In any given industry it is difficult to appraise appropriate profits until we know more about existing
plant capacity, measured against the capacity required for
maximum employment and output. The statement that agricultural prices are too high needs to be tested by a more discerning look at farm standards of living; coupled with a more
comprehensive analysis of the farm production necessary for
world trade, for our own industrial demands at maximum
employment, and for decent diets for every American family.
And shortages of some basic raw materials require immediate
attention.

Since the end of the war, there has been an understandable
slackening of interest in this whole matter of productive capacity, national requirements, and goals. There is need to
speed up this vital line of inquiry, not to restore the forced
drive of a war economy, but to marshal every acceptable incentive toward an economy of maximum production for
peacetime plenty.

These improved economic guides will not only help enterprise; they will also enrich the perspective of the government
in the performance of its own inescapable and in some respects
expanding functions. These functions will include a tax program which, until defense expenditures can be reduced
greatly, will draw in a minimum of more than 30 billion dollars a year in revenue; management of a national debt approximating a quarter of a trillion dollars; manifold money
and banking functions; social security, minimum wage, and
other protective or adjustment programs; the established
regulatory activities; and necessary public spending for defense and veterans, resource development and agriculture,
housing, public works, health, education, and welfare at total
levels far above the prewar rate.

The range and flexibility of these public undertakings make
them enormously powerful weapons for combating deflationary forces. They can furnish production incentives, affect
the size of the labor force, and redress imbalances in the
economy by withdrawing or adding purchasing power at
strategic spots. But the specific adjustment of all these govern-

mental programs to a consistent national economic policy and objective should not be ignored until depression appears, and then hastily attempted. As we learned from the last depression, such a course leads to inconsistency and lost motion. It will be far more profitable and less costly if these programs are constantly and temperately co-ordinated with all other efforts —especially those of enterprise—to maintain continuous prosperity. It is easier to hold fast to prosperity than to recapture it. An ounce of prevention is worth a pound of cure.

This co-ordination of all governmental programs does not imply a "regimented" economy or ever-increasing government intervention. The people who have complained most frequently about lack of consistency in government policy have been conservative businessmen and taxpayers, and harmonizing various undertakings pares down rather than increases the total size of the government structure. It weeds out duplications. It puts the spotlight on what is vital and what is superficial.

The Role of All   Transcending all these specifics, the campaign for continuous prosperity must be affirmative and aggressive. Defense will not win the war against unemployment. Economic Maginot Line strategy would have ruinous consequences. The people of America need to be electrified by our limitless possibilities, not frightened into action by prophets of disaster.

Our national income (1944 dollars) now is about two-thirds greater than it was in the last year before the war; almost three times what it was in the depression year 1932; about three-quarters greater than it was in the peak prosperity year 1929. During the war we made enormous strides in producing faster and more cheaply. If we apply these techniques, our national income can mount steadily in the years ahead. Nothing but folly can prevent us from attaining extraordinary and generally enjoyed standards of living and opportunities for self-development. There can be so much for all that the removal of unmerited poverty will remove the threat to merited wealth.

Prosperity is ours for the doing. In the light of the foregoing discussion, these five lines of activity, relevant to the current anti-recession effort but aimed mainly against the terrible threat of a major depression some time in the fifties, should be carried forward with relentless vigor and determination.

(1)   We need to set goals reflecting America's maximum productive capacity, based upon our resources and skills. We need to divide these goals into at least a few major classifications, so that production may be related to the optimum satisfaction of human needs, and so that incentives may be applied where shortcomings become apparent. These goals will provide an affirmative impulse to national effort and a frame of reference for testing the validity of specific economic policies. This is a task primarily for engineers, economists, and students of human needs.

(2)   We need to gain and apply more knowledge bearing upon the kind of income flow to producers and consumers that will stimulate and sustain this maximum production and the maximum employment that goes with it. This involves the wage-price-profit policies of enterprise. It also involves the fiscal and regulatory policies of government, for every important government program (for example, taxation, social security, rate making, tariffs, aid for education, agriculture, health, or housing) affects the flow of income to and from producers and consumers and therefore balances or unbalances the economy depending upon the wisdom of the application. This fitting of separate actions—both private and public— into the whole picture of economic equilibrium might be called the problem of maintaining maximum purchasing power. It requires still further advances in the science or art of economics, and greater acceptance of this tool by businessmen, farmers, workers, and public officials.

(3)   We need to define more clearly the respective roles of enterprise and government in maintaining maximum production, employment, and purchasing power. In order that enterprise may exert a powerful stabilizing role, our thinking about the size and practices of business and labor organizations needs to be brought into harmony with the size and complexity of the modern economy. In order that government may complement the stabilizing efforts of enterprise, we need ever increasing co-operation between the two and we need to weld all national economic policies into a consistent program.

This calls for public statesmanship and industrial statesmanship.

(4) We need to cultivate an ever growing understanding and co-operation between management and labor because their actions so largely affect the whole economy. This depends upon the leaders of both. It depends upon specific machinery for cooperation, which the government can encourage, as well as upon public good will.

(5) We need, above all, to achieve the popular agreements and consents without which there can be no effective action in a democracy. This is a challenge to all who help to mold public opinion or disseminate information through the written or spoken word. It calls for practical application of the highest gifts of political science.

These five main lines of concentration are virtually a summary of the purposes of the Employment Act of 1946. This act, approved by a majority of both parties, calls for an annual inventory of the nation's economic condition and an annual program to achieve the declared policy of continuous maximum employment, production, and purchasing power. Under the act, the Joint Congressional Committee on the Economic Report and the Council of Economic Advisers to the President have been established, and those charged with responsibility are enjoined to consult with industry, agriculture, labor, and consumers. This affords an unprecedented opportunity for the President, the Congress, and the people to participate in shaping the kind of future that we want.

But neither those "liberals" who betray nostalgia for the New Deal of the thirties which accomplished much but not nearly enough, nor those "conservatives" who would reincarnate the brutal and reckless economic philosophy of the twenties should be allowed to say the last word. Starting with a distillation of our long and varied experience, all those of good will who accept as the first tenet of their faith that political democracy and economic justice are inseparable, that economic progress and economic stability are compatible, can move forward together in the recognition that we have all registered both splendid achievements and disastrous mistakes in the past and that we all need to do a better job in a future filled with such enormous problems and with such infinite promise.

No great nation ever succumbed to the pressure of competing ideologies or forces unless it first weakened itself by self-inflicted wounds. If we make the most of our own resources and talents, we have nothing to fear in the course of world events. We hold within our hands the capacity to retain leadership in a peaceful world through the strength of our matchless native endowments.

PART THREE

Resources and Their Development

Introduction

by Seymour E. Harris

Demand and Resources   Support of demand alone will not bring nor sustain prosperity. If treatment of demand alone sufficed, then India might raise its $30 per capita income to $1,500, the United States level late in 1947. The tragedy of the thirties was that despite available resources adequate to yield a national income of 100 billion dollars, the actual income was but 60 per cent as large. Classical economics, with its excessive emphasis on the behavior of the individual entrepreneur and with its failure to deal with aggregate demand and supply helped becloud the issues.

Resource development serves as a bridge between the discussion of demand and supply. Wasteful use of resources, all too common in the American economy, ultimately will bring a reduced standard of living, a renaissance of the Malthusian difficulties, and finally strong governmental measures to assure fair distribution in malprovisioned markets. Messrs. Cooke and Nau have been primarily associated with the movement to conserve and develop our resources; and in this volume they dwell upon their special fields of interest. Garnsey adds an illuminating essay on regional development in the West. All these writers know that regional development offers a productive outlet for excess savings including government funds, and this not only helps solve the supply problem but also that of demand; and they are also cognizant of the fact that in determining how far these programs should be pushed, the government needs to take account of gains accruing gen-

97

erally to the nation, as well as the narrow gains directly to be allocated to the enterprise.

Need of a Blueprint   Information concerning our use of mines, farms, forests, and water power provides a useful background for discussion of policy. The reader will, I hope, profit more from the stimulating essays in this part for having gone over the lengthy survey contained in this introduction.

The source of much of our difficulties is the unsatisfactory time use of our resources. The cotton farmer, unmindful of the rights and interests of future generations in the use of top soil, takes what he can out of the soil and moves on. He leaves a trail of abandoned land, raped and valueless land, as he moves from Carolina to Georgia to Mississippi to Oklahoma, and finally to Texas and California. Similarly the oil man, pressed by twenty-five million automobile owners, takes the oil from the earth in a manner, however profligate, which will yield him the highest profit. He, too, is unmindful of the need of oil for his grandchildren, and indifferent to whether the cost will be twenty-five cents or twenty-five dollars a gallon; and he is not concerned that today's jaunt to Nigeria may be at the expense of tomorrow's defense of his country.

To formulate a time pattern for the use of our natural resources requires answers to some questions. How much should the present generation be asked to give up to future generations? Are we taking an undue share of lumber, oil, iron and steel, topsoil, and so forth? Are we exploiting our resources in a manner which can only be detrimental to John Jones born in 1950? Just before the war the United States, with a population of about two-thirds of the U.S.S.R., had a reserve of iron of but forty-eight tons per capita, as compared with ninety-four tons per capita for the U.S.S.R. Can we justify six million new automobiles per year under these circumstances?

Our planners should have a blueprint for 25, 50, and perhaps even 100 years. We clearly have a responsibility to plan for the next 25 or 50 years, and many would say for 100 years. We should make the best possible estimate of our resources; of the optimum allocation between alternative uses and between present and future uses. We shall indeed have to rely on guesses—informed guesses—as to population, age distribution, effects of new resources and improved technology, and the like. But an imperfect blueprint is better than none at all. In so far as this planning can cross national boundaries so much the better. If we do not want to be charged with robbing our grandchildren and great-grandchildren of their national heritage, we had better get busy.

If we cannot make headway in planning the use of today's resources, can we expect much success in planning the future allocation of resources? Our practice of allowing the individual, out for personal gain, to misuse economic resources in a manner that increases his profits but reduces the net gains for society is short-sighted and unintelligent. (The economist would say that in such instances there is net marginal *private* gain but a net marginal *social* loss.) An example of this costly planlessness is the British industrial movement from southeast to northwest and then back again to southeast. The loss in terms of additional congestion, extra cost of social services, vulnerability to attack, can scarcely be over-estimated. Today, however, there is much evidence that the British are determined to bridle the selfishness of those who act exclusively in response to opportunities for private gains.

The Malthusian specter of over-population in relation to economic resources no longer stalks us. According to the Malthusians, the *tendency* of population to grow excessively would be corrected by starvation and losses due to war. Actually, events have not borne out these gloomy forebodings: we have had both large increases in population and phenomenal gains in our standards of living. In the period from the Civil War to World War II our national income rose about 11 times; and our per capita income, about 4 times. Apparently this country had solved the problem of the relation of man to his natural resources, for this fourfold increase in per capita income took place despite considerable decline in the death rate and a very large rise in population. But we are beginning to be concerned about the depletion of resources it entailed and about the effects of continued absence of planning.

It is necessary to put a large part of the costs of planning, of discovery, and of conservation upon the government. Even when the individual farmer, for example, may profit directly from proper conservation practices, it does not follow that he will proceed in the public interest. The Department of Agriculture has observed:

> There are many who will argue, however, that when agriculture is prosperous farmers themselves should make the investment that is necessary for land maintenance and improvement, either out of their own savings or through loans for conservation. There are necessary conservation jobs on privately owned land in almost every community that farmers cannot afford to do, and should not be expected to do, because the benefits accrue primarily to the public and not to the individual. . . . The public clearly benefits from almost all conservation work, particularly as it controls erosion and prevents floods. At the same time, it is doubtful whether even owner-operated farmers are much interested in conservation farming in cases where they get no perceptible immediate increase in returns from investment in conservation.[1]

Minerals   Because of the strategic importance of minerals, the government necessarily takes large responsibilities for finding alternative sources as known supplies diminish. For example, the Strategic Materials Act of 1939 and the Stock Piling Act of 1946 put large tasks upon the Department of the Interior. "During the seven fiscal years from July, 1939 to July, 1946 more than 9,000 engineering examinations were made, about 900 development projects were conducted, many miles of trenches were dug, hundreds of thousand feet of holes were drilled, tens of thousands of samples were analyzed, and hundreds of beneficiation tests were performed." [2]

The broad objectives of the strategic and critical minerals program of the Bureau of Mines was to "improve the nation's internal position in respect to those minerals . . . essential to the common defense and the industrial needs of the United States, . . . the qualities or grades of which are inadequate from known domestic sources." [3] In 1947 the program covered

---

[1] U. S. Department of Agriculture, *Long Range Agricultural Policy and Programs* (Washington, D. C., 1947), Part IV, p. 3.

[2] *Investigation of National Resources*, Hearings before Senate Committee on Public Lands (1947), p. 38.

[3] *Ibid.*, p. 39.

about fifty metals and minerals on the strategic and critical list of the Army-Navy Munitions Board.

It is clear that Congress is not prepared to appropriate adequate sums for this important task: The estimated appropriations for 1948 are 1.6 million dollars as against minimum requirements of 5 million dollars.[4]

Many items essential both for peace and war purposes are not available in adequate amounts. Chart 2 compares the commercial reserves in proven deposits of 41 commodities in relation to annual consumption and production. During the years 1935–44 the reserves of 15 of these 41 minerals shown were adequate to meet more than 50 years' requirements at the 1935–44 rate of consumption. Included in this group are coal and iron ore and the fertilizer minerals, phosphate rock, potash, and nitrates. Reserves of magnesium derived chiefly from sea water and underground brines are virtually unlimited. Nitrogen, to be had from atmospheric nitrogen, and salt, available in undersea deposits, are also unlimited. Twenty-three of the commodities, including bauxite, zinc, copper, petroleum, lead, tin, most of the ferro-alloy minerals, and several non-metallic minerals are not available in supplies adequate to cover 25 years of consumption at current rates. According to statistics presented by the Department of Interior, virtual self-sufficiency, actual or impending, was assured for a long time for 13 minerals, complete or virtual dependence on foreign sources for 10 (including tin, chromite, quartz crystals), and partial dependence on foreign sources for 16 (including copper, iron ore, lead, mercury, zinc, tungsten, buaxite, vanadium).[5]

Shortages in petroleum and iron are especially important.[6] It is not likely that reserves of iron ore in the Great Lakes region will last more than 25 years if present rate of use, estimated on the basis of 1935–44 consumption, is continued. It will be necessary then to depend on beneficiation of low-grade ores. The rapid exhaustion of petroleum is evident in the fact that proved reserves of petroleum account for but 0.2 per cent

[4] *Ibid.*, p. 43.
[5] *Ibid.*, pp. 179–80.
[6] J. A. Krug, *National Resources and Foreign Aid* (1947), pp. 11–14.

ESTIMATED "COMMERCIAL" RESERVES AS OF 1944, IN KNOWN DEPOSITS, COMPARED WITH 1935-1944 ANNUAL RATES OF PRODUCTION AND CONSUMPTION

Figures indicate only order of magnitude of estimated reserves. They do not imply that production at rates indicated could be maintained for the full period shown. Estimates do not include allowance for future discoveries.

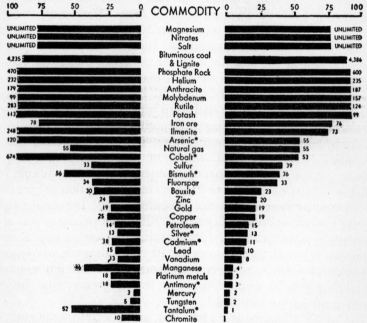

Reserves in Terms of Years of Production	COMMODITY	Reserves in Terms of Years of Consumption
UNLIMITED	Magnesium	UNLIMITED
UNLIMITED	Nitrates	UNLIMITED
UNLIMITED	Salt	UNLIMITED
4,235	Bituminous coal & Lignite	4,386
470	Phosphate Rock	600
232	Helium	235
179	Anthracite	187
99	Molybdenum	157
203	Rutile	124
113	Potash	99
78	Iron ore	76
248	Ilmenite	73
120	Arsenic*	55
55	Natural gas	55
674	Cobalt*	53
33	Sulfur	39
56	Bismuth*	36
34	Fluorspar	33
39	Bauxite	23
24	Zinc	20
19	Gold	19
25	Copper	19
14	Petroleum	15
13	Silver*	13
18	Cadmium*	11
15	Lead	10
13	Vanadium	8
48	Manganese	4
18	Platinum metals	3
18	Antimony*	3
3	Mercury	2
5	Tungsten	2
52	Tantalum*	1
10	Chromite	1

RESERVES NEGLIGIBLE—QUANTITATIVE COMPARISONS NOT SIGNIFICANT

I	Mica (strategic)	I
I	Asbestos (long-fiber)	I
I	Graphite (flake)	I
I	Nickel*	I
I	Tin	I
I	Industrial diamonds	I
I	Quartz crystal	I

*Obtained chiefly as byproducts. Output dependent on rate of production of associated metals.

SOURCE: U. S. DEPARTMENT OF INTERIOR.

CHART 2

of the estimated heat value of all fuels and yet in 1939, domestic crude oil accounted for 29.9 per cent of the sources of energy in the United States.[7]

It is not easy to estimate how long reserves will last. Reserves may be "measured," "indicated," or "inferred"; and exploitation depends on costs, prices, and changing technology. A portion of the reserves are in bodies of such size, grade, purity, and geologic and geographic distribution as to suggest exploitation in the foreseeable future—other portions are not of commercial interest at present. But with a reduction of costs or a rise in prices they may well prove to be.[8]

Adequacy   Adequacy depends upon the rate of exhaustion, economy in the use of materials, the success in finding substitutes (for example, plastics), and discovery of new resources and sources of supply (for example, nuclear power). An interesting example of economy is the saving on coal in the production of power: whereas in 1920 it required 3.39 pounds of coal to produce a kilowatt hour, in 1943 it required but 1.31 pounds. An instance of a new material is a "chemical" wood, "compreg," which gives a cheap wood the qualities of heavy, dense teakwood, comparable in strength to steel but somewhat higher in cost.[9]

In view of the large rise in output, the scarcities prevalent today are shocking: they reflect not the niggardliness of nature but the growth of the population, the demands of war, and wasteful methods of exploitation. Chart 3 presents the trend of mineral production from 1880 to 1945. From 1880, when total output amounted to 426 million dollars, there was a rise with some interruptions to 6.2 billion dollars in 1926, a decline to 2.5 billion dollars in 1932, and a rise to 8.4 billion by 1944.[10]

Table 1 summarizes the situation well.

Important shifts occurred from 1929 to 1940. Output of certain new metals and materials increased greatly, in part to replace older and bulkier metals, and in part to meet new

[7] Twentieth Century Fund, *America's Needs and Resources* (1947), pp. 588, 590.

[8] For the difficulties confronting geologists in estimating reserves, see *Investigation of National Reserves*, pp. 184–90.

[9] *America's Needs and Resources*, pp. 574–79.

[10] *Statistical Abstract* (1947), p. 730.

TRENDS IN VALUE OF MINERAL PRODUCTION IN THE UNITED STATES, 1880-1945

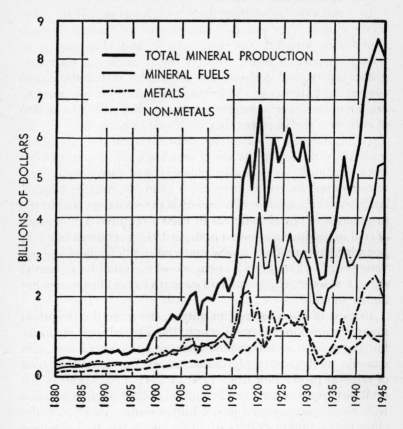

SOURCE: U. S. DEPARTMENT OF INTERIOR.

CHART 3

needs. Declines in the older items reflect depletion, shift to newer minerals, and economies in the use of older materials. Thus, from 1929 to 1940, the output of pig iron declined by 1.5 per cent, of copper by 9.2 per cent, of lead by 35.6 per cent, and of anthracite coal by 30.2 per cent. But there was a rise

TABLE 1

INDEXES OF PRODUCTION OF MINERALS, RAW MATERIALS,
LUMBER, WATER POWER, ELECTRIC POWER FOR PUBLIC
USE, AND MANUFACTURED GAS 1919, 1929, 1932, 1944

(1940 = 100)

Year	Total Minerals and Raw Materials	Refined Metals	Non-Metallic Minerals	Mineral Fuels	Non-Metallic Minerals Excluding Fuels	Lumber	Water Power	Electric Power	Manufactured Gas
1919	58.5	70.1	54.7	56.3	48.3	119.7	34.0	26.8	108.7
1929	93.8	98.8	92.1	90.3	99.3	127.7	73.6	66.1	136.3
1932	50.9	24.5	59.6	63.2	45.5	35.3	72.5	56.8	102.7
1944	130.2	145.3	125.3	130.2	105.8	112.5	152.5	159.2	120.5

SOURCE: Adapted from *America's Needs and Resources*, p. 578.

in the production of aluminum products of 81 per cent, of magnesium sold or used of 1,308 per cent, of crude petroleum of 34 per cent, of potash sold of 578 per cent.[11]

Land   In 1945, about 60 per cent of the land of the United States was in farms, but crop land harvested accounted for only a scant third of the farm land. The remaining two-thirds were about equally divided between non-plowable pasture and plowable land put to some other use or left fallow. By far the largest part of non-farm land was in forest or woodland—624 million acres, one-third of the country's total acreage.[12]

Over the last generation, the amount of land in use per farm has not varied greatly, but output rose by about 60 per cent from 1914 to 1946. Daily *per capita* food consumption seems to have fluctuated within 3 per cent of 5 pounds over the last 30 to 40 years. Indeed, eating habits have changed greatly with large per capita reductions in consumption of grains and potatoes and substantial rises in consumption of milk and cream, edible fats and oils, citrous fruits, vegetables, and sugar. Output of *total* (not per capita) grains in 1943 was at about the

[11] *America's Needs and Resources*, pp. 578–580.
[12] U. S. Census, *Land Utilization of the United States* (Washington, D. C., 1947), pp. 2–7.

1909 level; but production of fruit and nuts had increased 133 per cent, of truck crops almost 300 per cent, of meat animals almost 60 per cent, of poultry products, 116 per cent, and of dairy products, 100 per cent.[13]

Governmental guidance has been very effective in agriculture. Conservation measures in recent years contributed to an improved output; and in fact the significant rise in the years 1940 to 1946 may be associated with improved technology and greater use of machinery, development of more productive crops, adoption of improved feeding and cultivating practices, and the guidance of government. All of these, coupled with the rise of demand and prices and with favorable weather, accounted for an expansion of output reminiscent of the 1870's and 1880's, when the gains were associated with the bringing into cultivation of vast new lands.[14]

Our problem in the future is to make the most effective use of the resources now available. It will not be possible to bring into cultivation large additional amounts of land. What will be required is continued improvement in technology and culture, a still greater use of machinery, a frontal attack on erosion, and discouragement generally of wasteful exploitation of land. Indeed, it may be possible to bring into cultivation 10 million acres through irrigation, and 50 million more through drainage; but the amounts involved are small. As the Department of Agriculture says:

> Our land resources are under our feet today. That is, from now on, we must live with the resources at hand, and because we are steadily allowing our resources to wash away and overcutting our timber resources, the need for a comprehensive permanent conservation policy can no longer be ignored.[15]

The seriousness of the forestry situation is suggested by the following:

> This area of available forest-producing land in 1945 was only 56 per cent of the 820 million acres which comprised the original forested area of the United States. The area in forest at that

[13] *America's Needs and Resources*, pp. 599–602.
[14] *Land Utilization in the United States*, p. 1.
[15] *Long Range Agricultural Policy and Programs*, Part IV, p. 2.

time was tremendous in size but the forests themselves possessed many unsatisfactory characteristics compared with forests only a half century ago. Only about one-tenth, concentrated in the Western States, was old or virgin growth. About two-thirds of the area was in stocks of saw timber and pole dimensions. The remainder represented seedlings and saplings, and poorly restocking and denuded areas in about 50–50 ratio.[16]

Summary: Government and Resources In summary, future policy, discussed ably by Messrs. Cooke, Nau, and Garnsey, requires planning by government, much larger public spending to finance geological surveys, the advance of technology including new ways of economizing our resources, and conservation measures. An appropriation of one million dollars for the Department of Interior to further its efforts to provide more adequate minerals is absurd. Our industrial and military future depends on the adequacy of our mineral supply. Greater development of water power is required; at potential sites it is only about one-quarter developed. It is primarily the responsibility of government, not private enterprise, to assure the next generations adequate resources through the best use of our mines, agricultural lands and forests. An adequate job is not being done, though in agriculture there has been substantial improvement.

[16] *Land Utilization in the United States*, p. 4.

CHAPTER VII

Resources

by Morris Llewellyn Cooke

The Meaning of Resources in a Changing World   Our concept of what constitutes resources has changed markedly and constructively in recent years. When the term "natural resources" was coined it usually signified such items as captured oil, or coal and minerals in place in the earth, or other exhaustible assets. The ownership of such things in the early days spelled fairly quick and easy wealth and usually constituted a social passport. The seemingly inexhaustible store of natural resources within the nation excited both the energy and cupidity of go-getters decade after decade. Establishing these claims in most cases was almost like getting something for nothing. The process was attended by all the socially baneful excitations of "loot fever" as they call it in the Navy. The idea that trees could and should be harvested like a crop had not been born. So when virgin stands of timber were taken over the practice was often to cut and slash and burn. Too frequently the appropriation of these exhaustible and usually irreplaceable natural resources involved little more than the taking possession for private gain by individuals, or small groups, of something already in existence with at best only a modicum of social value added. Exploitation was easy and unopposed, for the citizens of the country, not considering the consequences, were not aroused to protest. Natural resources like the fairies "stood to reason."

But gradually through the years the concept of what the

totality of our resources really is has widened until resources have become "all those aspects or phases of man's endowment and surroundings upon which people depend for aid and support." [1] And even this definition is not broad enough because to be complete it must include people themselves—men, women, and children—the one resource of a free and developing people to which all other resources must be subordinated.

Fortunate it is that our attitude toward resources is in a continuous and an expanding process of change for the better. For one thing we no longer envision a given resource as a single asset standing by itself neither influencing the world about it nor subject to modification by its environment. Each such asset is looked upon increasingly as a strand in a seamless web of availabilities with its rating in the total scheme of national, and even international, well-being changing day by day in the light of myriad needs and influences playing upon it. It is this recognition of the ebb and flow in the intrinsic worth of the various items in our vast category of resources, running all the way from coal mines and oil wells to the school system and grand opera and even to our aggregate of moral and spiritual values, that makes the complexity of the modern world and is the key to progress.

When once the view is taken that the whole range of resources is a matter of general public rather than restricted private concern, money or market or exchange value must increasingly give ground to social value. Only so can the competitive initiative inherent in our free-enterprise system be supported.

Technology, born of modern science, has helped immeasurably to broaden our concept of resources. Indeed, one might almost say that technology creates resources, for what is coal if man has no means other than his hands to take it from the earth, or water power if he cannot harness it; what are acres of grain if they cannot be harvested in season, converted into food, and carried to those who need it? Nor is the end of technological advance yet in sight. It is the lever by which men can lift themselves to higher standards of living and thus,

[1] Erich W. Zimmerman, "What We Mean By Resources," in *Texas Looks Ahead* (1944).

by transcending physical urgencies—goods, clothing, shelter—
enhance the dignity and freedom of the individual.

The moment one abandons the idea of rigidity and the
status quo in this matter of resources to be liberal, to be democratic, even to be religious, one must adopt with deep conviction the idea of possible and continuous progress and with it
that never-ending adjustment of resources to need which
makes valid progress feasible.

The world becomes less static day by day and both groups
and individuals must try to adjust wisely thereto. This is a
simple idea but one on which realization of a full life for the
individual depends. Those who will serve best in this world of
flux will be as free as possible from bigotry and bias; to achieve
this freedom their minds must be open to what are sometimes painful readjustments in their thinking and acting and
circumstances. With the rise of science and global relationships, what is best for today may be very far from the best for
tomorrow, and a move which may advance the interest of
Sector A may have the opposite effect on Sector B. This involves constant re-evaluation for the individual, the group, the
community, and the nation.

The standard of living can be made within limits pretty
much what we have the will to make it. Through education,
the removal of obsolete and traditional barriers, and the doing
away with special privileges which benefit the few at the expense of more general interests, most of the indices of well-
being can not only be raised but continuously raised.

One of the most important lessons America learned through
World War II is that we do not have to wait forever to get
things done. Both in making the U. S. A. the arsenal of
democracy and in giving battle, the policy of "delay, linger,
and wait" had no place. We know now that we do not have to
drift to desirable ends. We first decide what is to be done and
then by deliberately thought-out steps we can bring it about.[2]
In all this the will of individuals, groups, and of the nation as a
whole played a determining part. When the vitality of a people
means so much it too must be listed among major resources.

[2] Bowles develops this point further, Chapter 2.

In nation building, as in character building for the individual, warfare against inertia is strategically important.

To advocate the withholding of loans or even gifts to nations devastated by war on the ground that we will be gearing their people to a scale of living that cannot be maintained is a self-defeating type of internationalism and shows a woeful lack of understanding of what modern science makes possible. It is even possible that countries relatively poor in irreplaceable "natural resources," oil and metals for instance, by a dynamic use of recent scientific developments such as synthetics, plastics, and cheap power and by co-ordinated planning may build a type of life not found in some countries abounding in natural resources but lacking the zest for a constantly bettered life for all the people. Resource building is not always dependent on money expenditures. The finances of Mexico at the moment do not permit the employment of teachers needed for a wide attack on illiteracy, so under legal compulsion those who can read and write are required to teach those who cannot—or hire someone to do it for them.

The attitude toward resources here advocated reflects the relative uselessness of painstaking lists of "natural resources." Even inventories by quantity and quality lose much of their value except for war and other short-term purposes and then only for items that are actually or potentially scarce. Such scheduling of "natural resources" in the past has seemed to blind us to the vast storehouse of other resources ready at hand. We Americans, individually and collectively, have benefitted so greatly by the accident of taking over a continent with all its natural assets intact that today we still suffer from an easily understood tendency to keep up predatory practices which in the light of modern scientific developments are out of date and usually quite unnecessary.

Soil and Water   Having recognized man himself as in the topmost bracket in our listing of resources let us turn next to two complementary resources—soil and water. It has not yet been proven that civilization permits the continued fertility of our soils. Evidence to date in all areas, and tragically exemplified in the Near East, in China, and over vast regions in Africa, would suggest a negative answer. Here again modern science affords the basis at least for an enlarging hope. We have learned more about the details of soil science in the last fifty years than in the previous millenniums of human history. But with the world's population more than four times today what it was 300 years ago [3] and the rate of population increase growing all the while, it is obvious that the tax on our soils is increasing. In this matter of soils we in the United States are in a quite favorable situation but only in comparison with other continental areas. In spite of much progress made in recent years in soil-erosion control the United States is still slipping; our soil situation is constantly being worsened. Unless we devote increasing thought to this area of supreme national interest nomadism for a once great people will be history's verdict.

Bearing on this tragic situation, one of the most important scientific conclusions of recent years has to do with the intimate and quite complex relationship between the control and conservation of soils and the control and conservation of water. Until recently the engineering attitude toward water was to get rid of it in the shortest possible time. Through cemented culverts and roadside ditches—six million miles of the latter—we had no other thought but to hasten the water to the sea. But the fall of the water table involving the catastrophic lessening of our underground water storage over a large part of the country indicated that something was wrong. This, together with the discovery of the interdependence of soil and water, has suggested that we take a new attitude toward water—hold the raindrop where it falls, allow it to sink in and in doing so have its impact with the ground such as to maintain the soil and its fertility.

Here as elsewhere the important development is the recognition of a problem or, as is usually the case, of an expanding series of problems. W. D. Ellison's fascinating investigation by highly scientific methods of splash erosion by raindrops, and various other inquiries attacking the problem each from a

[3] See "The Land and the People" by Walter C. Lowdermilk in *The Nation* (October 4, 1947). The population of the world in 1650 was 545 million. In 1945 it was 2.25 billion.

different angle represent an inspiring advance over our knowledge as it was in 1908 when at the White House Conservation Conference the official representative of the Department of Agriculture referred to our soils as imperishable and eternal.

The creation within the last ten years of nearly 2,000 wholly independent soil-conservation districts, each free in its own way to make use of newly discovered soil-conserving practices, areas which taken together cover one-half of the total area of the United States, must be considered an important step ahead in nation building. This is the most notable instance under our government where all the people of an area are banded together under state law specifically, and under their own initiative, to apply the best that is known about safeguarding a priceless national resource and in so doing advance their own interests. The Rural Electrification Administration cooperatives, without being so distinctly an arm of government, follow much the same democratic model by studying on their own the application of electricity to agriculture. We have education aplenty from the top and even assuming that it reaches the nooks and crannies—which it rarely does—unfortunately only a small percentage of it sticks. To have the rank and file organized in neighborly groups to assume responsibility to work out and apply specific disciplines certainly fits Woodrow Wilson's thought:

> When I look back on the processes of history, when I survey the genesis of America, I see this written on every page: that the nations are renewed from the bottom, not from the top; that the genius that springs up from the ranks of unknown men is the genius which renews the growth and energy of the people. Everything I know about history, every bit of experience and observation that has contributed to my thought has confirmed me in the conviction that the real wisdom of human life is compounded out of the experience of ordinary men. The utility, the vitality, the fruitage of life does not come from the top to the bottom; it comes like the natural growth of a great tree, from the soil, up through the trunk into the branches to the foliage and the fruit. The great struggling unknown masses of the men who are the base of everything are the dynamic force that

is lifting the levels of society. A nation is as great and only as great, as her rank and file.

With soil and water under increasingly beneficial control, a real start can be made on a scientifically directed agriculture, recognized as a resource since time immemorial. Research is developing new types of plowing, novel designs for simple and multi-purpose machines, widely varying mulches designed to meet specific needs, constantly improved cover crops and seed varieties, new fertilizers and test controls, and nitrogenous and phosphatic additions to the soil as aids to its maintenance, to the preservation of its fertility, and to the more efficient production of food. Except in the field of atomic fission one might have difficulty in locating an area where science, invention, and technology are so radically remoulding an age-old resource so that it can better serve man and, through our concern for his well-being, the ends of democracy. Possibly nowhere else is dynamic change affecting the lives of so many people as in agriculture. And the end is not yet!

Industrialization—a Necessity? The idea is very rapidly gaining ground that a high standard of living cannot be supported by agriculture in the absence of some measure of industrialization. In fact the figures indicate that the higher the percentage of the population engaged in industry the higher will be the per capita income. For instance in the United States where practically four out of five are in industry and other non-agricultural pursuits the average annual income is over $1,500, while in China where 80 per cent of the population are agricultural workers the per capita annual income is not much over $20.[4] These international comparisons have significance within each nation. There are areas within the United States—the Southeast and the Far West for instance—where industrial development is needed not only to stimulate agriculture but to utilize their other resources.

Of course energy is a resource absolutely essential to industrial development and for this reason the possession of energy resources has become a master index to national and regional self-sufficiency. The United States through its vast

[4] See Morris L. Cooke, "Some Observations on World Industrialization," *Mechanical Engineering* (May 1946).

coal deposits and to a lesser degree through its actual and potential water power is very advantageously situated. Here again it is not so much a question of possessing resources as of developing them and then learning to use them most advantageously. Applied to energy this always means low consumer rates with wide distribution.

The delegation of authority to a single agency charged with responsibility for widely varying but interrelated resource development on a water-shed basis, so splendidly exemplified by the Tennessee Valley Authority, is a unique method of achieving maximum resource use and has attracted worldwide interest and study. Even more important, it has enlisted the support of the people of the area. Such measures do make it possible to break down the responsibilities of government into territorial units of workable size. But it is the intimate and on-the-ground approach to interrelated resource values, both natural and human, which makes TVA tick. Natural resources have there begun to come to life and to glow in the fire of intensified human interest as they never can under colonial types of administration. A closeness of view points the way to both the administrator and the people of the region for the creation of new, vital, and integrated resource utilization. Even a partial list of TVA's accomplishments to date makes it appear that mere humans—Norris, Roosevelt, Lilienthal, and a long list of their associates—must have had access to some titanic Aladdin's lamp which yielded miscellaneous and important resource values for the rubbing.

One key to all this, of course, is plentiful and low-cost energy, and this is recovered through impounding the flowing waters of the main stream and its tributaries which otherwise would continue their age-old and useless, and in flood times their devastating, path to the sea. Many-sided research plus electrical energy has given rise to new industries and industrial aids to interests already established both in industry and agriculture. TVA has given birth to numerous gadgets, such as the barn hay dryer [5] which is now a best seller wherever men grow alfalfa or other varieties of hay. But under

[5] *Barn Hay Drier: Principles of Design, Installation, and Operation.* Agricultural Engineering Publication No. 6., Tennessee Valley Authority (1945).

honest and efficient administration, standing free from baneful political influences, and through close association with the desires and ambitions of the people of the region, TVA has laid the foundation for a type of life in the Tennessee Valley to be enjoyed by all the people—a type of life not built wholly with bricks and stones and not wholly directed toward the values of the market place.

More and more our people, including the business community, are realizing that our princely equipment of physical and financial resources does not answer many problems pressing for solution, such as "scarcity in the midst of plenty," the parlous situation of minorities, and the degradation of much of our political life. That the great majority of our people lead simple lives does not prevent them from dreaming of a nation well housed, well clothed, and well fed, and with access to adequate medical care for everybody. The conviction grows that through adequately financed and otherwise promoted science—both physical and social—the way must be cleared and is actually in process of being cleared for a new birth in freedom. This may be called the doctrine of acquired resources. Here a resolute people taps a storehouse without limitations.

CHAPTER VIII

Electric Power

by Carlton L. Nau

An abundance of low-cost electric power is crucially important in our economic and industrial life. It is a starting point for the full production so essential to domestic stability. It is basic to our great mass-production enterprises which will enable us to supply the world's tremendous needs for manufactured goods. The maintenance of a broad energy base as the support for international trade will advance the cause of peace.

To point up our problem, in 1850, usable goods valued at 23 cents were produced by the average worker each hour, with the average amount of draft-animal and machine assistance available in that day. Of the total physical energy expended to produce that 23 cents worth of wealth, the animal's share was 79 per cent and the machine's share was only 6 per cent.

Today that same combination of man plus animal plus machine produces per hour goods with a value of $1.36—more than five times as much as in 1850—but man's physical share in this production has shrunk from 15 per cent to only 3 per cent. The draft animal's share has dwindled from 79 per cent to 1 per cent, and the machine's share has increased from 6 per cent to 96 per cent.[1]

Or, to summarize the matter more succinctly, prosperity depends on increasing productivity per man hour. Produc-

[1] *America's Needs and Resources*, Twentieth Century Fund Survey, as excerpted by *Life* (May 12, 1946).

tivity is increasingly dependent upon the machine. And the machine, as we all know, is dependent upon energy. Unhampered development of the nation's power resources becomes then a goal for all progressive Americans.

Our discussion falls naturally into three principal categories: (1) Constructive work yet to be done. (2) The framework by which we can achieve these ends. (3) What policies will assure full benefits to the people?

Work To Be Done   Only one river valley—the Tennessee—has been fully developed, co-ordinating power production, flood control, navigation, soil conservation, etc. Here the interdependence of these functions is recognized in actual operation. Control of water begins when the first drop hits the ground back in the hills.

Results are self-evident. Twenty-six major dams control the waters of the region's rivers. A 650-mile navigation channel carried more than 260 million ton miles in 1947. Installed generating capacity exceeds 2.5 million kilowatts, which produced over 15 billion kilowatt hours of electricity in 1947.

Other valleys stand waiting, nature's challenge to man's ingenuity and capacity to co-operate. The mighty Columbia in the Pacific Northwest, snow-fed in summer and surging with winter rains, is potentially capable of producing 40 per cent of the nation's potential hydro-electric power. Only a start has been made, with two major dams in production—Bonneville and Grand Coulee. Foster Creek and McNary dams are under construction. Differences between the people of the region and the government over methods for development have been delaying factors. About 1.5 million acres of fertile land in Central Washington will be put under agriculture with water from the Coulee. The importance of hydro-electric power to this area comes into focus when we realize it has no coal, oil, or gas. Falling water is its only source of energy.

That the Missouri Valley should be developed with public funds has already been decided. Various multi-purpose projects have been built or are under construction as a joint undertaking of the Bureau of Reclamation and the Army engineers. Recurring floods, with staggering property losses and soil erosion, must be stopped. A substantial segment of public opinion—in the valley and in the nation holds that the TVA administrative pattern will work best there. Although defeated in the Senate in 1948, the St. Lawrence Seaway and Power Project may be approved eventually as necessary to our national defense and as a self-liquidating undertaking. The New England area has steadily been losing population and industries to other regions. As a section, it has extensive undeveloped hydro-electric resources and the highest power rates in the nation, a strange situation in the territory which gave birth to American Industry.[2]

Following World War II, the Secretary of War called New England a "power deficit area," pointing out that the St. Lawrence represents "a large source of cheap dependable power which can be generated without the use of coal or other critical combustibles and without use of crowded rail or highway transportation facilities." [3]

Some progress has been made towards harnessing the Colorado, the Arkansas, the White, and other lesser rivers. In the West, water for industrial, municipal, and farming purposes overshadows power generation, but future western growth will be in direct proportion to electric-power development. In the Southeast, extensive water-power developments are feasible, rivaling those in the Tennessee Valley.

Power is more than a commodity or service. It is a tool for community development and industrial progress. It is a creator of wealth, of new business, of new income. The Bonneville Power Administration has established the fact that contributions in taxes on new private investments equal the 280 million dollars already invested in the Columbia River. These returns can be traced directly or indirectly to Columbia River power.

The co-operative method for bringing electric power to America's farms has proven itself beyond all doubt. Lines financed by REA have increased the number of consumers indirectly as well as directly; their competitive pressure has resulted in more liberal line-extension programs by private

[2] Typical Bills Report of the Federal Power Commission (1946).
[3] Letter to Congress dated February 16, 1946.

companies. With about 35 per cent of our farms still unserved, much work remains to be done in this direction.

Framework for Development   In a modern state, technological advances are far ahead of man's capacity to administer and control for social and economic progress. This is true of electric power. It is only within the last several decades that we have begun to sense the stimulating effect of vast quantities of cheap power on the establishment and growth of private industry. The social and economic problems of over-centralization of industry can be avoided by the decentralizing process, already in operation, aided and abetted by electrical energy. New chemical and metallurgical plants, some stemming from research conducted by power suppliers, have opened new horizons. Thus how we go about our job—the administrative techniques to be applied—offers wide opportunities for initiative and the best of scientific management practices.

The Tennessee Valley Authority has clearly demonstrated what George Norris, that great liberal intended it should. It possesses the authority of a government corporation for developing the resources of a region, subject to Congressional direction but retaining the flexibility of private enterprise and freedom from political interference. The governors of the seven valley states have signed a joint statement attesting to the success of TVA and refuting assertions that the sovereignty of their states has in any way been abridged.

One way to strengthen TVA might be to select the board of directors from representatives of the power distributors, from whom TVA gets the bulk of its revenue. This would increase local authority and responsibility.

The writer is a strong believer in local autonomy. Our power resources should be developed as close to the people as possible. For fifteen years following 1920, the private utility industry demonstrated the evils and weaknesses of absentee ownership and management. Where conditions permit, and local authority is willing and able to do the job, it should have that opportunity. Similarly, it should be allowed to acquire and operate existing projects. Where the size or scope of the program precludes local management, either by a city, power district, or state agency, the next most desirable method is the government corporation, raising its capital by the issuance of revenue bonds rather than depending upon Congressional appropriations, which may fluctuate rather widely and make budgeting an impossibility.

By way of example, power facilities in Nebraska today are completely under public operation, either by state agency, power district, municipality, or rural co-operative. The security which these projects enjoy may be contrasted with the annual uncertainties faced by others.

The proprietary phase of the federal power program is handled principally by the Department of the Interior, through the Bureau of Reclamation. Outside of the eleven western states under the jurisdiction of the Bureau, the Army engineers of the War Department have constructed quite a few dams where hydro-electric energy is produced. Power, however, is marketed by the Interior Department. This pattern developed because power is a natural by-product of dams for flood control, navigation, and irrigation. Administration of these programs as an executive function of the federal government will continue for some time yet, adjusted and decentralized, however, to meet pressure caused by demand for local control. It is not inconceivable that ultimately they may by law become a part of a regional or state development.

Municipally owned systems are the oldest form of public power systems, having originated in 1882, the same year that two private power systems were established. By 1900, there were 732 municipally owned properties.[4] These were highly successful operations before the federal government ever undertook to produce power. For example, the Lansing, Michigan, project was established in 1892; that of Austin, Texas in 1895; of Tacoma, Washington in 1893; and of Columbus, Ohio in 1899.

Over 900 operating electric co-operatives serving about 1.6 million rural families are today firmly established as locally owned enterprises. When the Rural Electrification Administration began, in 1935, to serve a need largely disregarded by

[4] U. S. Department of Commerce, *Special Census Report on Central Electric Light and Power Stations* (Washington, D. C., 1902).

profit power systems, some 10 per cent of the farms had the benefits of electricity. This is the world's most highly industrialized nation. Ninety per cent of our farm homes were lighted by flickering oil lamps, which had experienced one major improvement since the days of the Roman Empire— the addition of a glass bowl. And water was brought by hand from a well in the yard.

Power on the farm is a producer, not a luxury. It means less muscle, more machine; less drudgery, more leisure; better health and higher incomes. Electric co-operatives have demonstrated their value. They have tremendous popular appeal and the strongest bi-partisan support of any federal power activity. Completely self-liquidating, they should have the backing of all liberals until every farmer who wants it has service.

Policies to Achieve Fullest Benefits   Now that we have discussed the job to be done and the framework for action, let us examine the policies which should be applied in order to assure the greatest good for the greatest number.

Progressives agree that water and power resources should be developed to the full. Failure to do so because of controversies over method, current high price of materials, or so-called economy measures would be a serious long-range error. Power from falling water saves our irreplaceable stocks of oil, coal, and gas. Hydro-electric plants require less manpower, an important consideration in times of emergency. Transportation facilities are not needed to move fuel. Our experience in World War II showed how difficult it is quickly to expand generating capacity.

Our two atomic energy plants were located on the lines of the Tennessee Valley Authority and the Bonneville Power Administration. This decision was not political. They were the only two spots in the nation where power was adequate in amount and dependability. How might the atom bomb have fared if private utilities had been successful in preventing the establishment of these two power projects?

Most of us agree that the federal government should limit itself to generation and transmission. Distribution is properly within the province of local bodies. Where states or public authorities prefer to handle transmission, they should do so. With this one exception, at no time should the ability to transport energy from the dam site to the load center be restricted. Following World War I, private companies sought to contract for all energy which might be produced at Wilson Dam on the Tennessee River. The plan was to purchase it at three mills and sell it for about 10 cents per kilowatt hour. This proposal was defeated. Instead, a policy was followed which assured public transmission and gave preference in the sale of power to cities, co-operatives, and public groups. To sell all energy at wholesale at the dam means that the company and its stockholders reap the benefits of cheap production costs.

Many of the West's most feasible multi-purpose projects have already been built or are now under construction by the Bureau of Reclamation. Those undertaken in the future should be examined carefully to assure that they are economically sound. None should be built solely for the purpose of perpetuating this function. As the margin of feasibility decreases, power will be asked to bear so much of the costs which the irrigators cannot carry that the original purposes may be defeated. Related benefits such as fish and wild-life control, navigation, flood control, soil conservation, silt and salinity control should not be charged to water and power users. If as a matter of policy, it is decided to subsidize irrigation features, the subsidy should be provided for by direct legislation, and interest payments from power users should not be diverted for these purposes. Interest rates ought to remain as low as possible and be made uniform on all projects. Unnecessarily long amortization periods should be avoided.

In some areas, the federal government has assumed responsibility as the sole supplier of electric power, to the exclusion of all others. Having done this, it must plan and build for the expanding needs of the area. In its own interests and for sound business reasons, it must provide adequately for capital requirements. Projects once begun should be finished at the earliest moment, and become revenue producing. To delay or reduce appropriations makes final costs higher, and may eventually defeat the original purposes approved by Congress.

There are several thousand municipal power systems, most of which are in smaller cities and towns. The Los Angeles system is the largest, grossing almost 50 million dollars annually. The long record of successful operation of these undertakings proves there is no monopoly of good management. Cities can and do provide this essential service directly, rather than farm it out, via a franchise, to a private company. They can employ skilled talent and managerial abilities as readily as any private organization. Furthermore, the city gains in several direct ways such as:

(1)   Electric service can be geared to community economic progress and public objectives rather than principally to private profits and private advantage. Rates can be designed not to get the most money out of customers, but to advance the common interests of all groups.

(2)   Many additions to plant are financed out of earnings, and debt is retired as rapidly as possible, thus permitting a lighter burden on the consumer.

(3)   Surpluses are not siphoned off to absentee owners but accrue to the benefit of the people, through lower rates, improvements in the power system, and contributions to the general fund.

(4)   Operating expenses are lower. As in water service, gas, transportation, etc., municipal power systems are exempt from federal taxation, as instrumentalities of the state performing a governmental function.

(5)   With private financing at low interest rates, either through revenue bonds or general obligation bonds, they are not dependent on political factors in Washington, D. C., for their capital. The high standing in financial circles of municipal revenue bonds attests to the wisdom of the safeguards built around them.

Liberals everywhere should fight for the right of the people to decide these issues free from heavily financed, highly organized outside pressures. Actually, under our concept of government, this right is inalienable, but in practical application it has been circumvented and thwarted. Every franchise election puts this issue in focus. In Pennsylvania and Michigan, for example, there is no legal authority under which a city can issue revenue bonds to acquire or build an electric system. Sacramento, California, was tied up in the courts for eight years after a majority of its citizens had decided to serve themselves directly. Let us see to it that a favorable body of law is established within the framework of constitutional authority whereby the public will is not frustrated and majority rule is not just an academic theory.

Lines financed by REA should be constructed to carry heavier power loads, even though it means higher costs per mile. Low-priced energy is being used in unexpected quantities in the farm home and its applications to farming operations are reaching unprecedented proportions. More applied research is needed here. It should be conducted by REA, the agricultural and engineering colleges, and equipment manufacturers and private utilities.

Wherever it can be feasibly arranged, electric co-operatives should band together and establish control over their power source. Some 60 per cent are now dependent on wholesale contracts with private companies. As long as the antagonism between public and private power distributors exists, such an arrangement must produce insecurity. Further, the experience of the municipal distributing systems bears out the desirability of owning the power source.

Any extension of the amortization period beyond the present thirty-five years should be discouraged. Borrowers should be urged to pay off their debt and stand on their own feet. Through adequate educational programs they should be prepared to operate without government assistance at the earliest practicable date. Their problems are local and their boards of directors, composed of farm people, should assume responsibility for the business which they own.

Regulation Versus Competition Progressives interested in taking a long step forward should *insist upon* more effective regulation of the private electric utility industry but *depend upon* competition from public power to guarantee good service, low rates, and the protection of the paramount public interest. Mr. Justice Brandeis had this to say about regulation: "No system of regulation can safely be substituted for the operation of individual liberty as expressed in competition. . . . Human nature is such that monopolies, however well intentioned, and however well regulated, inevitably become, in course of time, oppressive, arbitrary, unprogressive, and inefficient." [5]

There exists ample proof of the failure of state regulation. The pyramiding of holding companies in the twenties occurred under "regulation." Millions of people lost money in stock issued under "regulation." The Federal Trade Commission investigation begun in 1928 revealed some startling practices indeed in an industry supposedly "regulated" in the public interest. The period of holding-company dominance (1921–1929) was a barren period so far as growth in average residential use was concerned; in the eight years there was an increase of only 13 kilowatt hours or less than 2 kilowatt hours per year.

In Michigan, the regulatory body had staff and funds only sufficient to analyze 7 out of 28 major companies in order to determine what was a fair return. The remaining 21 provided the data by which they were regulated.

It was not until teeth were put in the Federal Power Act and the Securities and Exchange Commission was created that the industry was cleaned up. The FPC has squeezed out 1,237 million dollars worth of water from utility accounts, with only three cases out of 160 taken to the courts. The commission was sustained in those three cases. The SEC has insisted upon high standards of corporate finance and under the Holding Company Act has forced the dissolution of many non-integrated and unnecessary units. But the urgent need for better state regulation is apparent when it is realized that 144 electric utilities, with assets of 4.25 billion dollars, have already passed from the jurisdiction of the SEC to local regulation.

A new concept of rate making can be adopted by regulatory bodies, which would stimulate management by offering a higher return for more efficiency. The practice of basing rates on the static concept of yesterday's sales could be changed so that they would be fixed on the assumption of substantial in-

[5] Alpheus T. Mason, *Brandeis: A Free Man's Life* (New York: The Viking Press; 1946), p. 181.

creases in use each year. The net effect would be a higher per cent return on capital invested.[6]

Support from organized labor, consumer groups, and all organizations concerned with public welfare should be obtained to protect existing public power systems and prevent the adoption of laws and policies which would make a farce of the regulatory process. A people's council might be formed in each city, representing the citizens. Aspirants to office on regulatory basis should be supported or rejected on their record as defenders of the public interest. Politicians should be asked to take a stand on these issues before they are elected. Federal power projects should get ample funds to carry out the law which created them.

Electric power is not a partisan issue. Water power, developed as a by-product of multi-purpose federal projects, is government property under the federal Constitution. The Supreme Court has so held in all late decisions. The public interest in this type of property should be duly safeguarded. President Lincoln enunciated this principle in connection with the first land laws. New York's Governor Charles Evans Hughes said, in 1907, that water powers "should be preserved and held for the benefit of all the people and should not be surrendered to private interests." [7] Theodore Roosevelt restated this principle in his Rainey River Power veto message of 1908. Gifford Pinchot, one-time governor of Pennsylvania, faithfully carried on the tradition of the "conservationists."

Despite propaganda to the contrary, there is nothing alien or un-American about public power. As an inherent power of sovereignty, a state or its political subdivisions possess the right and obligation to supply its citizens with water, electricity, police protection, etc., and to perform other activities directly related to public health, safety, and welfare. In so doing, they are exercising essential governmental func-

[6] For more details on this point, see the address by Leland Olds, member of the Federal Power Commission, before the American Public Power Association, Memphis, Tenn., May 9, 1946, entitled "New Concept of Rate Making for the Electric Industry."

[7] *First Annual Message to N. Y. Legislature* (January 7, 1907).

tions, which must be performed, even at a loss, if society is to continue to function. Some have delegated these functions and this authority to a private corporation as a public trust, allowing it to earn a fair profit, exercise the power of condemnation, and enjoy a monopoly. Some have performed this governmental function directly from the beginning, as we have noted before.

To argue that the decision of the people in these matters is not in accord with true democratic principles is in itself an expression of a viewpoint we fought two great wars to wipe out.

The undercurrent of popular thought has been accurate on this issue for a generation or more. The thinking on schools, toll roads and water service, for example, began over at the right, gradually shifting to the left as it became apparent that regulation was not satisfactory in the absence of competition, and operation as a public undertaking was essential in order to protect the public interest. The trend in the field of electric power has followed this same pattern—toward more public ownership.

Atomic Energy   The Atomic Energy Act, passed in 1946, declared it to be the policy of the people of the United States that "subject at all times to the paramount objective of assuring the common defense and security, the development and utilization of atomic energy shall, so far as practicable, be directed toward improving the public welfare, increasing the standard of living, strengthening free competition in private enterprise, and promoting world peace." This program very clearly provides for public ownership and control of the production and use of fissionable material. It anticipates cooperation with private enterprise but public interest is so paramount that it cannot be left wholly to private development.

As for its use in the production of electric energy, experts predict that it may be at least ten years before we have atomic-energy power plants in operation. A pilot plant has been built at Oak Ridge, Tennessee. Others are in process of construction elsewhere. Such plants will, of necessity, have to be large and designed to serve urban areas. They will be costly to install and they require a new type of expertness to operate. The most straightforward procedure will be to use the atomic reactor to heat steam to a high temperature and then use this steam in a turbine in the conventional manner. Basing their calculations on this method, engineers consider it feasible to develop atomic power plants that will be roughly equivalent in cost of operation to a standard coal-burning plant and considerably cheaper to operate in regions where coal is scarce. This program should be supported and the rights of the public in this vast new force eternally safeguarded.

Summary   Summing up, America's liberal power program should include:

1. A continuation of multi-purpose river valley development, designed to produce as much electric power as feasible. But the important thing is to market the power in such a way that it lifts the total economy of a region, promotes higher standards of living, and encourages greater industrial development. This includes the right to build transmission lines to power markets. It also includes local autonomy in relation to the part technology may allocate to it.
2. Completion of the job of rural electrification.
3. Positive action to assure the establishment of a favorable body of law within which public power can serve.
4. Insistence upon better regulation of private companies but dependence upon competition, through yardstick plants and otherwise, for protection of the public interest.
5. If private companies fail to carry out their responsibilities as *service* organizations, the delegation of authority to them should be withdrawn and the function performed directly by the public.

CHAPTER IX

Economic Policy for the West*

by Morris E. Garnsey

The rain stops where the West begins. East of the ninety-eighth meridian the mean annual fall of rain and snow is sufficient to grow crops. "West of '98"—except in the high mountains and a narrow strip along the Pacific—annual precipitation is twenty inches or less, as compared with thirty to fifty inches to the East. Crops must be irrigated, or farmed with special dry-land techniques. Water is precious, and wherever it does not reach there is only open range or desert.

And the West is big. Nearly half of the United States lies west of the ninety-eighth meridian which runs through the middle of the Dakotas, Nebraska, and Kansas. The West looks big, too, because of its high peaks, wide sweeping valleys, and forested mountain slopes. Of these valleys a single one in Colorado is larger than Connecticut, while all of New England plus Pennsylvania and New Jersey could be slipped comfortably inside the borders of New Mexico.

The West is a complex area, divided into at least twelve distinct sub-regions in three major areas: the Great Plains, the Intermountain West embracing eight states in the Rockies, and the Pacific Coast region of California, Oregon, and Washington.

The West, so vast in area, is also vast in undeveloped re-

---

* The data upon which this essay is based will form part of a larger study of the economy of the Mountain States, upon which the author is currently engaged while holding a Guggenheim Fellowship. A grant from the University of Colorado Council on Research has further assisted the project.

sources. Agriculture is its chief source of wealth. Yet only half of its irrigable land has yet been brought under the water which is available to enrich it; and two-thirds of its water power is still unharnessed. The West produces nearly all of our copper, mercury, molybdenum, and vanadium, and more than one-fourth of our petroleum. Western Colorado provides our only domestic source of uranium. Billions of tons of phosphates and coal await chemical and engineering developments which will release chemical and oil supplies sufficient for many generations.

The Changing Position of the Western Economy Nevertheless, with such vast resources waiting to be utilized, the West is still sparsely populated. There are fourteen million people in the three Pacific Coast states, but the other eight contain only four million persons. Thus only eighteen million people, one-eighth of our total population, inhabit one-third of the entire area of the United States.

This very uneven distribution of population indicates internal basic economic divergences within the West. Hence from this point on, any generalizations about the region must distinguish between the Pacific Coast and the Mountain and Plains areas.

Recent economic changes have been quite different on the Coast than elsewhere in the region. First of all, the Coast states have experienced a phenomenal gain in population from 1940 to 1947—a gain of 38.9 per cent, which constitutes the major population shift in the nation for the present decade. By contrast the Mountain states have gained only 3.9 per cent in population in the last seven years. Since the country as a whole has gained 8.7 per cent it follows that, relatively, the Mountain states have lost adult population. Indeed, Montana and Idaho have experienced an absolute loss of 13 per cent. Four of the Plains states also have registered a net loss of population since the last census.

In general the people who have left the Mountains and Plains have gone in search of greater economic opportunity elsewhere—the more numerous job openings, better pay, and higher incomes available in the Eastern industrial states and in Washington, Oregon, and California.

Per capita income is a very good indicator of relative economic status, and here, also, interesting changes have taken place. Per capita income has been higher in the Coast states than the United States average since before 1929, while in the other Western states and in the Plains states it has been substantially lower than the national level. In 1940, for example, California's per capita income was 40 per cent above the average for the United States, while in the Mountain states it varied from 62 per cent to 105 per cent of the national average.

From 1940 to 1946 the Mountain states improved their relative income position noticeably, although five of them (and all of the Plains states except one) remained below the national average. These income gains have resulted largely from the great increase in agricultural income since 1940. On the West Coast, however, the gains have been more general in origin, with a particularly noteworthy increase in manufacturing wages and salaries. In this category the Far West made substantial gains in food processing, nonferrous metals, rubber, furniture and transportation equipment—all denoting a relative shift of these types of manufacturing from the older established areas to a new, rising one.

From 1940 to 1946 the Pacific Coast raised its percentage of total national manufacturing payrolls from 6.59 to 7.87 per cent. But the same years saw virtually no improvement in the manufacturing position of the Mountain states. In 1946, these eight states, with 3 per cent of the nation's population, had only nine-tenths of 1 per cent of the country's manufacturing payrolls.

Thus the great Western region has developed unevenly during a period of expansion and national full employment. The rapidly growing Pacific Coast offers a sharp contrast to the slow progress and relative decline of the outdistanced Mountains and Plains states. This lack of balance between the Western economy and that of the nation deeply concerns many economists and observers. A slackening of economic activity, particularly a decline in agricultural prices and output, would bear heavily on the Mountain states. Nevertheless, these states possess great potential sources of wealth, and substantial possibilities for employment. The Pacific Coast states, also, have tremendous undeveloped resources, despite their recent rapid growth. It appears, therefore, that a sound economic policy for the West should be directed towards achieving a better internal balance regionally and nationally by means of an effective and integrated program of resources development.

An Outline of Economic Policy   The keynote for a liberal Western economic policy is conservation and development. Our wealth lies in our great resources which we must develop to the full. Yet these resources can be wasted and exhausted, so that we must use them with economy and with thought for the welfare of future generations.

Here is a twelve-point declaration of policy:

(1)   To extend soil-building and anti-erosion practices to every acre of Western arable land. Failure to do so will mean silted-up dams, and dust storms which again will deposit Western topsoil in Washington, D. C.

(2)   To intensify productive use of our forest and range reserves, with intensified opposition to wasteful exploitation by over-cutting and over-grazing.

(3)   The continued maintenance of large areas of "wide-open space" for recreation and wild-life protection.

(4)   To implement a twenty-year program of exploration for minerals, using the most advanced techniques of geologic mapping, aerial survey, and geophysics.

(5)   To expand physical and economic research to discover new techniques and new markets for utilizing low-grade ores.

(6)   Construction of a greater network of dams, reservoirs, and ditches for the optimum utilization of our scarce water resources.

(7)   Exploitation of every potential kilowatt of hydro-electric energy, plus extension of transmission lines into new areas and new markets.

(8)   Development of locally managed, locally financed manufacturing industry to process Western food, fiber, and minerals.

(9)   Sustained and vigorous attack on institutional barriers to Western development—freight rates, monopoly control of natural resources and industrial processes, and absentee ownership both private and federal.

(10)   Vigilant opposition to the anti-social policies of Western minority groups—of which the wool tariff, the silver-purchase pro-

gram, and recent attacks on forest and grazing conservation are notorious examples.

(11) The preservation of human resources by the extension of adequate facilities for education, technical training, and public health to all of the people of the region.

(12) The effective implementation of all of the above policies by research and planning and by the better co-ordination of present programs of conservation and industrial development.

This statement of policy can command wide agreement and wide support. But the Western liberal cannot be satisfied with a declaration of objectives to which everyone is willing to give pious lip service. The policy must be complete and concrete, with a detailed program of action springing from it. Here, of course, major difficulties arise, notably that of developing adequate research to arrive at sound methods of development, and the practical difficulty of harmonizing divergent interests and points of view to secure agreement on specific activities. Also, since this is a comprehensive and long-run program, agreement must be reached on the order of urgency of the various proposals.

Nevertheless, experience indicates many details that are sufficiently tested to provide a basis for Western liberal policy. These would include, in agriculture, the continued encouragement of homestead farming by maintenance, in most cases, of the 160-acre limitation on reclamation projects and the expansion of the water-facilities loan program of the Farm Home Administration. Both are important to improve the technical efficiency and competitive power of the family-sized farm. In forestry and grazing, first on the agenda would be to resist the selfish attempts to weaken public regulation which prevents over-grazing, and preserves the natural grandeur of scenic areas. The agenda also would include reforestation, shelter belts, and reseeding of range lands.

In the mining industry, liberal policy would advocate the gradual abandonment of subsidies and tariffs as the energy now devoted to lobbying for these ends is successfully diverted toward the enactment of state and federal legislation designed to finance and stimulate exploration, and technical and economic research.

Industrialization of the West In the field of industrial development, first steps would be to create state, regional, and area Committees for Resource Development, to stimulate locally owned processing plants by providing research facilities, technical assistance, and financing on a co-operative, fee basis. One of the first of these projects should be the development of a Western fertilizer industry utilizing our extensive deposits of phosphate and potash. Another would be the establishment of local plants for the grading, sorting, and processing of wool. The committees also should set up production and marketing standards for indigenous manufactures, and establish Research and Development Corporations to provide venture capital for new enterprises in certain fields; financed, perhaps, by means of mixed corporations. They might also work for an independent Western steel industry, to provide the best possible foundation for successful Western industrialization.

In the attack on institutional barriers against industrialization, the West gained a substantial victory in 1947 when the Interstate Commerce Commission Freight Rate Order of May 1945, became effective. This already famous decision provides ultimately for a uniform system of classification on class-rate commodities for the entire United States. Thus it is a first step toward breaking down the historic freight-territories basis for rates, which favors the Northeast and discriminates against the West and South. With this good beginning Western liberals should be encouraged to demand further investigations designed to remove commodity-rate and exception-rate discriminations and to extend transportation into neglected areas.

In the field of monopoly the first strategy seems to be that of specific attacks on particular monopoly barriers. Whenever a new Western firm, founded to fabricate or process a Western material, finds that patents or monopoly controls block its path, then negotiation should be brought into play; followed where necessary by anti-trust prosecution by a strengthened Department of Justice. The main attack on monopoly, however, will come from a positive program for providing capital, research, and technical assistance to small new enterprises through private, semi-public, and public agencies such as commercial banks, co-operatives, and development corporations. It is well to observe at this point that the program is not aimed at regional self-sufficiency. The aim is to achieve regional balance, not regional autarchy. Accordingly, branches of national concerns are welcomed, and the subsidization of high-cost local enterprises is not contemplated.

Power and Water   All these policies for agriculture, mining, industry, and recreation are important. Yet the real key to Western development is in the optimum utilization of its resources of water and hydro-electric power. During the next half century the Western irrigated areas should be increased from 21 million acres to the economic maximum of 43 million acres; and installed power capacity should be increased by 15 million kilowatts. Projects embracing 11 million acres and 10 million kilowatts should be completed within 25 years. This would provide the base for Western industrialization and minerals development, and the framework for soil and forest conservation. In fact, power and water constitute the central core around which can be built the simultaneous and integrated development of the West's varied resources.

Regional Authorities for the West   It follows that the effective utilization of our Western resources will require multiple-purpose projects, which simultaneously control the water, enrich and protect the land, generate power, develop new industries, train industrial and farm workers, provide recreation facilities, and safeguard health and wild life. Experience has shown that the "authority" type of administrative organization greatly facilitates the multiple-purpose scheme of development. Consequently, the Western liberal vigorously supports the creation of regional TVA's in the West. Logic indicates such a policy. Moreover, this point of view is strengthened by the apparent inadequacies of the Pick-Sloan Plan for the Missouri Valley which falls so far short of achieving optimum, over-all resource use as to be tantamount to the sabotage of the timely achievement of a genuine multiple-purpose development.

Western liberal policy will not oppose such modifications of the TVA pattern as will strengthen regional autonomy or assign an important role to state government. However, the Western liberal insists upon a policy which is based on rational efficiency and integration, and not on the perpetuation of private or governmental vested interests. He also insists on a policy which calculates the costs and benefits of a resources-development project in terms of social goals and social responsibilities, and not merely in terms of the accounting calculus of private enterprise. The regional authority can, and must, allocate part of its costs to the achievement of social objectives such as flood and erosion control. Equally, it must calculate its benefits not only in terms of dollars of revenue in the till, but also in terms of a rising per capita income, and a rising standard of living for the people of the region and the nation.

Finally, it cannot be emphasized too strongly that the above proposals represent a minimum program. If these instruments fail to break the restrictive barriers of rates and patents and lack of capital, more direct and vigorous measures will be necessary. Moreover, some way must be found to persuade the Congress to see the wisdom of effective federal policies of expansion, and to abandon the restrictionism implicit in its recent curtailment of reclamation development in the West. The Western liberal takes this position because he is determined that the colonialism of the West must end. But even more important is the belief that the very survival of a free, liberal, democratic society will depend upon our finding a way to achieve and maintain a balanced, expanding economy.

Western Policy and the Nation The proposed economic policy for the West obviously impinges directly upon national policy. In the first place, Western development directly depends upon the federal government in many respects. The federal government owns and administers 54 per cent of the area of the Western states. It controls the navigable streams. Its various regulatory agencies supervise transportation, communications, and many aspects of economic activity. Its developmental agencies, such as the Bureau of Reclamation, are engaged in improving the West's resources. It follows that the achievement of Western economic development will depend largely upon national policies. The liberal

West asks, therefore, for a sympathetic understanding of its problems by Americans everywhere.

In return the West offers to the rest of the nation its very substantial contribution to the national welfare. Its development will contribute a very significant amount to the nation's wealth, which will help to raise per capita income, not only in the West, but in the nation as a whole.

Equally important, development of the West will help to stabilize the national economy, by providing an economically sound outlet for investment of capital funds, by stabilizing regional incomes, and by reducing regional under-employment and unemployment. These gains will result, in turn, in the more equitable distribution of national income, which is a primary requisite of economic stability.

Finally, developing the West can contribute to national welfare because of its emphasis upon the principle of decentralization. Physical decentralization is a necessity of the atomic age. But the philosophy of decentralization has much broader implications than the physical. The West can accommodate several million more people with no loss in the present high enjoyment of life by Westerners, and with better and happier living for many inhabitants of the typical congested urban area. More important still, development of the West by regional authorities, firmly based on the people, will do much to push back upon the region, the local government, and the individual citizen the responsibility and opportunity for self-government and for democratic control of our economic destinies.

The West is still a land of opportunity. It is large and underdeveloped. It particularly lacks manufacturing, and its economy is unbalanced and unstable—too dependent on the whims of Nature. An economic policy for the West should be directed toward conserving and developing its great resources, and particularly toward the processing of its own food, fiber, and minerals. Such industrialization should be encouraged by state and regional committees for research, financing, and other services; and by locally inspired attacks on the institutional barriers to economic expansion. In particular the semi-arid West must expand the use of its water and power resources, through the establishment of regional authorities. If properly implemented, these policies will result in population growth, greater stability in the regional economy, a rise in per capita income, and an increase in the region's contribution to the wealth and security of the American people.

CHAPTER X

Public Spending and Resources

by Seymour E. Harris

Deficit Spending—Pros and Cons Since chapters seven through nine deal with the development of resources, this may be an appropriate place to summarize the results of these chapters and to introduce a discussion of public spending and deficits. Later, we shall discuss the problem of keeping demand up by governmental aid and intervention; [1] but in the next section we must take note of a problem raised by Schlesinger—the danger of competing with private enterprise. We shall also suggest the province of government activity. Opposition to government spending stems from the effects on the public debt and the uneasiness caused by government competition.

A growing public debt raises serious and difficult problems, which lead to what may be called a debt neurosis. Those who are excessively concerned over the public debt should compare our 40-billion-dollar economy in 1933 with an annual federal debt charge of about half a billion, and the 200-billion-dollar economy of 1947 with a debt charge of 5 billion. They should also distinguish between a public debt incurred in the process of destruction (for example, in 1941–46), and one incurred to put unemployed resources to work (as in the thirties), contributing to growth of income and providing permanent assets, against which the new charges may be put. They should also consider whether this country, in the absence of public deficits, would have had an income for the years 1941–

[1] See Part V.

47 of close to 1,000 billion dollars, averaging annually more than 140 billion; or of 409 billion for the years 1935–40, an annual average of 68 billion, in contrast to an income for the three years 1932–34 of 143 billion, at an annual average of 48 billion dollars. In the forties, from 1941 to 1947, the average annual income has been 80 billion dollars above that of the thirties; even allowing for price changes, the average was at least 100 per cent higher than for the thirties, and for the second half of the thirties it was substantially above that of 1932–34. Public spending and government guarantee of markets were the most important single explanation of the rise. It is regrettable indeed that in 1941–46 the money could not have been spent for more useful purposes.

The reader should not construe this discussion as a plea for larger government deficits, and particularly not for an increase of debt at the rate of recent years. It is rather a plea for sober judgment in these matters, for a consideration of pluses as well as minuses, for relating the growth of debt to that of income, for weighing the evil of debt against the even greater evils of unemployment, distress, and wasted resources.

Fear of Government Competition Fear of government competition is a second objection to government deficit spending. Many economists reflect their distaste for this competition by urging as the depression medicine the reduction of taxes rather than deficit spending. Many arguments can be adduced against a tax-reduction policy, not the least of which are that (1) it offers relief to the well-to-do, that is, the taxpayer, not to those in distress, for example, the unemployed; (2) it may not be effective in stimulating the economy because reductions may go into monetary hoards instead of spending and investment, and meanwhile the government must function with less income, thus running up the deficit anyway. Many economists nevertheless would choose the tax-reduction route to full employment because they fear government competition more than they fear public deficit. A rise of spending, in their view, may intensify that competition.

Public Spending Complementary as Well as Competitive
Yet these fears are greatly exaggerated. The TVA dramatized government enterprise in competition with private industry;

but it also highlighted the enterprise too large for any private agglomeration of capital to handle, and with stakes too large to be entrusted to private capital. The St. Lawrence Seaway project is another case in point. In the twenties, a combination of large business interests tried to buy the power rights of the St. Lawrence project, offering free navigation rights as part of the price. Governors Smith and Roosevelt saved this project for the people and refused to sell their rights for private profit. Now private enterprise is doing its utmost to prevent the development of the seaway on the grounds that it is not practical or would involve the federal government in vast subsidies.

It is indeed probable that the government may be able to spend enough to keep demand at a sufficiently high level without trespassing significantly on private domains. Punitive spending to force business away from restrictive practices, as suggested by Bowles, is another matter.[2] Bowles, Berle, and Cooke list many of the non-competitive areas which government may exploit. Public disbursements in these areas would raise the income of the country and thus contribute to the gains of business enterprise. How much business is done by private interests depends not only upon the *proportionate* activity in the public and private sector but also upon the *total*. Surely no one would contend that private enterprise suffered as a result of TVA or the Coulee Dam.

Test of Gains Accruing Generally   Public expenditures of a non-competitive type should meet certain tests. The main condition is that a significant part of the gains should accrue to the economy generally. No corporation, not even General Motors, can afford to spend, say, a billion dollars *for the general welfare;* for since its receipts are much less than 1 per cent of the nation's income, General Motors would receive back much less than one cent per dollar spent. Government expenditure of a billion dollars may well, in the appropriate conditions and through the stimulation of demand, raise the nation's income by 2 to 3 billion dollars: what the government spends comes back to the nation.

Our ability to maintain a free system with a minimum of controls will depend upon how well we plan, and upon the

[2] See above, pp. 24–25.

effectiveness with which we use our resources. There is no greater threat to freedom than wastage of resources through unemployment or misuse (for example, war). There comes a time in periods of unemployment and unproductivity when the public is prepared to barter freedom for bread, clothing, housing, and urban redevelopment. Of these, housing is by far the most important, if for no other reason than that in this field we have sorely lagged behind. In a stimulating essay on housing, Abrams shows the need of government subsidies in housing (as did Bowles). Housing costs are so high, and the industry is so permeated with monopoly that it has priced itself out of the market. A large proportion of the potential buyers or renters are unable to buy or rent adequate housing. Abrams points the way to building 20 million homes in the next 10 to 20 years: federal aid, local planning, and exercise of the right of eminent domain will yield attractive and comfortable houses, contribute to reduced costs, and yet not dispense with ultimate private ownership. In the immediate crisis, I would propose also allocation of scarce materials; and I would point out that federal and local governments might induce a timing of building that fits in well with the requirements of the economic situation.

Urban redevelopment, a related problem, is the theme of Greer's paper. Here again there is no alternative to the use of federal funds for solving the problem of city slums and blights and of regional planning. Land values are so high that private enterprise could afford to pay them only by replacing slums with tall buildings, thus even increasing the degree of overcrowding. But finance is not the only problem, as Greer so well shows; nevertheless, the physical decay of metropolitan areas will not be arrested until federal financial aid is forthcoming. A more radical proposal, accepted by the British Government, is a writing down of excess values, in part inflated on the unjustified assumption that all areas not used or badly used will ultimately find profitable use.

Cooke, one of the leading proponents of the public interest in the nation's resources, is eloquent and convincing in his discussion of resources, in his plea for the implementation of market with social values, in his urging that our vital resources be renewed rather than depleted.[3] He reminds us that even as late as 1908, the Secretary of Agriculture assured the country that our soil could not be depleted or eroded; and that 6 million miles of ditch roads are depriving us of vast and indispensable reserves of water. It is incumbent upon government to spend public funds in order to exploit our resources as well as to conserve them; in order to assure their availability tomorrow as well as today.

The federal government can spend large sums of money productively on hydro-electric enterprises. The resulting increase in power will help prevent the depletion of irreplaceable sources of energy—oil, natural gas, and coal, which we are now using up at a rate vastly more rapid than current production by the rays of the sun. Hydro-electric enterprises are too large and the public interest too much involved to allow their exploitation by private business. Machinery is a *sine qua non* for a rising standard of living, and energy moves the machine. Nau deals fully and well with the place of public power systems in our economy.

Depletion of Resources and Government Responsibility Geologists warn us that our known reserves of oil will last only 20 years and total supplies about 40 years; that our rich iron ores will be gone in a generation; that the reserves of nonferrous metals are in an even more precarious state; that deforestation exceeds the rate of afforestation; that our coking coal will be exhausted in 65 years; that our top soil is being washed off to sea at a dangerous rate.[4] Yet we do little about these impending crises, depending perhaps on miracles like the recent discoveries in wood plastics which make soft wood previously not usable as hard as teak wood.

Indeed, this country seems to have licked the Malthusian devil, as is apparent in a doubling of income every 15 to 20 years; yet the wastage of non-renewable resources, the failure to put them to the most essential uses, the tendency, under excessive reliance on market prices, to rob the future generations, bring us once more face to face with the Malthusian problem of inadequate supplies. To some extent, however,

[3] Cf. Chapter 9.
[4] See the introduction to this part.

emphasis is shifted from foods. Pressure from abroad to share our resources further underlines the reappearance of the Malthusian specter.

Private versus Public Responsibility for New Discoveries Experimentation is the province of the government. We can no longer depend upon private enterprise to carry on the research which will yield the products required by 140 million Americans, or by a world with four times the population it had 300 years ago. There is no assurance, on the past record, that private enterprise will spend enough on research or that the results of research will be made generally available. The very fact that a large part of the gains accrues to others than those who invest in research tends to discourage research expenditures. Total business research expenditures amounted to about 0.5 per cent of the nation's income in 1947, a fraction of the percentage spent in the U.S.S.R. That the investment in research is likely to be profitable only in so far as special privileges accrue to the company making the discoveries militates against exclusive reliance on private research.

For example, the government should be spending vast sums on experimentation with the large veins of low-grade ores in the Great Lakes areas, which are almost indispensable for a great industrial nation. One might even say that the survival of this country as a high-income power depends on successful exploitation of the low-grade iron ore. Yet we are content to allow private companies to carry on most of the research, and at a level woefully inadequate to meet the needs of the country. These companies oppose the St. Lawrence Seaway on the ground that it may make importation of foreign iron ore profitable; fearful of increased competition from foreign ore, they further contract experimental work. The solution of the problem would be to carry on federal research, subsidize private research on condition that the results be made available to all, and also to build the Seaway.

Limits of Public Spending We have justified public spending when the gains accrue largely to the nation, when essential commodities and services cannot be obtained under free-market conditions, and in order to carry on research to assure adequate resources in this and later generations. The spending involved is largely non-competitive. It may well be that when allowance is made for the multiple effect upon income of public expenditures of a stimulative type, for the possibility of timing expenditures according to fluctuations of spending in the private sector, and for other measures which might contribute towards stabilization at a high level of income, then it may not be necessary to spend greatly in competitive areas in order to assure adequate total spending.

Keyserling well shows that the limits to be put upon public spending will depend on how well the private sector of the economy succeeds in achieving workable arrangements. In order to confine public outlays to non-competitive areas, it will be necessary to introduce improved policies in the private sector of the economy. In the postwar years, this part of the economy should account for at least 75 per cent of demand; and, therefore, the exclusion of government from competitive areas rests upon improved price, wage, and output policies and better co-operation among the interested groups.[5] In summary, sound management of the private economy may largely exclude public spending in competitive areas.

Special Arguments for Public Enterprise   A strong case can be made for government competition with private enterprise when the stakes are sufficiently high. Nau, for example, suggests the need of public competition in power to implement public regulation. Thus there are persuasive arguments for public enterprise in competitive and non-competitive areas. The gist of the argument is that spending may be kept at an adequate level by having recourse to non-competitive spending by government. Should this prove inadequate, however, then the government should spend competitively if the alternative is vast amounts of unemployment and wasted resources.

There is also a powerful argument for complete government control of developments such as atomic energy. Atomic energy is so vital to the country's defense, its unregulated use so dangerous to the health of the nation, and its positive contribution to power development and to the advance of medicine so great, that the government has taken the unprecedented

[5] Cf. also Chapters 13 and 19.

step of assuming complete control of fissionable materials from the raw material to the finished product; and ownership at every stage beyond the original exploitation. In this manner, the government is responsible for experimentation, for the use of the fissionable material, for the control of relevant information, and for accelerating or retarding the use of the materials for energy.

Regional Development an Outlet for Surplus Funds   In economic structure, the United States with about one-half the world's income is more like a continent than a country. Competition among areas is keen, with newly developed regions striving to overcome the advantages of the older regions, favored by early leadership, low unit costs associated with command of markets and large-scale output, and monopolistic practices militating against emergence of potential competitors.

Regional development is a matter of importance not only to the South and West but also to the rest of the country. Bowles, Berle, Cooke, and Nau all comment on the outlets for public funds in regional development. Garnsey's entire essay deals with the problems confronting an under-developed region, the growth of which will contribute to the advantage of the country. This essay deserves the careful consideration of every reader, for what Garnsey has to say applies equally well to other under-developed regions.

Regional development is, in part, a problem of finding outlets for surplus funds; but it is also a problem of allocating resources in the most effective manner—thus combining the Keynesian and the structural approaches. By the latter we mean dealing with specific weak spots in the economy through encouraging movements of the factors of production, improving technical methods, finding markets, and so on. What then are the vital issues?

Outlets for Savings   A cardinal point is that in a peaceful world there may not be sufficient outlets for savings. Conservation of water, the fullest development of hydroelectric power, afforestation, the provision of capital for indigenous development of industries, to obtain, among other things, a better decentralization of industry as required in an atomic age—all of these will provide profitable outlets for our surplus savings. Garnsey's blueprint for the next fifty years calls for an increase of Western irrigated areas from 21 million acres to a maximum of 43 million, and a rise of installed power capacity by 15 million kilowatts. Investment, moreover, should be pushed beyond the point where it is self-liquidating on an accounting basis; for to some extent the gains in better forests, recreation, and diversification, as well as the resulting stability and higher incomes, will all accrue to · the nation, not to the various TVA projects.

Equalizing Competitive Conditions Between Old and New Areas   Development of regions should be based on their comparative advantages and on their ability to support new industries in competition with other regions. Although this criterion does not exclude multiple-purpose developments which might be subsidized because large gains accrue to the nation (inclusive of those resulting from the industrialization of some areas), it does exclude special subsidies by government to foster particular industries unable ultimately to make effective use of the factors of production.

New regions suffer from the competition offered by older regions that have had the advantages of an early start, as the East, particularly, and of monopolistic practices, such as patent control, price discrimination, restriction of output, and the like. The most productive allocation of economic resources can be obtained only if older regions abandon or are forced to give up their special privileges. It is the task of government to allow newer areas a fair chance to establish their position in agriculture and manufacturing. Foreign countries, prepared to counter the advantages of older manufacturing areas with protectionist devices, are in a much more favorable position than the South and West which cannot have recourse to protection on a substantial scale. The South indeed frequently offers tax incentives to new firms; but since older firms are taxed more heavily to offset exemptions granted to the newest, with the passage of time these tax concessions prove largely illusory.

To put new regions into a fair competitive position, it is necessary not only to eliminate the monopolistic advantages of older industries and regions but also to give the newcomers positive help. The TVA programs, research help, provision of capital—all of these may be means of putting industry in the newer areas on a fair competitive basis with the East. Expenditures of public funds are clearly not justifiable, however, unless industry, once grown up, is likely to stand on its own. In the South and West, many industries requiring much labor, which is available in large quantities (especially in the South), may profit so much from cheap power and proximity to raw materials that they should thrive.

Orderly Adjustment for Older Regions   Growth is the problem of new regions; decline that of the old. As the South and West gain in manufacturing, the East will have to make difficult adjustments. In New England, for example, manufacturing declined steadily during the forty years preceding World War II; by the twenties there were serious areas of decay. Wartime prosperity and its aftermath have tended to blind her leaders to the long-run problems of adjustment. For the shifting of markets to the West and South, the exhaustion of crucial raw materials in the East, the improvement elsewhere of manufacturing techniques and management threaten New England's relative and, to some extent, its absolute position. Instead of taking a Domesday or inventory of industries and services which, on the basis of her peculiar advantages of skilled labor, plentiful capital, long experience in advanced techniques, high scientific standards and the growing importance of tertiary industries, are likely to prosper, and to chart her course accordingly, her leaders are frequently inclined to put economists to work to prove to the world that all is well in New England, that the region is growing faster than others, and that it is the land of the future. Many of her leaders devote their major energies to fighting the St. Lawrence Seaway because, though it might profit the country, it will (at least in the views of the Boston Port Authority and New England railroads) injure New England; to plumping for the Boston Airport and seaport as though these were the one and only road to prosperity; to proclaiming the ascendancy of New England at the same time that they export capital to the South and West.

New England has a great future, as do the Middle Atlantic states; but it is a future beclouded by losses in industries which cannot bear the high cost structure in these states; and a future darkened by adjustments which necessarily follow the ups and downs and transfers of resources in a dynamic society. These regions can continue to grow and to play a large part in the economic life of the nation; but they must reform their tax system, study their balance of payments with the rest of the country and with the world, concentrate on industries which can afford their high labor and power costs, facilitate the transfer of resources to growing industries, reduce the costs of those which are declining, and impose a greater flexibility of wages. That adjustments are being made is evident from a recent national survey of manufacturing industries. Despite very high wages, the Pacific industries were continuing to gain; and the effects of years of losses were evident in the tendency of New England to become a low-wage area.

> Only 1 of the 29 Pacific industries had average earnings lower than the national average, whereas in the Southwest only 1 of 35 industries came above the national average. . . . New England's industries were almost equally divided (15 below and 18 above the national average), whereas more than two-thirds of the industries in the Middle Atlantic and Great Lakes States had average hourly earnings that exceeded the national average.[6]

Summary   To government falls the task of making the best possible use of the country's resources, and of sustaining the level of demand. Development of the country's resources, to the extent that the task cannot or should not be performed by private interests, provides a significant outlet for the country's excess savings and a means of pushing the nation's income upward. Non-competitive spending of this kind by government may well yield the stimulus required of public spending. At times, however, it may be necessary to go beyond non-competitive spending. In the next two parts, we turn to the related problems of Planning and Controls and Stabilization of Demand.

---

[6] *Labor in the South*, Bureau of Labor Statistics Bulletin, No. 898 (1947), p. 60. See also S. E. Harris, "New England's Decline in the American Economy." *Harvard Business Review* (1947).

PART FOUR

Planning and Controls

Introduction

by Seymour E. Harris

Before turning to a discussion of the crucial issue of demand, we pause to analyze the problems of planning and controls. Experience has taught us that the interests of business and society, or even of labor and society, are not necessarily harmonious; that not all goods produced are taken off the market; that unless the government protects the interest of the nation, the greedy few will despoil our resources, or these resources will remain undeveloped.

As Merriam shows, planning is a "must" if there is to be organization in our economic life and if the best use is to be made of our resources; but there is a stopping point short of socialism. Co-operation among the large groups making decisions which take adequate account of the public interest will reduce the amount of central planning required as well as delimit the area of controls. Gilbert and Fainsod are both hopeful that groups will mature and mellow, and learn how to get on together and be reasonable. That our economy increasingly tends to be operated largely by monopolists militates against the return to nineteenth-century liberalism. Either the onward movement of monopoly must be arrested, or, in so far as the groups do not act on behalf of the public interest, controls by the state will have to increase. Berge proposes a direct attack on monopoly.

It is an easy transition from Part III (Resources and Their Development) to Part IV (Planning and Controls). In order to develop resources, it is necessary to plan for the economy as a whole; for obviously a program for regional development is related to the needs of the economy as a whole, and has to be considered in that framework. Government spending for development or for offsetting fluctuations in the private sector of the economy, constitutes planning of a sort. How far the country will have to go in the direction of more comprehensive planning, including direct allocation of economic resources, will depend upon the success with which private enterprise functions, the contribution of programs of conservation and development, and in general the scope and effectiveness of monetary and fiscal policy. Through monetary policy, the government and the central banks seek to adapt monetary supplies to the needs of the economy, whereas fiscal policy proposes direct attacks on demand through variations in public receipts and expenditures.

Planning on the March All over the world planning is on the march—in Russia and the Argentine with their new Five-Year Plans, Poland and France with their Four-Year Plans, Czechoslovakia with her Two-Year Plan, Great Britain with her Four-Year Plan still in the gestation phase, and even the United States with its Economic Budget.

As Merriam points out in his spirited defense, planning is not necessarily undemocratic; it is compatible with liberty; and with the increasing complexity of modern life it is not only necessary but indispensable if we are to be spared collapse and regimentation.

Opposition to planning arises not only from its association with totalitarianism, but also (and related) from the wide acceptance of the view that there is no stopping place short of a completely controlled economy. Merriam, Gilbert, and Fainsod all take pains to refute this popular misconception, showing that in theory all-out planning is not required, in practice a mixed system frequently prevails, and that the test of extension or non-extension is largely a pragmatic one. Gilbert well says that the surrender of lesser liberties may be the cost of maintaining the larger freedoms.

As Gilbert shows, economic planning has advanced from the treatment of cyclical indispositions to more ambitious programs to assure full employment and the best allocation of economic resources. In this country, the progress has been from almost exclusive reliance on monetary policy through the twenties, to increased dependence on fiscal policy and an extension of direct controls in the thirties, and the development of the latter with the advent of war.

Problems of a Full-Employment Economy   One of the crucial issues facing the country in 1948–49 is whether or not fiscal policy can be used effectively enough to make direct controls dispensable. It is clear that full-employment economies are not the economists' Utopia that was envisaged in the thirties. In the high- or over-employed economy, inflationary pressures haunt the policy-makers, who may overlook them and allow them to create distortions, maldistribution, political turmoil, and economic collapse, or they may do something about them. Various alternatives are open if one refuses to accept the inevitability of boom and bust, and alternate cycles of over- and under-employment.

First, the country may depend upon co-operation on the part of the large bargaining groups—labor, capital, farmers, and government—to arrive at fair and workable solutions of distribution and related problems; and as Keyserling shows, the greater the success achieved, the less the need for government help. Government's task might then largely be that of an arbiter, although failure to achieve agreements, with the interest of the public protected, might be countered with government intervention. Gilbert and Fainsod, as well as Keyserling earlier, express the hope that large groups will somehow consummate reasonable agreements. But on the basis of past performance, they should not be too optimistic. Failure of the interested groups to agree on fundamentals will inevitably bring the second alternative—compensatory fiscal policy and then controls in periods of high employment or, alternatively, the boom and its aftermath.

How far may it be necessary to extend controls? Monetary and fiscal policies are in a measure a substitute for direct (that is, precise) controls. In 1947–48, this means credit control, higher taxes, and reduced public spending. In so far as these, the Keynesian medicine, suffice, it will not be necessary to control prices, allocate supplies and labor, and to ration. The appeal, to Keynes and to others, of monetary and fiscal measures, which would influence the rate of interest, prices, consumption, and investment prospects, was that they would allow capital and labor to respond to economic incentives, and would free them of direct controls. In short, fiscal policy vigorously and wisely applied, may yield the level of demand, not alone in periods of inflation but also in periods of deflation, which may save the country from government allocation of resources and control of prices.

Attacks on the rate of interest and compensatory finance are *general* measures which may fail to treat specific distortions in the economic system. For example, in 1948, no practical fiscal policy will solve the problem of meat shortage though a severe tax and monetary policy might reduce income sufficiently to curtail demand greatly. But solution through induced depression is not a wise one. In other areas, also, fiscal policy alone may not suffice. Planners have to contend with excesses of labor in one section or occupation, and deficiencies in another, with maldistribution of investment funds, with failure to adapt supplies to the changing demand pattern. The higher the demand and the more satisfactory the economic conditions, the less immobility (that is, relative failure of capital, management, and labor to move in response to incentives, either because of ignorance of alternative opportunities, or because of institutional or other deterrents to movement) interferes with the desired movements. In depression, the movement of labor and capital is for obvious reasons sluggish. Even under the most favorable conditions, there remains a residual of structural readjustment; and in a completely planned economy with the government, not the consumers, determining what is to be produced, the problem of proper distribution of resources also is acute.

Importance of Incentives In both the semi-planned and the fully planned economy, incentives may play a decisive part, and may make compulsory measures unnecessary. That is clearly the case under democratic planning. Instead of forcing the capitalist to invest in housing, he may be induced to do so by tax remissions; instead of compelling the workers to go into the coal mines, they may find it to their advantage

to do so, when good housing and special social-security benefits are provided and (where moderate controls are in use)
they are given special rations. If it is necessary to carry planning beyond fiscal and monetary policy, incentives, in part
the components of sound fiscal policy, may be used instead of
compulsions. It should rarely be necessary to force movements of capital and labor, except when, under the stress of
war, speed is necessary and the response to economic incentive is too slow. Government, as Fainsod suggests, may
provide numerous incentives, and yet not be over-zealous in
their use.

In short, monetary and fiscal policy, wisely and courage-
ously used, may well suffice in a system of democratic planning, and may make advanced planning unnecessary. In
periods of high activity, it may also be necessary to impose a
measure of control, but a combination of wise fiscal policies
and incentives may suffice to keep direct controls down to a
minimum.

Some Lessons from Russian Experience   In some respects, we might learn much from the Russian system, though
its excesses, particularly its denial of liberties, would have little
appeal in this country. That system approaches the egalitarian principle in that differences of income as great as are
common here are eliminated; and yet it condones the use of
incentives, particularly for raising output of labor and management. Many will be critical of the excessive allocation of
resources for war and capital equipment in Russia, although
the large outlays for capital may be justified by its scarcity.
In the Russian economy, scarcity is reflected in low man-hour
output, explained in part by small capital investments per
worker. In some respects, however, the allocation of resources
commands approval: with the government determining the
use of resources primarily, there is a tendency to put first things
first—workers' housing before luxurious hotels; bread before
cake; essential clothing before luxuries; education before
travel.

In our country there is a tendency to spend too much for
distribution. Surely one-third to one-half of our income should
not go for distribution as long as a large part of our popula-

tion lacks the essentials of life. Our distributive system is wasteful of resources. The Russians set up objectives and fit their resources into the production pattern as determined by the objectives. Unemployment is a relatively unimportant problem. We, on the other hand, suffer much unemployment or obviate it in part by using resources unproductively: by buying gold with exports; by making public investments which to some extent are wasteful; by finding work in the inflated distributive employments.

The world needs a system which will combine the best features of the Russian system (for example, an approach to fair distribution, full use of resources, and the mobilization of incentives for workers) with the attractive features of our system (for example, political and other freedoms, the maximum scope of freedom of choice by consumers, investors, and workers consistent with high levels of employment and fair distribution, and the *general* application of incentives).

CHAPTER XI

The Place of Planning

by Charles E. Merriam

In the necessarily short space allotted to me it is of course impossible to do more than make a token payment on account. To attempt to cover the history of planning, the content of planning, its technical aspects whether governmental or otherwise, the nature, interrelations, and limits of planning agencies—all this is out of the question.[1] My own experience began with the city plan of Chicago in 1907 and has extended over a wide range of contacts with various planning agencies and problems down to the present time.[2]

Background of Planning In order to bring about closer co-operation between the political order and the social order it is necessary to provide for the reorganization of planning agencies, both public and private. It is true that planning is a red rag to some, but this is primarily due to a misunderstanding of the word. Planning, as the term is used in America, does not involve principally economic planning, or total economic planning, or totalitarian planning. Here planning

[1] George B. Galloway and associates, *Planning for America* (New York, 1941); Lewis Lorwin, *Time for Planning* (New York, 1945); Oliver Franks, *Central Planning and Control in War and Peace* (Cambridge, Mass., 1947); Cleveland Rodgers, *American Planning* (New York, 1947); Proceedings of the American Society of Planning Officials.

[2] See my *Systematic Politics* (Chicago, 1945); "The National Resources Planning Board: A Chapter in American Planning Experiences," *American Political Science Review*, XXXVIII (1944), p. 1,075; *On the Agenda of Democracy* (Cambridge, Mass., 1941), Part II. See also numerous reports of the National Resources Planning Board from 1932 to the sweeping plan for the development of national resources in 1943.

is employed in quite a different sense. It indicates institutional provision for intelligent and systematic analysis and forecasting of the most efficient use of resources and the choice of the best alternatives in a balanced program. A good housewife is a good planner; a good farmer is a good planner; and no one thinks either the housewife or the farmer is a Communist because of his or her planning. On the contrary, those who do not plan are likely to be called slipshod and careless. In this day of closer technical analysis of the factors of efficiency, all social groups, whether public or private, tend to set up arrangements and instruments which taken together constitute what we now call planning.

If someone wishes to use another term such as "policy" or "development," the outcome is the same. He can change the name of the Chicago Planning Commission to the Chicago Development Commission—of Chicago, New York, or a hundred other cities. There are now around 2,000 city planning boards in the United States. In many states the planning boards have been rechristened development boards or reconstruction boards, but the function is much the same. There are now planning boards (under various names) in almost every state. The name of the national planning agency has been changed many times and is now by the recent act of Congress called the Council of Economic Advisers. We have a National Planning Association in Washington, a private organization made up of many distinguished representatives of business, labor, and agriculture. There is a large and flourishing organization known as the American Society of Planning Officials. There is also the American Institute of Planners. There are schools of planning in Harvard University and the University of Chicago.

It is quite true that as far back as 1884 a distinguished sociologist, Herbert Spencer, discredited governmental regulation as "the coming slavery." Likewise in more recent times the economist Friedrich A. Hayek, attacked all forms of planning as the "road to serfdom." Doubtless these well-intentioned critics have their value in so far as they challenge the validity of particular plans. But having heard from Doubting

Castle, we may proceed in full confidence that we are on the road to freedom.[3]

One of the surest roads to totalitarianism is unwillingness to trust ourselves enough to build up an adequate planning structure. Those who oppose planning are unintentionally making planning necessary, but not democratic planning. The alternative is not between planning and no planning, but between democratic planning and autocratic planning, between planning in a free society and planning under a dictatorship, whether Fascist or Communist. Doubtless many well-meaning persons who are critical of all planning believe that they are contributing to freedom. On the contrary they are helping to make it impossible. It cannot be too strongly stated that the real foes of freedom are those who refuse to co-operate in setting up machinery for democratic dealing with the difficulties of our time. Planning is coming. Of this there can be no doubt. The only question is whether it will be the democratic planning of a free society, or totalitarian in character.

Planning agencies in government and other organizations serve primarily as a general staff rather than as operators. This does not mean ignorance of or indifference to the practical problems of operation, but involves an over-all point of view such as may be taken in any large going concern. A city planning board in a municipality does not "run the town"; in the national field a national planning board is not for the purpose of "running" the nation. These agencies develop conclusions which take the form of directives, but the actual directive comes from the policy-making agency and the actual operation from another group.

When a group of such planning agencies is set up in various public and private governments, it is relatively easy for them to work out ways and means of co-operation through interchange of information, analysis, and clearing of plans. It may well be that such agencies are not formally designated as

[3] See Edwin G. Nourse, "Serfdom: Utopia, or Democratic Opportunity?" *Public Administration Review* (Spring, 1946), a review of Hayek, Finer, and Wootton.

planning mechanisms, but if planning techniques are employed and the general purposes of planning kept in mind, the same results are reached. Observation and experience which lead to forecasting in agriculture, industry, labor, fit in with a like type of forecasting by the government. A step in this direction has been made by the recent act of Congress setting up a Council of Economic Advisers consisting of three members to survey the state of the national income and to make such forecasts and recommendations as seem appropriate.[4] The functions of this body are advisory only. They advise the president of the United States. Furthermore, their advice and recommendations go to a committee of the House and Senate, set up for the purpose of receiving such recommendations and of taking such action as may be judged expedient.

It is clear that no national planning agency can deal successfully with all the ills that flesh is heir to. It cannot settle all the problems of the government and the economic order. If it undertakes too much, it will accomplish very little. In the nation as in the city the role of planning is primarily a long-range one, looking backwards, to be sure, at trends, looking around at current developments, but primarily looking forward to problems and possibilities emerging in the future. Thus a city planning board may deal with the long-range questions of urban redevelopment, of housing, transportation, metropolitan expansion, encouragement and expansion of local industries, improvement of local working and living conditions, recreation, housing, etc.[5] In like manner in the national field national planning agencies may consider proposed possible development of national and human resources in various areas and on various frontiers. They may help to build up neglected areas by programs of reclamation and conservation. They may develop and apply and use resources in the form of hydro-electric power and for other purposes. They may help to increase the fertility of the soil, the output of the factory, the welfare of workers in certain

[4] This was in fact the purpose of the Employment Stabilization Act introduced by Senator Wagner and passed in 1931 with the approval of President Hoover.

[5] See Chapters 14 and 15.

situations. They may consider the expansion of trade beyond national boundaries and the ways and means of adjusting our economy to imports from other lands. They may plan to set a floor under wages or place a curb on monopoly or to restrict unfair trade practices, to stabilize industry. Or they may deal with health, housing, recreation, education or welfare. The planning process in short involves a high exercise of human intelligence and it is important that the intelligence of the governmental order co-operate with the intelligence in the economic order and the other social orders to attain the maximum results.

It is a common error to conclude that we must plan "everything or nothing." Precisely the opposite is true both in theory and in practice. Planning requires integration, to be sure, but it also requires decentralization, functional and territorial, on many levels of government and of other private governments alongside the public. Our choice need not be made between anarchy and autocracy in planning anymore than in other areas of human behavior in a democratic society. Creative power in a system of the consent of the governed is found at the grass roots as well as the top, and is flexible enough to provide for phases of diffusion as well as of concentration of community directives and their application. What Franks calls "woolliness" of administration may be found in any system; it is not peculiar to democracy.[6] On the contrary, participation, discussion, and consent, the democratic bases of efficiency, are the soundest yet discovered by human intelligence.

I should like to discuss the work of the National Resources Planning Board, of which I was a member for some ten years, but time and space will not permit. I can only say the board's conferences with the President were the most vital and fruitful part of our task, alike in the determination of projects, the canvass of progress, and the disposition of results. The origin of the bill of economic and social rights and the GI Bill of Rights, two of the most important projects of the NRPB, are of special meaning in this connection. Obviously, printed reports are not the only activities of planners, on any level of

[6] Oliver Franks, *op. cit.*

government. Some day I hope to analyze these materials for the benefit of students of planning techniques on the federal level. The 1943 final report of the board gives a full statement of a broad program covering natural and human resources.

New Problems for Planners   In more recent times planning has entered upon new phases of responsibility, overshadowing the older tasks. These are planning in the light of global problems and planning in the light of the atomic age. Thus the United Nations Charter and organization provide for a social and economic council and for a commission on human rights. Both of these are high responsibilities full of import for the future of mankind.

The atomic era, using this as a symbol for the rapid development of science and technology in our time, has also brought problems of vast significance to the modern planner—so tremendous and startling that many planners have not been awakened to their real meaning for all agencies of government on all levels. Planning has won its difficult way over many obstacles, but must now face the greatest problems ever confronting those who tried to peer into the future and lay out courses of human effort.

Above and beyond all traditional and ordinary politico-economic considerations is the new development of atomic energies and modern science. Neutronics is likely to compel a reorganization of politics in the not-too-distant future. Much of the ordinary discussion now going on may be out of date within the next, shall we say, twenty years, or even earlier. While the time and the form of application of science to industry may be speculative at the present moment, let there be no doubt as to what is on the way. Our economy of abundance, which is replacing an economy of scarcity, may bring revolutionary changes in our whole social-industrial system, supplanting much of the current speculation regarding political economy or politics and economics.

It is idle to proceed as if nothing had happened. We may well be in the midst of the greatest revolution mankind has ever known and its implications are the most important thing in human life at this time. We have seen the blinding flash of the bomb, but the roar and surge of power have not yet really reached our peacetime ways of life. We are passing through a revolution in man's control over physical nature and approaching a revolution in man's control over himself in the setting of nature. Not to realize this and to act accordingly is to miss the meaning of the time, and the urgency of far-seeing plans. Science has amply demonstrated that the productive possibilities of mankind stagger the imagination. The real struggle is to attain, before it is too late, such social, economic, political organization and attitudes as enable men to use effectively these newly found powers. Otherwise the new science may bring the new slavery rather than the new freedom, and panic instead of planning. Without the recognition of these far-reaching changes, discussions over planning are merely the beating over of old straw.

We move into a world of new knowledge and aspiration in which free intercommunication and interpenetration of human experience, interests, ideas, might provide a new basis for general understandings regarding the common good and the welfare of human personalities.

We may say that the span of association in the developing community moves higher up and farther around, is lifted up, so to speak, to envelop perhaps more, but paradoxically to control perhaps less. It is as if a new pattern of arrangements and adjustments were being created—one in which we may be more at home than ever, and also more secure than ever before. This new network is not merely governmental or economic, but social, scientific, and in a sense ethical. For this we must plan.

The personality is not continuously re-enslaved or re-exploited, but progressively emancipated and enriched in life possibilities and actualities. New understandings, new expectancies, new attitudes and principles are the basis of new behavior patterns which planning must interpret. Whether these patterns are termed governmental, economic, social, is of relatively little importance in the larger view of the over-all situation. The outcome is not "governmentalization" or "socialization" in the old sense of these terms, or radicalism, reaction, or liberalism, but rather new forms of reciprocal adjustment, which outreach the capacity of the older formulas.

For example, a jural world order is a part of the new patterns, but so is an economic world order and a cultural world order.

The new science in its applications to social affairs may produce new patterns which may be interwoven into new forms of social order and advance. Nuclear energies, medicine, and education make new writings on the wall. Communication and transportation make new types of association and lead to new types of interchange of experience. New patterns of human relationships are in the making which we are not yet able to discern or describe at all clearly.

But all these gains are conditioned upon sound planning for the responsibility and accountability of those who hold the vast new forces, upon general understanding of the meaning and implications of rapidly developing science, upon maintaining the consent of the governed under new and difficult conditions, upon maintaining the supremacy of the civil over the military power in periods of stress and strain. An agenda of planning which omits these important items is scanty and temporary. Looking backward only we may find ourselves overwhelmed by the titanic forces the mind has set loose.

Possibilities of Planning   Gloomy as the outlook sometimes seems, we are on the high road to peace, prosperity, freedom, in richer measure than the world has every enjoyed before. Slavery and serfdom rested on contempt of man, on poverty of resources or inability to utilize them, on lack of inventiveness and imagination in social as well as in mechanical affairs. We are not at the broken end of a worn-out way. We are on the upward road, challenging fears with science and with hope and trust. Democracy, liberty, equality, can now rise triumphant throughout the world, if our courage, faith, and judgment do not falter in the race with opportunity.

We are learning how to be at home in a larger house and a broader community; how to be at home with large-scale organization and tremendous mechanical power and yet without losing liberty, or falling back into anarchy. We can learn how to keep the channels clear for the onrushing stream of new life, new ideas, new enterprise, industrial, political, scientific; how to integrate the political, the economic, the scientific, the social, and religious orders; how to avoid the transformation of specialization into clannishness and narrow likemindedness; how to find and use a language and a means of communication for democracy, adapted to the changing world we live in; how to find the new symbols of association, new types of education, for a new type of human life; how to find a faith and a vision and a way which rises from the hopes and ideals of the past and present, and arches up to the future.

The emerging order could be scientific in the highest sense, political and economic in the richest sense, moral and religious in the finest sense, and crowned with truth, liberty, and justice.

What we are struggling for and could attain transcends the bounds of region, class, or race, or the limits of nineteenth-century economics, and weaves their permanent values together in new values, new institutions, new faith. The role of planning in the next period is greater than ever before in the history of mankind, more complicated and more imperative. That many of the clichés of liberalism and of reaction may soon be obsolete or inapplicable complicates the task of the planners. Careful examination of the ends and means of planning becomes more important than ever.[7]

[7] I hope to discuss some of these emerging problems in a forthcoming study on "Government and the Economic Order in the United States."

CHAPTER XII

Controls

by Richard V. Gilbert

The beginning and end of wisdom, for those who wrap themselves in the tradition of laissez-faire, is embodied in the cliché, "our system cannot continue half free and half controlled." In this they are more royal than the king, for the true classicists, from Adam Smith through John Stuart Mill, knew better. They were concerned, not with ideal types—pure anarchy and pure statism—but rather with determining the degree of state intervention which, under the economic circumstances of the day, would yield the maximum of freedom for the individual consistent with the general welfare. And it is this which constitutes the basic problem for sensible men today.

It is generally recognized that the operations of the free market within the framework of governmental intervention as we have known it result in serious and sometimes violent fluctuations of production, employment, and income. It is also now generally recognized that mass unemployment is no longer politically, socially, or morally acceptable. Our problem, therefore, is to find that degree of intervention, that set of governmental controls, which will preserve the maximum degree of freedom of enterprise consistent with sustained full employment. And the test, as it always has been, is pragmatic. We must go as far as is required, but no further, to make our system work effectively and in the interest of all our people.

Liberals are quick to see that government intervention must

not go beyond what is necessary. It is equally important, however, to understand that government intervention must not stop short of what is necessary. If there is one thing clear from economic experience, it is that when governments do too little they are invariably driven to do far too much. For crises demand action and the more severe the crisis and the greater the unpreparedness for it, the more drastic and authoritarian the action is likely to be. What is more, if the responsibility for maintaining full and effective use of our resources—a responsibility which it cannot discharge—is placed upon free enterprise, when the crisis comes the result is a general discrediting of free enterprise. Businessmen are held responsible not only for their own sins, but also for the sins of the system, of which they are only a part. The end result of inadequate governmental responsibility and intervention is thus to undermine the very foundation of private enterprise. Experience both here and abroad demonstrates that the government controls necessary to make our system work are a prerequisite for the healthy functioning, indeed, for the very survival, of the free elements of our system.

The Evolution of Fiscal Policy   Concern about the business cycle goes back a long way. Almost every decade since the Civil War has witnessed a wave of intense public discussion of the causes of and possible cures for this basic disease of our system. In the earlier part of the period the discussion ran principally in terms of the influence of the supply of money on prices and general economic activity. Later this was broadened to include the influence of the level and structure of interest rates. The advocates of government intervention stressed the need for federal control over both the supply of money and the level of interest. With the establishment of the Federal Reserve System, what had once been regarded as statism became orthodox doctrine.

The onset of the Great Depression demonstrated that these controls were inadequate and the focus of attention gradually shifted from the supply of money and the rate of interest to the flow of spending and its determinants. It was natural that emphasis should come to be placed on the role of fiscal policy, which was at first conceived in terms of government spending to revive markets, production, and employment. It was not long, however, before a more sophisticated version was developed, emphasizing the role of fiscal policy not only to bring the economy to levels of full production but to keep it there by offsetting the ebb and flow of private spending. In this case, too, it is remarkable how short was the step from radical innovation, decried as statism, to orthodoxy. Within ten years we passed from the alarms and excursions of the Committee for Constitutional Government to the sober policy statements of the Committee for Economic Development. Even the National Association of Manufacturers has felt required, in resubmitting its archaic proposals, to use the sophisticated language of the new body of theory.[1]

Thinking on fiscal policy today, however, goes beyond the use of government surpluses and deficits to offset the ebb and flow of private spending and to sustain total demand at a level sufficient to clear the market of the goods produced at full employment. It is recognized that the fiscal instrument is a device for redistributing income. By graduating taxes to cut into incomes in the upper ranges of the income structure and by directing the flow of government spending to supplement consumption in the lower ranges of the income structure, it becomes possible, without incurring a continuing deficit, to secure the necessary balance between our propensity to save and our opportunities to invest.

The Limits of Fiscal Policy   Even this thinking is no longer regarded as bearing the mark of the cloven hoof. There are differences of opinion as to the degree of income redistribution which can or should be secured by fiscal policy, and there are those who warn that redistribution may, by cutting into the rewards of enterprise, choke off risk investment. These warnings should not be lightly dismissed. It is a question of balancing the effects upon risk investment of a curtailment of rewards on the one hand and the elimination or reduction of the risks of business fluctuations on the other. Once again the test is pragmatic. It may well be that some deficits

---

[1] Cf. *The American Individual Enterprise System* published by the N.A.M. (New York, 1946), Chapters VII (Savings and Capital Formation in the Enterprise System), XVI (Business Fluctuations), and XX (A Program for America).

on a continuing basis must be accepted in lieu of a balanced budget in order to provide adequate incentives to the entrepreneur.

Like control over the supply of money and the rate of interest, fiscal policy is no panacea. It is being increasingly recognized that a level of spending sufficient to clear the market of the goods produced at full employment creates strong inflationary pressures which may result in a wage-price spiral that can end only in a collapse of prices, production, and employment. It follows that a level of spending consistent with stable prices may entail production and employment seriously below capacity. If we restrict government intervention to fiscal policy, therefore, we must face the unpalatable alternatives of partial employment on the one hand and continued and perhaps violent economic instability on the other. Some form of control of prices and wages, to supplement fiscal policy, naturally suggests itself.

There are some who take the position that we could break out of this dilemma if we were prepared to destroy the concentration of economic power and to restore a reasonable facsimile of atomistic competition. This view, of course, has long been held on the anti-trust front. More recently, and notably in the Taft-Hartley Act, it has been carried over to the labor field as well. In my judgment, the view is a delusion. The truth is that an atomistic system, with wages and prices completely sensitive to the ebb and flow of demand and expectations, would be extremely volatile in its behavior. Even, therefore, if the concentrations of power could be broken down without destroying the productiveness of our system, which is open to the most serious question, the result would be to eliminate such elements of stability as our system now possesses. We must never lose sight of the fact that security and stability rank with monopoly profits as objectives of organized and concentrated economic power.

Administered Prices and Wages   Today, throughout the greater part of our economy, prices and wages are administered and they are administered with at least one eye cocked on stability. Throughout the area of durable-goods production, and in a large part of the nondurable-goods area as well, prices are not determined by the impersonal forces of the market; they are determined by men, a relatively few men, who either fix prices in collaboration or set their own prices in full awareness of what price action to expect from their few competitors. And, coextensive with the area of administered prices, there is the area of administered wages. Here again, a relatively small number of men, sitting around a table, set the national level, and in considerable degree the national structure of wages.

This is machinery that places enormous power in the hands of a small number of men. This power may be abused, but it is equally true that it can be used to great public advantage. Indeed, it is not too much to say that without such machinery a stable and balanced structure of wages and prices would be beyond our reach. Were such machinery not already in existence, it would be necessary to create it. But it is of the utmost importance that the power to determine the price and wage structure be used wisely, for it is this structure that determines the distribution of the national income and the balance or lack of balance between purchasing power and output. Without proper balance between prices and wages, and proper balance between purchasing power and output, sustained full employment is simply impossible of achievement.

What is the likelihood that we can get this wise use of power by voluntary means? Frankly, I do not pretend to know. The drive for quick profits, the difficulty of taking the long view, so clearly demonstrated since the premature ending of price control, provides little ground for optimism. On the other hand, there is an increasing understanding of the basic mechanisms and requirements of our system. The policy statements of such organizations as the Committee for Economic Development and the National Planning Association set a high standard, and if the practice falls short of the precept this may only represent a lag which time can cure. I may be wrong, but it is my feeling that the business community, if it could relive 1946, would not repeat the blunders it made that year.

In any event, prices and wages constitute a crucial area of policy which must be watched with the greatest care. In the future we must have a national price and wage policy, modified in the light of changing economic circumstances and designed to contribute to the basic national objective of full employment. If this cannot be achieved under predominantly private responsibility, some form of price and wage controls will have to be developed. It is too early as yet to say whether this will be necessary, and liberals should be very reluctant to discount the possibilities of voluntary arrangements arrived at under more nearly normal circumstances than those of the past few years. It is equally important, however, that liberals not hestitate to press for such controls, should it become apparent that nothing less will serve. For, to repeat what I said at the outset, too little governmental intervention must inevitably lead to too much.

Investment, Stability, and Growth Quite apart from the necessity of securing a proper balance between purchasing power and output and an appropriate distribution of income, without which that balance cannot be sustained, it must be recognized that there are elements in our economy, particularly in the investment field, which are highly volatile. Investment has in the past always proceeded by fits and starts and this has been equally true of all the basic components of investment—plant and equipment, housing, inventories, and foreign lending. The question arises whether economic stability can be secured without some form of direct control of the flow of investment. Beveridge, for one, believes that it cannot and that control is required.

On this score, too, I am in doubt. It is too early to say whether stabilization of the economy, if continued long enough to be taken by businessmen as a given fact, would not permit of investment planned for stability, thus choking off at its source the most basic impulse to economic instability in our system. Some degree of government intervention, particularly in the fields of housing and foreign lending, designed for quite other purposes, but serving the purposes of stabilization as well, might be all that is required. Time will tell.

One final point: The level of investment in crucial areas of the economy is in the hands of a relatively small group of men. In the past, they have used their power not only to release investment by fits and starts, but, in the interest of monopoly profits, to damp the level of investment as a whole. This has restricted the production of vitally needed goods; it has also resulted in unemployment throughout the economy. If this behavior should be continued, government investment can of course be used to offset the swings of private investment and to supplement its total volume. But this gives rise to the questions whether the government, under such circumstances, should leave to private enterprise the most productive and socially useful areas of investment and confine itself to those areas in which private enterprise cannot or will not operate. Many liberals are unwilling to accept this alternative. Some suggest government ownership in certain industries as the remedy. Others suggest government investment in yardstick plants which could serve both to supplement private capacity and to set the pace in pricing.[2] Still others suggest a combination of the two, with direct control of investment thrown into the pot as well.

There is no easy answer to any of these questions, and this for the very reason that the issues are not of a kind but of degree. The test should be pragmatic—what will work? And the attitude should be experimental—we do not know everything yet. The liberal, with his abiding faith in the values of individual freedom, will be reluctant to sacrifice any part of that freedom unless the circumstances leave no practical alternative. On the other hand, the liberal, ever conscious of the basic requirement that our system serve men rather than men the system, will not hesitate when achievement of the larger freedom requires diminution of the lesser.

[2] See Chapters 8 and 9.

CHAPTER XIII

Government and Business
in a Mixed Economy

by Merle Fainsod

A decade ago, when New Deal hopes still glowed brightly, mixed economy as exemplified by Sweden's "Middle Way" was being saluted as the shining pole-star of America's future. Today, in the full swing of the reaction against war controls, mixed economy is being denounced in influential circles. It is widely heralded as the "road to serfdom." Our efforts to mingle public ownership, government controls, private and co-operative enterprise, we are told, must end in disaster. Either we must choose wholly unrestricted and uncontrolled private enterprise or submit to dictatorial regimentation. There is no middle way.[1]

This "either-or" line of argument has an obvious polemic value. It is intended to make us hesitate before we entrust any additional functions to government. Yet as a matter of practical choice, it is doubtful whether any substantial body of opinion in the United States, Republican or Democratic, would be prepared to recognize the alternatives of laissez faire or dictatorship as very real. We maintain our attachment to civil and political liberties. We retain our faith in private enterprise as a mainspring of economic activity in many important sectors of our economic life. But, particularly since the Great Depression, we have also come to accept a new re-

[1] This observation has been made by others in this volume; it is important enough to stand repetition.—Ed.

sponsibility on the part of government for the economic well-being of the nation. There are certain basic securities, such as protection against unemployment and provision for the aged and the destitute, which are increasingly recognized as a primary concern of government. We can be certain that if mass unemployment should again be with us, it will be to government that people will turn for action.

Does this mean that we are committed to a future in which government grows more and more powerful? Will we in our drive for security create an all-powerful bureaucratic Frankenstein which ends up by telling us where we shall work, what we shall eat, what we shall produce, how much we shall earn, and what we shall think? Or is there middle ground between complete private and complete public enterprise in which we can combine the civil and political liberties which we cherish and the basic economic securities to which we aspire?

The Meaning of "Mixed Economy"   The term which we use to describe such middle ground is mixed economy. The phrase "mixed economy" may cover a considerable variety of possible permutations and combinations. In this country, for all of the legacy of New Deal controls, it still refers to an economy in which private enterprise is of major importance. By far the larger part of our heavy and light industries and distributive trades falls within the area of private ownership and control.

A mixed economy of this kind means that responsibility for the economic welfare of the nation is decentralized. Over most of the economy we look to businessmen to make the important decisions determining output, prices, and profits. Their decisions are in turn affected by the demands and bargaining strength of labor, by the prices paid for raw materials which farmers and others produce, and by the public policies which government pursues. The policies of government are particularly important in the area of fiscal policy and over the whole range of publicly owned or regulated industries. But our "mixed economy" does not operate with a centrally directed plan. Business, labor, agriculture, and government all divide and share responsibility for making the important economic choices which, taken together, spell prosperity or depression.

The Dangers of Mixed Economy   Here lie both the
great danger and the grand opportunity of mixed economy.
The danger consists in the fact that each group may make its
own economic decisions with an eye only on what it conceives
to be its own short-run interests. That danger is vividly illustrated by inflationary developments since the collapse of
the wartime stabilization program. Some businessmen who
should have known better have driven for higher prices in
order to make excessive profits in a scarcity market, regardless of the impact on the rest of the economy and the long-
term consequences of boom and bust. Some farm groups, too,
have exploited shortages and have sought to perpetuate them
against the day when consumer demand begins to fall off.
Certain labor leaders have resorted to monopolistic restrictions and paralyzing strikes to win compensatory advantages
for themselves. A mixed economy operated in this fashion
becomes very mixed up indeed, particularly when, as part of
the reaction against war controls, government abdicates its
responsibilities and allows the pulling and hauling of the great
economic groups to prepare the way for catastrophe.

These dangers are real. But the opportunities for constructive statesmanship are no less apparent. A business community
concerned with its own survival must appreciate that public
responsibilities go with leadership, and that these responsibilities extend beyond the short-run profit and loss position of the
company. Business needs to recognize that its own health is
dependent on the economic health of the other large economic
groups in the nation—farmers, workers, and consumers. The
relationship by the same token is reciprocal, a fact which
the more far-sighted farmer and labor leaders give increasing
evidence of understanding.

The Task of Government   Government too has its
obligations to meet. Its basic problem is to achieve a fruitful
working relationship with the great economic groups so that
each can make its contribution to the national economic well-
being. If a mixed economy is to produce maximum employment, production, and purchasing power, government and
business dare not fall into the error of regarding each other as
hostile antagonists. The legacy of bitterness which we carry

over from the thirties does not ease the task of making a mixed economy work. The New Deal expansion of the economic powers of government represented in the main a response to the demands of disadvantaged farm and labor groups, which used the instrumentality of government to improve their positions. Controls, such as the Securities and Exchange Commission, and the National Labor Relations Board, which were imposed on business, inspired resentment. Many business leaders viewed the New Deal as an enemy determined to displace private enterprise by a socialist state. The frictions and cleavages produced had destructive results. Despite unprecedented governmental activity during the New Deal era and very real social gains, substantial portions of our resources of capital and labor remained idle. The full possibilities of synchronizing governmental and business efforts to overcome economic maladjustments were not adequately realized.

Can they be effectively meshed? If we are to operate a mixed economy with any hope of success, we must exercise all our ingenuity and inventiveness to devise a scheme of interrelationships which will avoid locking business and government in sterile combat. We must find ways of inducing both business and government to give their support to public policies which spell high production, full employment, economic stability, and equitable distribution.

The Employment Act of 1946 with its provision for a three man Council of Economic Advisers, whose function it is, among other things, "to recommend to the President national economic policies to foster and promote free competitive enterprise, to avoid economic fluctuations or to diminish the effects thereof, and to maintain employment, production, and purchasing power" is a useful start in this direction. But it is only a start. The analyses and recommendations of the council are essays in persuasion, rather than policies which carry their own implementation.

As we grapple with the economic problems of the postwar years there are certain lessons of our past experience with government regulation of business which it is important for us to keep in mind. Typically, the regulatory agency in this country has not been concerned with such issues as maximizing production, or employment, or securing the most efficient utilization of resources. Typically, as in the railroad field, we have embarked on regulation to stamp out specific abuses such as unreasonable or discriminatory rates. It was important that such abuses be eliminated. But a regulatory philosophy which puts major emphasis on a system of negative restraints inevitably generates friction between regulators and regulated. It is difficult in such a climate to develop public policies in which government and business contribute their efforts as collaborative instrumentalities working toward a common goal.

It may well be that there are situations in which direct controls of the traditional type are unavoidable. Short of public ownership, it is difficult to visualize any alternatives in those areas of the economy in which monopoly factors have taken firm root. Moreover, in a full-employment economy threatened by run-away inflation, where fiscal controls have proved inadequate, direct controls over prices, wages, and allocations may have to be invoked as a last resort. But it should be recognized that the imposition of such controls is almost certain to accentuate hostility between business and government.

Effective Compromise   Can terms be found by which government and business can join in building a full-employment economy without wasting their energies in useless friction? Some indications that the problem is not insoluble are provided by the public utterances of such business leaders as Mr. Paul G. Hoffman, chairman of the Committee for Economic Development. Mr. Hoffman and those for whom he speaks agree that it will take the collective wisdom of government, business, labor, and agriculture to stabilize our economic system. He has declared himself ready to support a considerable expansion in the coverage of unemployment insurance, the management of the public debt and credit policy to achieve greater economic stability, the timing of the construction of public works so as to provide for expansion when the level of private business activity is low, a vigorous anti-monopoly policy to insure competition, and a tax system recast to stabilize spending and to encourage investment in risk enterprises. It may well be that the conceptions of government's responsibilities shared by Mr. Hoffman and his collaborators fall far short of the views of liberals who are prepared to press for higher minimum wages, for vigorous programs of regional development, for slum clearance, for health insurance, and the guarantee of a basic minimum diet below which no American family should be allowed to fall. But at least there is common ground within which it is possible to work together. With a minimum of recrimination on each side, it may even be possible to widen the area of agreement.

If public policy is to be oriented toward dynamic economic expansion and, if business leadership is expected to play a significant role in achieving such expansion, we cannot afford to accept the dreary either-or dilemma that there can be no compromise between private and public enterprise and that their essential purposes are always and necessarily hostile. The challenge is rather that of devising the means and inventing the techniques by which both government and business can make a common contribution to the prosperity of the nation.

Too little attention has been devoted to meeting this challenge. That the task is not impossible is indicated by the imaginative work of the Department of Agriculture in developing the food-stamp plan during the thirties. Here was an administrative invention by which subsidies were used to expand consumption, rather than to restrict production. Farmers benefited by reduced surpluses. Since the surplus items disposed of in exchange for food stamps moved through commercial channels, processors and distributors benefited by the increase in their business. Those on relief benefited, of course, as a result of the improvement in their basic diet. Here was an emergency expedient for sustaining purchasing power which enlisted wide-spread support from government, farmers, and the business interests affected. If the need should arise again, can we not devise other equally effective techniques to support purchasing power and expand consumption and production, while minimizing potential business opposition by utilizing the channels of private enterprise to achieve the desired results?

Regulation by incentive has its dangers. Carried to a *reductio ad absurdum*, its logic trends toward a demand for universal subsidization. But it is a mistake in public policy, as in other areas, to seek to discredit a device on the ground that it can be abused. The more important question is whether there are areas of public policy where it can be effectively used to achieve the goals of economic welfare upon which there is wide-spread agreement. If incentives can be employed at strategic points in the economy as seed to produce a richer crop of national economic well-being, then their use should not be too difficult to justify. From this point of view there is much to be said for careful experimentation with this technique of regulation, not only in periods of depression when consumption needs to be expanded and new investment encouraged, but also in periods of relative prosperity when resistance to the expansion of the capacity of bottle-neck industries such as steel cannot otherwise be overcome.

The problem of using government creatively and effectively to make our mixed economy work promises to be a continuing challenge from which there is no turning back. We enter the postwar period with a probable peacetime federal budget of 35 billion dollars a year. This constitutes a substantial percentage of the national income. It means that decisions on government revenues and expenditures are bound to have important effects on the level of economic activity as a whole. The management of the public debt, tax policy, credit policy, and the direction of government expenditures will all have a profound impact on general employment, production, and purchasing power.[2] The wise guidance of fiscal policy becomes of crucial significance in determining whether a mixed economy can function effectively.

New technological developments mean that government will become an increasingly important factor in the economy. The Atomic Energy Act of 1946, for example, outlines a program for government control of production, ownership, and use of fissionable material. New vistas are opened up which we can as yet only dimly apprehend. This new source of energy, provided we find ways of holding its destructive

[2] Cf. Chapter 6.

potentialities in leash, may have profound consequences on the organization of our civilian economy. The responsibilities imposed on government controllers are awesome in their magnitude. There have been few periods in our history when the need for an able and responsible public service has been more urgent.

Do these increased governmental responsibilities spell the omnipotent state and the end of individual liberties as we have known them in the past? No one can vouchsafe a certain answer. In a political system such as ours in which organized economic interests find free expression, no single pattern of relationships between government and the great economic groups can be forever ordained as fixed and unalterable. But while the bulk of the American electorate retains a vigorous and lively faith in democratic processes and our economic system provides high employment, production, and just distribution, the danger is not great. The immediate problem which faces us is not the menace of a totalitarian state or the loss of our political liberties. The challenge is rather that of using government creatively, not as a threat to private enterprise, but as a positive guiding force to strengthen the economy and to adjust it to the needs of the basic economic groups—consumers, farmers, laborers, and businessmen—to whom it is directly responsible.

CHAPTER XIV

Housing—The Ever-Recurring Crisis

by Charles Abrams

America has faced seven housing emergencies in the last 25 years:

1917–18—A shelter shortage in World War I upset the production time-table, menacing the war effort. A war housing program was initiated.

1922–26—A postwar housing shortage caused homelessness and overcrowding. Rents rose sharply. Rent controls were imposed, and tax subsidies given by some cities to speed home building.

1933–36—Lack of home building was linked to the unemployment emergency. Home building was made the object of vast federal aids in an effort to revive construction and promote economic recovery. More than a dozen federal housing agencies were set up to tackle various phases of the program.

1937—"One-third of a nation" was found to be living in slums. Emphasis in housing shifted toward recognition of a "social emergency" and adoption of a slum-clearance program entailing 800 million dollars in loans and 28 million dollars in annual subsidies.

1940—A defense housing emergency was declared as we belatedly realized that there can be no efficient defense program without shelter for the defense workers. With workers living in box-cars, pews, and jails, a number of federal agencies were empowered to build housing with federal funds.

1941—World War II brought us face to face with production problems caused by labor turnover due to housing shortages in war-production areas. An extended war housing program was undertaken to keep the war effort from bogging down.

1946—War ended. Veterans returned and faced a postwar housing emergency more serious than that which followed World War I.

Whenever one of these emergencies arose, an emergency measure was authorized to meet it. But a new crisis followed soon after. It has become evident that without a national policy aimed at removing the causes of housing crises, the housing problem in America will continue to be one unending, ever recurring emergency.

A New Emergency Ahead While still in the throes of the postwar housing emergency, it is already possible to see another looming ahead. The aging of our housing plant, the increase in the number of our families, the drop in home building during the depression and war years, the failure of the building industry to meet accruing needs, and the large number of marriages after World War II have joined to bring on the most pressing need for housing in our history. The postwar shortage was only the first pang of that crisis.

Depending upon the period in which we undertake to meet the need, the number of dwellings required per annum will be as follows: under a ten-year program, 1,860,000; under a fifteen-year program, 1,420,000; under a twenty-year program, 1,200,000.[1] Whether we build in ten, fifteen, or twenty years, two things are clear: (1) Housing equalling about half the existing supply of forty million dwelling units need to be built. Not since the opening of the frontier has a greater opportunity therefore confronted America. For this accumulated need makes home building today an opening wedge into the comprehensive replanning of our cities. We can either choose to build solvent new neighborhoods, or allow the pent-up demand for this housing to be released without guidance into the same haphazard patterns that have characterized American city development from the start.

[1] For the basis of these estimates see my *The Future of Housing* (New York, 1946).

(2) We cannot meet these housing needs under the present private-building formulas.

We have the land, the labor, and the materials. We have the energy and the genius to utilize them. But blockading the production of our housing is the small-home builder upon whose capacity and willingness to tackle the job the whole operation depends. Home building functions or idles at his pleasure. Even effective demand cannot arouse him to rise above his physical limitations. He is unequipped to build more than half a dozen houses a year. Between the two World Wars, the industry could average only 500,000 dwellings annually and none of them were for the lowest income families. At best the home builder can do no more than a small part of the home-building job—providing houses for the well-to-do.

Around his limitations, as around an undersized sieve, has collected a residue of waste, ineptitude, irresponsibility, concentration of power, and unfair competition that is unparalleled in any other industry. All too often these evils are looked upon as causes of the builder's limitations when in fact they are effects. The housing need will be met neither quantitatively nor qualitatively so long as this little speculative industry continues to block up the flow and hold down the quality of homes for the American people. Greater efficiency would follow if the builder were set up as a large-scale producer on a parity with the automobile manufacturer.

This failure of American housing production is responsible for the slums that have undermined the health of our people. The poor quality and high price of new homes have made home ownership a hazard, while recurring housing shortages have become an ever imminent threat to our social and economic well-being.

Fifteen billion dollars of federal funds and commitments have been poured into housing undertakings since 1933 and billions of dollars of cash and credit will continue to be poured into the bottomless pit that housing is today. Despite these vast outlays, little has been accomplished. The housing problem will persist, stubbornly impervious to private effort or public aid, unless we acknowledge the failure of the private

building industry to meet the housing needs of the people
and unless the government evolves a workable program to
meet those needs.

A New Approach to the Problem   The magnitude of
the problem demands a new approach to the planning process in housing. It entails a shift from negative to positive city
planning. The new approach would acknowledge that in
providing housing and rebuilding our cities, restrictive legislation such as zoning, dwelling laws, and other controls are
obsolete as primary weapons. The main instrumentality must
be the eminent-domain and spending powers. Putting it less
legalistically: (1) extensive acquisition of land by the cities
is essential to their proper replanning, (2) such land must be
acquired in connection with master plans laid down in advance, (3) after acquiring the land, cities must be prepared
to allot it for public and private redevelopment in line with
the master plan, (4) cities must be prepared, with federal
and state assistance, to build housing for *all groups* not served
by the private builder.

To avoid socialization of our housing the plan will recognize that the main prop under the private enterprise system is
private ownership which must be preserved and encouraged.
We should envision public ownership only in those enterprises
in which public operation is essential, such as schools and
post-offices. Since public ownership is not an essential part
of the public function in the building of homes, their ownership or control should be turned over to the tenants and other
purchasers as soon as feasible. The encouragement and formation of tenant co-operatives would be indispensable to such a
program. In other words, after assuming the positive approach
in planning and housing we must also shift the emphasis from
public building and public ownership to public building as
a means of assuring sound private ownership.

The Ideological Impediment   What holds us back
from undertaking a ten- or fifteen-year program to rebuild
America? Not the cost. A complete clearance of all our slums,
the largest phase of the operation, would cost no more annually than three days' cost of World War II, or less than 10
per cent of the current military budget. New York City could

clear its slums in about ten years without any federal aid by earmarking its current emergency sales tax for the task. If all three levels of government co-operated, the job could be done without great budgetary strain on any one of them.

The main impediment to a comprehensive program is a confusion over whether extensive operations by public agencies in the rebuilding of our cities would conflict with the philosophy underlying the private-enterprise system. If this issue were resolved we could proceed to rationalize the housing disorder, build dignified cities, have decent homes for ourselves and for the generations to succeed us.

Let us then submit the issue to four rigid tests—practicality, constitutionality, tradition, and conservative economics.

(1)   We are making huge commitments in our cities anyway, but doing it piecemeal and planlessly. The total cost of these haphazard and emergency efforts will be greater than would be a comprehensive undertaking boldly planned, envisioned in advance and systematically pursued to its completion. That slums are costly and that it is economy to clear them is well established too.[2] Since we are being called upon to build homes equal to half our existing supply, is it wise to make the expenditure piece by piece, when the end product will be only the ossification of the obsolete patterns and the perpetuation of crisis? Or shall we use this great opportunity to build twentieth-century communities befitting our wealth, our energy, and our culture, and at the same time solve the housing problem for ourselves and our children? The answer is plain.

(2)   The constitutional issue is easily disposed of. The Supreme Court and the high courts of twenty-one states have upheld the legality of publicly sponsored housing. Rarely has a reform received more passionate sanction from the American bench.[3] Public subsidies and eminent domain are authorized

---

[2] See statement of John B. Blandford, Administrator of the National Housing Agency, together with accompanying data filed with the Subcommittee on Housing and Urban Redevelopment of the Senate, 79th Congress, 1st session, Part 6, January 9, 1945.

[3] See Myres S. McDougal and Addison A. Mueller, "Public Purpose in Public Housing," *Yale Law Journal* (December 1942).

even to private companies for slum clearance. City planning, too, has long been recognized as a governmental function, and effective city planning is no less legal than our current ineffective city planning.

(3)   From the standpoint of our traditions, the purchase of land and its resale is in line even with the planning principles of the founding fathers. Washington, D. C., could never have been developed without actual control of much of the strategic land needed to carry out Major L'Enfant's plan. After the fulfillment of the general plan was assured, the land was turned back into private hands. The right of land acquisition for national uses has always been implicit in our American system. And often the land acquired has been resold when no longer needed. In the two World Wars for example, all the land needed for housing and other war uses was purchased, built upon, and then sold when the emergency was over. The logic that applies to a war emergency applies as forcefully to a postwar emergency.

(4)   The most effective, though not the most cogent, argument against comprehensive planning is that it would compete with private enterprise and threaten the capitalist society. This argument is effective because it plays upon the prejudices of a public not fully informed in all the ramifications of economic theory.

The fact is that public and private activities in housing have become so interdependent today that there is no longer a detectable cleavage. Private housing enters the public field by accepting vast public aid and even assuming public powers—FHA, the Home Loan Bank System, and Stuyvesant Town are recent examples. Every private development enforces vast public investment for streets, schools, and other public improvements.[4] Today's jerry-built house is tomorrow's slum, pressing for public intervention and expenditure. With almost 60 per cent of all home mortgages already underwritten by the federal government and the way paved for insuring most of the rest, separation of private and public effort into self-contained zones has become impossible. The gov-

[4] Streets, schools, and other public property in a neighborhood usually represent about 35 per cent of the total area.

ernment is now so deeply involved in housing, mortgage underwriting, and the security of home ownership that it is bound to intervene with all its necessary resources should the mortgage or home-ownership structure be again threatened.

Words like "socialism" and "communism" are being hurled about recklessly to the terror of the uninformed public, but above the din, the issue between the pressure groups contesting for government housing benefits gradually clarifies. One group, spearheaded by a lobby of builders and lenders, asserts that all housing appropriations should be channeled primarily through business groups without measuring the benefit accruing to the rank and file. Under a private-enterprise system, it argues, the dividends to the masses should be residual and subordinate to the benefit to business. Another group seeks to effect a "practical" compromise. It asserts that the appropriations should be dispensed for the benefit of the rank and file primarily, but to achieve its objective it is willing to compromise by allowing the lion's share of the benefits to business in the form of FHA and Home Loan Bank assistance, yield insurance, and other risk-lifting devices.

There is room for a third point of view not represented, one aiming to assure the maximum benefit to the rank and file while still giving the private-enterprise mechanisms in housing a greater opportunity than they have ever experienced in their history.

This becomes clear when we understand how the private builder operates. He usually has only a transient interest in the job. He buys the land, builds and sells the home. His interest in the transaction lasts for about six months. Though looked upon as an entrepreneur he is in fact little more than a contractor particularly in operations aided by the federal government. The predominant functions of private enterprise in home building are not his, but those of the materials companies, labor, the financiers, and the sub-contractors.

If, in the building of our twenty-one to twenty-four million homes, our cities, through local housing authorities, assumed the primary responsibility for building all housing not built by the private builder as well as for building the public works in connection with these developments, the private housing enterprise would not only not be harmed but would receive a tremendous impetus.[5]

The advantages of a positive program of decentralized public building are that (1) we could get housing built to meet our needs, (2) the city could determine where the new developments should best take place to meet the requirements of the city plan instead of simply conforming its investment to small, inefficient mushroom private developments, (3) the city could better secure the long-term soundness of the homes built, by building them in sound, durable communities that create their own environment, (4) under a comprehensive program, mass orders could be given and unified specifications drawn, resulting in a greater uniformity of parts; labor could be more effectively utilized and the defunct building industry might at last head toward rationalization and efficiency; (5) as a result of standardization of specifications and mass production resulting from mass orders, home building for the higher income groups served by the private builder would benefit, too; costs would be brought down, and the field of government building would be gradually narrowed as rationalization is achieved.

Such a program not only conforms with capitalist tradition but complies even with eighteenth-century conceptions of government function. Adam Smith recognized the duty of the sovereign to be "that of erecting and maintaining those public institutions and those public works . . . of such a nature, that the profit could never repay the expense to any individual . . . and which it, therefore, cannot be expected that any individual, or small number of individuals, should erect or maintain."

In housing policy, American liberals are not daring enough to demand a complete program, while the conservatives are not conservative enough to insist that the public-housing programs should assure private ownership. The ideological conflict in America on comprehensive planning and housing exists largely because of the confusion over the meaning of

[5] See my *Future of Housing* (New York, 1946), p. 360, and compare with Harold E. Stassen's proposal in *Where I Stand* (New York, 1947).

"free enterprise" and "private enterprise" in housing—a "free enterprise" which is being fashioned to become an enterprise free of risk and a "private enterprise" that in housing today is no longer either private or enterprise.

If we had a clear-cut policy under which cities assumed leadership for the rebuilding of America not only would it not be a challenge to the private-enterprise system, it can be the most effective bulwark for its preservation.

The Role of Local Authorities   Such a program would mean an expansion of the role of the local housing authorities. They should be reconstituted to explore new techniques, relate private to public undertakings, solicit private builders to build near their projects, and assemble the land required for both. Where a shortage occurs and the private builder does not fulfill his function, the public authority should step in. Just as war housing was within its province, the provision of veterans' housing should also be. The authority should originate proposals to anticipate and relieve housing shortages, give advice to the prospective home buyer and to the veteran against reckless dealers. In short, it should be responsible for all the housing problems and policies in the community rather than be merely the advocate of public housing.

Public housing should also strive to divest itself of public control and ultimately even of public ownership by lease or sale of the projects to the tenants. It is here that co-operative ownership can find its most important place. Public housing should therefore aim to educate its tenants and prepare them for assuming the responsibilities of operation and ownership.

Summary   If we adopted the above program we would be achieving our aims within the private enterprise system. We would be respecting and encouraging private ownership. We would be revitalizing our building industry by substituting mass operations for the small, sporadic enterprises of the speculative builder. We would be housing our low-income families and clearing our slums. We would be rebuilding our cities and replacing our blighted areas by communities fitting our culture and productive capacity. We would be establishing a sounder home ownership structure. We would be supplying adequate rental housing for those unable or unwilling to own. Our veterans could have homes that are sound both physically and financially. We would be stabilizing the patterns of our cities and thereby assuring greater safety of public and private investment. The drain on our municipal revenues caused by our uneconomic city patterns would be checked. We would be helping toward achieving higher employment by speeding up the building program when necessary and making it fulfill its role in the economy. Finally, we would be giving our people a real and a vital stake in democracy and demonstrating to the world that America can solve its housing problem within the framework of its present system.

CHAPTER XV

Urban Redevelopment

by Guy Greer

American cities and towns are a disgrace to America. That is what a sharp-tongued observer from Europe would be likely to tell you, if he had traveled widely over the country and looked both at and below the surface of things in our urban communities. If you should remind him that European cities—quite apart from war devastation—are nothing to brag about either, probably he would agree with you. But he might then retort that the cities of America have far less excuse than do those of Europe for the mess they are in, and that therein lies the disgrace.

To pursue further such an imaginary interchange of incivilities might be entertaining, but scarcely profitable. Nor would it be worth while to go very deeply into reasons for the present state of affairs, except as required to uncover and remove causes. The common-sense procedure is to take a candid look at the worst of conditions as they are, then to figure out what can be done to remedy them.

The Mess We Are In   Thanks to lack of forethought and planning—a lack attributable to several generations of exaggerated faith in the virtues of laissez faire—both the physical pattern and the administrative framework of our towns have become obsolete and hopelessly inadequate for modern requirements. Whether the city be large or small, it is being smothered by traffic and other congestion, and its efforts to breathe freely and healthily are hindered by the well-nigh insuperable obstacles of outmoded legal and fiscal arrangements. The makeshift outcome is described by the dread word "decentralization"—the flight of people and business and industry from the older sections of the town to the suburbs or the open country, where there is more room for living and making a living.

But since decentralization is unorganized and unguided, its consequences are already so fraught with evil that it is being called a disease. And it threatens to create all over again on the outskirts the same conditions that caused it to start from the downtown areas in the first place. Usually the new developments are as badly planned and as little controlled as was the growth of the original city. Hence the same overcrowding is likely to occur, and the same kind of blight and slum conditions. Moreover, the new suburbs or satellites are seldom well planned as to location—that is, in relation to the urban community as a whole—so that they often add to the already nightmarish difficulties of traffic and transportation in the urbanized region. Thus the decentralization movement, though based on wholesome instincts, tends to have the effect of merely extending over wider areas the very conditions it set out to get rid of.

Its most immediately serious effects, however, and the ones with which this chapter is principally concerned, are in the city proper. They are manifest in the blighted areas left behind and in the vicious spiral set in motion whereby the municipal government is obliged to take action that tends to make blight spread.

Generally the most prosperous citizens, those best able to pay taxes, are the ones who move out beyond city limits. They do so partly in order to escape city taxes. Then the city government, in its desperate efforts to make ends meet, must maintain or even increase taxes on those who remain, thus helping to drive more of them away. Assessed values and taxes on the properties left behind must be kept up, else the city government would go broke, though the owners (whether old or new) cannot afford even to keep the buildings in good repair, much less construct new ones. Land under the run-down buildings, however, is usually too high-priced to permit the kind of use the city needs. To redevelop it for residential purposes (generally its required use) with the small number of families per acre that would avoid another crisis of overcrowding, is out of the question for business enterprise; for, with rare exceptions, the project would not be a profitable investment.

False and True Remedies　　In an attempt to cope with the problem of blight, a dozen or more states have passed "urban redevelopment" laws. These start from the sound premise that land for successful redevelopment must be assembled in large parcels, and provision is actually made for purchase through condemnation where necessary. But in another way and for the most part, such legislation is totally inadequate, and often it even threatens to do more harm than good. This is so because, no matter how the land is acquired, its cost is likely to be as high as existing market prices or assessed valuations, or even higher; then in order for a redevelopment project to promise to justify the investment, so many big buildings must go up that overcrowding is sure to be made worse. In New York, for example (the only place where the new laws have as yet been extensively used), several large housing projects are being built to accommodate two or three times as many families as lived in the same areas before, thus adding to congestion in sections of the city that already were badly overcrowded.

A realistic approach to the problem must recognize the necessity, in most instances, of writing off or otherwise disposing of an excess of land values ranging anywhere from 30 or 40 to 80 or 90 per cent of present market prices. When this is done, in all probability private enterprise may be counted on to buy or lease the areas in question and build on them the sort of housing that will conform to a sanely conceived redevelopment plan. Failing this, however, nothing more can be hoped for—even when the land *can* be assembled in large parcels—than an occasional large project like those of New York. And if such projects really should become numerous enough to use up the bulk of the blighted areas, they would make present difficulties of overcrowding and congestion seem mild by comparison.

The Public Must Pay   The question arises, then, how to accomplish the necessary deflation of land values. Plainly there is no practicable way to do it except through having the cost borne by the urban community as a whole— which, rather than the individual owners of the property, is responsible for the neglect that allowed the drift into present conditions. And indeed a few of the more recently enacted state urban redevelopment laws do provide, at least tacitly, that the city itself may buy up the blighted land for subsequent resale or lease at prices lower than the cost of acquisition—if the city wants to and can. But there's the rub. Outlays on a scale large enough to solve the problem of blight are impossible for virtually every town in the country.

Here, greatly simplified but not distorted, is the essence of the problem of urban redevelopment. How are the local governments of the urban communities to be provided with the necessary funds, assuming that blight is not to be allowed to continue to spread? Either they must be put into a position to get at a larger proportion of the wealth and income their citizens produce, which means a nation-wide overhauling of our traditional arrangements for taxation and public expenditures, or else they must receive the needed funds from the federal government or from the state governments having jurisdiction, or from both sources.

Theoretically the state governments, through their power to levy income taxes, are in a position to solve the problem without federal aid. On principle, moreover, they ought to do it. But there are well-nigh insuperable obstacles in the way, for example, the reluctance of states to levy or to increase income taxes, the fact that in a good many instances an urban community extends into territory of two or more states. So, as a practical matter and for the time being, the funds in question must come from the federal government if they are to be made available at all.

The Taft-Ellender-Wagner Bill—and After   Such is at any rate the reasoning back of that section of the Taft-Ellender-Wagner bill of 1947 which purports to deal with urban redevelopment. Unfortunately, however, the T-E-W bill's approach is so timid and cautious that in all probability little or nothing can be accomplished under the relevant section of it. The appropriations envisaged are insignificant compared with what would be needed, and even these are hedged about with so many financial conditions to be met by the cities that the local governments will be reluctant to undertake operations of considerable size. At the same time, however, the conditions with respect to planning, and to the reforms in state-local governmental relations that will be needed for a genuine solution of the problem, are vague if not ambiguous. Passage of the urban redevelopment section of the bill, as now drawn, would no doubt be better than continued neglect of spreading blight; but if it is passed as it now stands, work should be started at once on amendments that would come to grips with the problem's fundamentals.

Needed is a co-ordinated attack on the three principal phases of the difficulty: (1) jurisdictional powers of the local government; (2) planning for the whole urban community (city proper and present and future suburbs); and (3) money to clear away the obstacles (excessive land costs) in the way of sound redevelopment. The third phase should become a responsibility of the federal government only on condition that the first two are tackled realistically by the state and local governments. Otherwise there could be no assurance that the spread of blight would not be resumed within a few years, for lack of power of the local communities to control its causes.

Jurisdictional powers of the local governments are matters of state legislation. They need to be redefined and expanded geographically. Permissive legislation (amendment of state constitutions where necessary) is required whereby any urban community composed of the city proper and suburban development beyond its corporate limits can superimpose over the entire urban area the degree of metropolitan administration requisite for over-all planning and zoning and for other governmental functions, such as arterial transportation, police and fire protection, water and sewer service, and so on, which are of greater importance to the area as a whole than to its separate parts. Probably a federated metropolitan government of limited powers, leaving all undelegated powers of the constituent local governments as before, would be the best arrangement—except that the power of local governments to buy and sell land should be expanded and clarified. And of course, in the case of an urban community extending over state lines, the permissive legislation would have to be passed by all the states having jurisdiction.

Enactment of such legislation by the states concerned should be made a condition precedent to federal financial aid for any community in the redevelopment of its blighted areas.

But this is not the only condition that ought to be imposed. Required also should be the actual use by the urban community of its new powers. Aid should be extended only when, through democratic processes, the constituent local governments have in fact set up the kind of area-wide controls needed and have at least drawn up and adopted both a satisfactory outline of a planning program for the community as a whole and a specific plan for redevelopment of the blighted area or areas in question. If necessary the federal government might help to defray the cost of the planning and, upon request, it might furnish technical assistance. But there should be left no doubt that essential decisions with respect to planning are matters of local responsibility.

Theoretically, of course, there might be danger that the agency charged with administering the federal aid would arbitrarily impose its own notions of good planning before releasing funds. But this danger could be overcome in practice by a suitable wording of the federal law, notwithstanding some very bad planning imposed upon certain cities by the U. S. Housing Authority.

Why Rely on the Federal Government? The foregoing is intended to present, in highly condensed form, a practicable procedure for using the financial power of the federal government to cause physically sane urban redevelopment (whether financially sane or not) to be started fairly soon, without waiting for the grand overhauling that is needed of federal-state-local taxation and expenditures. Let us look for a moment in conclusion at whether such a procedure would be socially and politically desirable. (Other chapters of this volume deal with the federal financial and fiscal problems that would be involved, as well as with the desirability of varying public expenditures to compensate for the ups and downs of private investment.)

It has long been evident to observers of our economic society that there is a growing volume of urgently needed functions requiring financial outlays that must be performed at public expense if they are to be performed at all. And it has by now become equally clear that removing the obstacles in the way of reshaping the obsolete physical patterns of our cities and towns is such a function. The only question that remains is whether this particular task should be undertaken by the federal rather than the state and local governments.

In theory, the states and localities should attend to it, for the best of reasons. Each community and each region should stand on its own feet, as far as physical development is concerned, except in matters affecting the welfare of the country as a whole. If redevelopment with indigenous resources is impossible, the region or community should shrink in population to a self-supporting level and the extra people should move to where indigenous resources are more abundant. Though education, public health, and perhaps housing are exceptions, it would make no sort of theoretical sense for the federal government, at the expense of the rest of the country, to pour public money into a community to supplement its own ability to pay for its plant and equipment.

But theory in this instance comes up against two very stubborn practical facts. The first is that unless the federal government provides the bulk of the public funds required to remove the obstacles in the way of sane urban redevelopment, the funds will not be provided any time soon. The local communities cannot do it, and the states will not. The other fact is less simple, since it involves concepts of fairness and justice, but no less real. It is that for a generation or more the people and business concerns of the urban communities have been paying almost all the taxes collected by the federal government, and may be expected for a long time to go on doing so, with strictly limited tax resources left for the local governments' own expenditures. Pending the fiscal overhauling that will result in a juster arrangement all around, therefore, it seems only fair that the federal government should aid the local governments to the extent necessary to cover their urgently needed outlays.

Such are the problems of policy involved in today's mooted question of urban redevelopment. Upon the decisions made will be likely to depend, for many years to come, whether American cities and towns must continue to deserve to be called a disgrace to America.

Summary Among the most urgent needs of the United States today are boldly conceived measures to cope with deterioration and obsolescence of physical pattern in the cities and towns, and to overhaul outmoded arrangements for taxation and public expenditures. Needed specifically are: (1) redefinition and expansion geographically of the powers of local government, in order that the decentralization movement may be guided and controlled; and (2) large funds wherewith redevelopment of in-town blighted areas can be made possible. The latter need is the more visibly urgent. It arises from the necessity of using public funds to acquire blighted properties, the land under which must usually be resold or leased for a great deal less than acquisition cost in order to get it used in accordance with a desirable over-all plan for the city. But the local governments cannot under present conditions raise the necessary funds, and the state governments will not. It is therefore proposed here that, in spite of valid theoretical objections, the federal government should furnish the money required, through improvement of the action provided in the Taft-Ellender-Wagner bill of 1947. But such action should be taken only when the state and local governments have done what is needed in the way of planning and of reform of the state-local administrative set-up.

CHAPTER XVI

Anti-Trust Policy

by Wendell Berge

Monopoly versus Free Enterprise   There is a strong tradition in this country against monopoly. This tradition has been expressed in the Sherman Antitrust Act and numerous other federal laws, as well as in state legislation. We repeatedly assert our faith in free enterprise. We believe in economic opportunity. We are against regimentation of business. We want businessmen left free to take risks, decide their business policies, and then to succeed in their ventures or fail according to their abilities and the whims of fortune.

This is the American philosophy. And yet despite the generality of its acceptance, it has not prevented monopoly from gaining ground. Indeed, concentration of economic control in the sense that a few companies control the major output of an industry is today the standard pattern of American business.

The trend appears to be toward greater concentration. Actually, in most major industries, control by three, four, or five corporations is the rule. To be sure there is a movement away from one-company domination. In 1904, twenty-six trusts controlled 80 per cent or more of the production in their respective fields. And there were at least eight concerns— American Can Company, American Sugar Refining Company, American Tobacco Company, Corn Products Company, International Harvester Company, National Cash Register Company, Standard Oil Company of New Jersey, and United Shoe Machinery Company—that controlled, at one time or another, 90 per cent or more of the output of some or all of their respective products. Today control is less often found in one company alone, although it is still the case in nickel, and until recently was true for railroad sleeping cars and the production of aluminum. The Sherman Act at least deserves credit for setting up the domination of the few as a substitute for the domination of the one in a number of industries. But domination by the few may be just as dangerous to the maintenance of a competitive economy, especially when the few customarily act together in matters of production, distribution, and price.

In 1909, the 200 largest non-financial corporations owned one-third of the non-financial corporation assets. By 1929, their share had increased to nearly 50 per cent. It was estimated in 1933 that the relative rate of growth maintained by the larger and smaller concerns from 1909 to 1929, if continued for another twenty years, would place 70 per cent of the nation's corporate wealth in the hands of the 200 largest in 1950. By 1939, the share of the 200 largest had actually increased to 57 per cent. In 1926, 316 large manufacturing corporations held 35 per cent of the working capital of manufacturing corporations; by 1938 the percentage had risen to 47.

This concentration presents a real problem in the maintenance of a capitalistic economy. In such an economy the questions of what kind of goods will be produced, the amount of production, who shall produce goods, where they shall be produced, means and methods of distribution and pricing are at least in theory determined by the free competitive action of individual businessmen. The motor that drives a capitalistic system is competition.

The impact of the increased concentration of power falls not only on those businessmen who are pushed out of business. It falls on all business and the community as a whole. When a small handful of individuals has absolute authority over entire industrial empires, we have the basic conditions for stifling economic expansion. The monopolistic practices of these industrial empires retard the rate of growth of our economy. They discourage investment and hold up technological advance. They provide major stumbling blocks to new and independent businesses.

When competition is eliminated from a capitalistic society, the system is in danger of breaking down. With competition, prices tend to find their fair level, and maximum production and employment result. But monopoly prices yield higher profits to businessmen than competitive prices, hence businessmen are under a steady temptation to suppress competition and raise prices. When they yield to this temptation, the result is that automatically consumption is reduced and production is restricted. If this process occurs in many industries the cumulative effect is depression and unemployment.

A prolonged depression induced by abuses of the capitalistic system results in the government stepping in with a spending program to relieve the unemployment tension. As long as the spending lasts, serious crisis can be averted. In our recent history the spending program of the 1930's was followed by war spending which provided the necessary injection to keep the patient alive.

But unless we can find a way to make private business function again as the major factor in providing jobs, the future of capitalism will be precarious. We must act effectively now to free our capitalistic economy from the restraints which threaten to strangle it. One of the factors which brought about the depression that began in 1929 was the success of businessmen and financiers in eliminating competition from large areas of our system. At the levels of management and investment private controls had been erected which made it possible for those operating them to restrict production. This systematic restriction of production finally became so great that private business could not provide employment for a sizeable part of our population. We were gradually pushed by monopoly restrictions into a downward spiral of falling production and employment, from which after much suffering we were partially rescued by a program of government spending.

In a soundly functioning capitalism no one engaged in production has the power to restrict it. The existence of real competition makes it impossible for selfish groups to enrich themselves by restricting production and raising prices.

Monopoly and Politics   Even more important to the future of our country are the political implications of this concentrated economic power. Our basic political institutions have not only survived the war; they have been strengthened by victory. The American people are more firmly convinced than ever before of the worth of government founded upon the rights and dignity of free men.

But our political institutions, strong and solid as they are in themselves, rest upon certain economic foundations. This country has always been favored by an abundance of natural resources. Its people have been reared and nourished in the traditions of freedom embodied in the Constitution. Above all, however, they have been economically free. It is this freedom of economic opportunity which has distinguished the American economy from many other economic systems of the world. It is this same freedom of economic opportunity which instilled into the American people the conviction that the right to follow callings of their own choosing, the right to engage in enterprise upon their own initiative, and the right to compete in the production of goods and services are essential elements of a true democracy.

Today America is the last major industrial country in which the system of private enterprise still operates as the major organizing principle of economic activity. If private enterprise is to be preserved in this country, the process of economic concentration must be stopped. (I leave out of account natural monopolies.) If it is not stopped, the time may come to us, as it came to some other nations that fell victims to their monopolists, when neither private enterprise nor political liberty any longer exist. Whether private monopolies manage the government or the government takes over and manages the monopolies will make little difference. Economic and political freedom would be left by the wayside.

We will not accept in this country the idea that an authoritarian economy operating under the close supervision of government is compatible with genuine economic advancement. Yet we must recognize that every increase in monopoly power invites a corresponding increase in government direction of industry. In the long run monopoly domination of economic life by the concentration of private economic power will lead to increasing control of the economy by the government.

The highest qualities of economic statesmanship and vision must be invoked to insure a constant and steady increase in economic opportunities and in the standard of living of the American people. This process is not that of "boom and bust" but rather a progressive widening of our industrial frontiers. It is upon this type of development that our industrial strength and continued technological advancement depends.

The Sherman Act   In the achievement of these aims the enforcement of the anti-trust laws is a key factor. By themselves the anti-trust laws cannot produce Utopia. Rather they are the symbol of a long-run policy which must prevail throughout government and industry if a free economy is to prosper. Both major political parties have consistently asserted their recognition of this fact. Their campaign pledges ever since 1890 abound in specific endorsement of the economic policies for which the anti-trust laws stand. In the course of events after World War II, much more than after World War I, something more concrete than proclamations will be required.

For more than forty years during which the anti-trust laws were on the books they were applied only superficially and for long periods almost not at all. The Anti-trust Division staff is composed of competent and faithful public servants. But the disproportion between the scope of the work which must be done and the means available to do it is and has been so great that the Sherman Act has been little more than a pious preamble to economic policy.

There is no mystery about why the Sherman Act lapsed into disuse. During the halcyon days of the twenties there was little public concern with monopoly. Indeed, size was accepted as the symbol of efficiency in industry. The pyramiding of mergers and combines was part of the game of business. The formation of international cartels and the mushrooming of patent pools were trends to be praised and imitated. The continuous elimination of small enterprise from many industrial fields was looked upon as a necessity in the construction of economic skyscrapers dominating the most important areas of our economy.

As we learned so painfully, such an economic situation was a house of cards. Its collapse ushered in a depression which seared the welfare of millions of people and set the world economy adrift. Governments both here and abroad sought drastic remedies for desperate circumstances. Thus the NRA was conceived with the best of intentions, but its economic premises were faulty because they were based upon the same fallacies of concentration which had in large part led to the collapse.[1]

After the failure of NRA a growing body of opinion came to believe that vigorous enforcement of the anti-trust laws was at least worth a trial. Somewhat larger appropriations were secured and a series of new cases was instituted over a period of several years immediately preceding World War II.

Nevertheless, it would be self-deception if we were to assume that the amount of anti-trust enforcement which we have had, even in recent years, is all that we need. Anti-trust enforcement is still woefully inadequate. Even now it is not possible, because of insufficient funds and insufficient personnel, to investigate with the thoroughness which they warrant many complaints which come to the Anti-trust Division.

The resources available for anti-trust enforcement in any one year since the passage of the Sherman Act in 1890 have been less than the sum of money expended by a single corporation to defend a single anti-trust suit. The entire appropriation for the Anti-trust Division for each of the years since its establishment, except for the year 1942, has been less than 2 million dollars and at least in one case, and perhaps in others, it is known that the legal fees for defense exceeded that amount.

Cost of Non-enforcement   The failure to enforce the anti-trust laws is more costly to taxpayers than an adequate program would be. For the fiscal years 1940 through 1946 anti-trust appropriations totaled $12,030,600. Fines assessed

[1] Cf. Chapter 5.

during the same period in suits brought under the anti-trust laws totaled 5.9 million dollars. Thus, anti-trust fines alone amounted to almost half the funds appropriated. It is not possible to estimate in all cases the enormous savings to the consumer resulting from the fact that competition was restored and maintained in many important industries.

But in some instances we do have direct, positive evidence of savings derived from anti-trust prosecutions. The direct saving on a single contract in Pittsburgh, because of an anti-trust investigation, amounted to 85 per cent of the annual appropriation. As a result of one other major anti-trust suit, royalties in patents were reduced in one industry by 50 per cent and the saving to the consumers as a result of that action exceeded 4 million dollars, or more than twice the annual appropriation for the Anti-trust Division. The accomplishments of the Anti-trust Division on a budget of less than 2 million dollars a year provide an effective sample of what could be done if more adequate funds were made available.

While it is possible that the substantive provisions of the anti-trust laws could in some respects be strengthened, the basic trouble is not with the law but with the inadequate resources for enforcement.

Sometimes the question is raised whether the law itself has "sufficient teeth" to be effective against large monopolies. The answer is that the teeth are there, especially in view of recent Supreme Court decisions. The Supreme Court in *American Tobacco Company, et al* v. *United States* (323 U. S. 781), made clear that possession of power to exclude competitors from the market, coupled with the intention to exercise such power, is illegal under the monopoly section of the Sherman Act (Section 2), even though the power to exclude is not actually exercised. Some previous Supreme Court decisions had thrown doubt on this principle, which is now settled by unanimous decision. As a result the Department of Justice need not be deterred from instituting actions against large monopoly groups merely because the conduct of such groups has not resulted in the complete exclusion of competition and even though their power to control the market has not actually been exercised. A defense commonly heard in anti-trust cases that a company's monopoly position was innocently attained, or was "thrust upon" such company, but that the power has never actually been exerted against competitors, cannot, under the American Tobacco decision, be effectively maintained. What we now most need is the will and the resources in money and man-power to enforce the anti-trust law.

The policies of government, the daily conduct and practices of business, and the development of an informed and decisive public opinion concerning economic affairs within the next few years will determine the success with which the American economy resolves the immense tasks before it. For free enterprise the test is crucial. We know that it can meet the test if it is not prevented from doing so by an accumulation of monopoly barriers to production and to the development of new industries. We know also that it will require a high degree of enlightened co-operation on the part of labor, management, the government, and the general public to give free enterprise a chance to work as it can. With this support we may look forward to a period of greater and more lasting prosperity than we have ever known. The fight to preserve that freedom of opportunity necessary to preserve capitalism is well worth while. But we must act promptly. At the present tempo of change in the world it may be later than we think.

PART FIVE

Stabilization of Demand

Introduction

by Seymour E. Harris

Planning may take the form of allocation of economic resources, including labor, by a central board operating on behalf of government. Contributors to this volume are hopeful that direct controls of this type might be kept down to a minimum, though some of us realize that in the absence of improved relations among the influential groups, direct controls may be the only way to stave off inflation.

Part V is devoted to the kind of planning which interferes a minimum with the underpinnings of capitalism (for example, consumers' sovereignty, the quest for profits, freedom to invest and work without central dictation). In periods of deficient demand it is necessary to pump money into the system, reduce taxes, and raise public expenditures; and in periods of excess demand, to withdraw money, raise taxes, and reduce public expenditures. The excesses and deficiencies may be cyclical (Hansen) or long run (Tarshis). Soule suggests some of the difficulties confronting government in working out compensatory fiscal policies. Chandler elaborates the appropriate monetary policies which are to be meshed with these fiscal policies.

Shift of Emphasis from Supply to Demand Scarcities in the nineteenth century, as well as the influence of Malthus, tended, until recent years, to emphasize the importance of supply. By the end of the third decade of the twentieth century, with the intensification of depressions and the growing ascendancy of Keynesianism, emphasis had shifted to demand. American economic policy in the thirties was concerned with insufficiency of demand. Keynes and his disciples had made it clear to the world of economists, journalists, and practitioners in economic policy that a large part of the economic potential of affluent societies may be wasted unless the demand is adequate to take the annual production of goods off the market. Rich economies tend toward over-saving; and the individual who seeks security through saving may well be behaving in an anti-social manner, in that he contributes to declining demand and depression.

Aspects of demand concern many contributors to this volume. Having been influenced by the course of events and by the new economies, they are all aware that demand must be sustained. In an earlier part of this book,[1] Bowles stresses the importance of supporting demand by public spending and in general by maintaining output where business fails to do so; Berle would not allow exaggerated fears of inflation to interfere with the expansion of money to support demand in periods of unemployment;[2] and though concerned with the object of public expenditures (a subject which we treat elsewhere [3]) Schlesinger also approves of the Keynesian approach.[4] Using aggregate statistics, Tarshis in the first chapter of this part of the book shows the origin of income, the uses to which it is put, and the relation of income to spending. A modern economy wholly dependent on consumer spending cannot survive as a prosperous economic community; and even one sustained almost wholly by spending on consumption and private investment will probably spawn much unemployment. It is necessary to rely to some extent on public spending. (Keynes had noted in 1936 that large expenditures on private investment may just put off the ultimate collapse.) Tarshis's figures reveal that from 1932 to 1937 only 65 out of 100 *additional* dollars earned were spent on consumers' goods. We might add that from 1937 to 1947, when gross national product rose by 145 billion dollars, only 91 billion of this incre-

[1] Chapter 2, pp. 24–31.
[2] Cf. Chapter 3.
[3] Cf. Chapter 10.
[4] Cf. Chapter 5.

mental income went into consumers' markets. Both the large savings in the war period and the abnormally low ratio of savings to income are revealed in Chart 4.

Approaches to Adequacy of Demand Obviously, additional outlets must be found. Hansen, Tarshis, Soule, and Chandler deal with the problem of finding supplementary sources of demand, and they all envisage significant contributions by government. While Soule would rely on agreements among business, labor, and other large groups to keep the economy on an even keel, as well as a *long-range* public investment program, Hansen, fearful of bunching of investments and the effects of the capricious business cycle, advises a long-range public-investment program, adapted, however, to the changing cyclical situation. Aware of structural maladjustments and the need of larger participation of government in spending, Hansen also warns that cyclical indispositions are still a serious threat. He would, therefore, lace both tax and public-spending policies with spending by the private sector of the economy; and he would achieve timeliness of public action by delegating to the executive the right to change tax rates periodically. Finally, Chandler's emphasis is on a monetary policy tethered to correct fiscal policy as outlined above; and in his analysis, monetary policy includes the activities of government, which are reflected in adding to or subtracting from the spending of the private sector of the economy.

Demand Problems in a Peaceful and a Bellicose World No one can predict with certainty that the fifties are going to be a period of insufficiency of demand. War and its aftermath have given us a breathing spell from concern over deficient demand. It is easy to keep demand up if we wage war and rebuild in every generation. Should we continue through the fifties on a semi-war basis and should we generously aid in world reconstruction, then the danger of stagnation will be substantially reduced. Yet even in 1947, clearly a period of excess demand, consumption accounted for but 160 billion dollars out of a gross national product of 230 billion dollars; and had domestic investment been substantially below the record level of 30 billion dollars (annual rate), and (or) had ex-

CONSUMER INCOME, SPENDING, AND SAVING

Spending increased more than income.

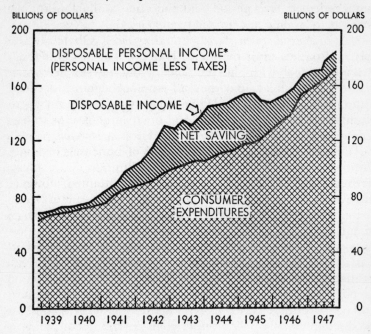

BILLIONS OF DOLLARS

BILLIONS OF DOLLARS

DISPOSABLE PERSONAL INCOME*
(PERSONAL INCOME LESS TAXES)

DISPOSABLE INCOME

NET SAVING

CONSUMER EXPENDITURES

Rate of net saving continued to drop.

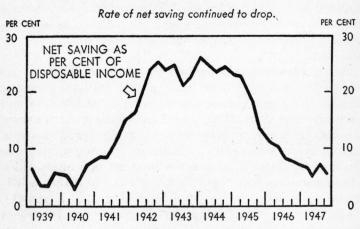

PER CENT

PER CENT

NET SAVING AS
PER CENT OF
DISPOSABLE INCOME

*Seasonally adjusted annual rates

SOURCE: U. S. DEPARTMENT OF COMMERCE.

CHART 4

cess of exports over imports been substantially below the unprecedented level of 10 billion dollars (annual rate), the recession generally anticipated would certainly have occurred. Government expenditures of around 55 billion dollars also contributed to the support of demand, although receipts exceeded outlays. In a peaceful world, and in the absence of vigorous measures to raise consumption of the masses through appropriate tax, social-security, wage, and farm policies, including public spending and public investment, it does not seem likely that our economy will realize its potentialities.

The immediate problem seems to be one of excess demand. Contributors to Part V are all aware of the dangers of excessive spending. But since the problem is not dealt with fully, I have added a chapter on inflation at the end.

The Relevance of Science and Leisure In the absence of measures along the lines suggested for dealing with deflationary situations, another possible way out, as briefly indicated by Bowles and Soule, is an increase of leisure and education. Ever since the days of Jean Sismondi, one of the precursors of modern socialism, and on through the technocrats of the 1930's writers have dwelt on the problem of excess production and periodic crisis. In part the explanation is rapid scientific and technological advance, with institutional adaptations proceeding at a snail's pace: the downward response of prices and the rise of wages and demand are insufficient.

Technological developments, in combination with the tendency to save too much in advanced economic societies, contribute to economic malaise. In an advancing society, machines increasingly displace men; and though it is proper to encourage scientific advances, we are much more aware of the fact than we were a generation ago that rapid rates of advance, not followed by adequate institutional adaptations, bring unemployment. No one seems safe in the modern scientific age.

Mr. Alt, of the Ballistic Research Laboratories, writes concerning a new high-speed computing machine:

This machine is designed to operate at night without requiring the presence of a human operator. If, during unattended hours, a trouble occurs—this may be either a failure of some part of the machine or an error of the operator who had previously set the machine up for a particular problem—the machine will wait a short time to see if the trouble clears up and will then automatically discontinue all computations in the present problem, and immediately start work on any other problem that has been prepared for it. . . .

Most important of all, the machine will be capable of storing hundreds of numbers which may be obtained as intermediate results in the course of a computation and which are almost instantaneously accessible for future computation. . . .

The availability of these machines will enable us to solve problems which have hitherto been inaccessible to numerical methods. It is believed that partial differential equations in three or four variables, integral equations, and problems in the values of variations are within the scope of the EDVAC.[5]

The prejudices in favor of private against public activity are still powerful in our society. Therefore, practical implementation of measures adumbrated above may well take the form of more leisure rather than higher standards of living, with interstices of depressions and long spells of resource wastage. Since the early part of the nineteenth century, the average per capita real income has risen by about 10 times. Clearly, the gains of progress have been taken more in rising standards than in a reduction of hours, more schooling, and earlier retirement. Even since 1900, hours of work have been reduced only from 60 to 40 hours, a period during which per capita income rose several times. If no more effective way of treating the deficiency of demand is to be found, more schooling and more leisure, and hence a better distribution of available employment and income, is to be preferred to long periods of unemployment, with the incidence of distress concentrated on an unfortunate minority. But if the average citizen prefers to work 40 hours a week for 50 weeks for 50 years, or 100,000 hours in all, and be rewarded correspondingly, the offer of 30 hours a week for 40 weeks for 40 years, or 48,000 hours, constitutes a second-best solution.

Productive Government Spending   Elsewhere we comment on the nature of spending by public authority. At this

[5] From the Bulletin of the American Statistical Association, Aug. 1947.

point, it suffices to say that spending should be of the most productive type. In the New Deal days, the government was unprepared for the heavy responsibilities for spending which were placed upon it, and consequently hasty improvisation was necessary. As a result of the lessons learned from that experience, the government should do a better job in the next depression. Unfortunately, despite all the energies expended by the Administration to prepare a shelf of public works, an intransigent Congress has refused to take the vigorous measures required to assure adequate plans. At the present time, the various levels of government of the United States are prepared to launch public-investment programs which, in terms of present incomes and possible declines, would make only a small contribution toward containing the forces of depression.

CHAPTER XVII

Needed: A Cycle Policy*

by Alvin H. Hansen

Two major fears haunt Americans, indeed, the whole world at the present moment. One is the great danger of another world war; the other is that the United States may not succeed in maintaining high levels of income and employment. These two problems are not unrelated. The future of all of the Western democratic world depends very much upon economic conditions in the United States, and as a reflection of these conditions, the extent to which adequate aid can be given to the reconstruction of the economic systems of Western Europe.

That we should be enjoying a period of postwar prosperity is not surprising to anyone. The backlogs of demand caused by the war insure high activity both in the fields of capital goods and consumers' goods; but how long it will last is the question. It could, indeed, turn out (this seems by now not improbable) that we might largely escape the immediate postwar recession —comparable to that of 1921—by a lucky combination of circumstances. Already, something of this sort has occurred. The considerable decline in inventory accumulation in the first quarter of 1947 was, fortunately, offset by a sharp rise in the net export surplus. In 1921, on the other hand, both declined drastically, together producing a sharp recession.

Recent Suggestions for Avoiding Depression   But, however events may unfold with respect to the immediate post-

* Reprinted, with changes, from an article in *Journal of Industrial Relations* (Ithaca, 1947).

war recession, no one, so far as I know, doubts that the back-log of demand, particularly in the fields of construction and business equipment, will in some few years come to an end. There is, moreover, widespread belief that this postwar era of prosperity is not likely to last as long as the seven good years from 1923 to 1929. There is nowhere evident currently (apart from the consideration cited below) the economic basis for so long a period of high prosperity.

To this statement one notable exception may be made, but it is not one that can be envisaged with equanimity. A world situation so threatening as to require very large and growing military expenditures, sufficient to offset the eventual decline in private capital outlays, might, indeed, give us an almost indefinite period of high employment. But this is a solution which would point to and probably eventuate in a world ca-lamity. Apart from such a consideration there are few, if any, who doubt that a severe depression is, sooner or later, in store.

Nevertheless, the discussions both from the economic left and economic right have, in recent years, run in terms which, more or less, rule out the business cycle. Thus, for example, Lord Beveridge in his *Full Employment in a Free Society* comes pretty close to arguing that a long-run planned program of expansion, such as he advocates, would, of itself, eliminate the business cycle; but he does not, in fact, go that far. On the other side, more conservative writers have been disposed to talk in recent years a great deal about depressions and un-employment as though it were wholly a matter of imbalance in the *structure* of the economy. Thus it has been argued that wage-price adjustments, improved basic tax structures, labor-management relations, etc., might be so ordered that no depression is necessary.

This is a dangerous illusion. Recent discussions indicate that it is high time that we revert to a serious study of the business cycle and the factors which underlie it. It is, indeed, true that structural reforms and adaptation to changed con-ditions are highly important for the functioning of the econ-omy, particularly from the standpoint of secular development and progress. But it is not true that these secular adjustments can prevent the short-run fluctuations of the business cycle. Lord Beveridge's position rests on stronger grounds, but it goes too far. It is, indeed, true that a long-run program of planned expansion will minimize the violence of cyclical fluctuations and, particularly, reduce much of the force of the cumulative process. Thus, the secondary and tertiary effects of the primary fluctuations in the rate of investment could certainly be very much minimized. But even with a planned long-run program of expansion the primary fluctuations in private investment would still remain to plague us. Bulges of investment would continue to come and go. Thus, to achieve economic stability, it is necessary not only to have a long-run program of planned expansion, but also to implement it with a short-run compensatory program to offset the short-run fluctuations in investment.

Conditions of Instability It may, in fact, be expected that the aftermath of the war will for some time intensify the business-cycle fluctuations in investment. Serious distortions follow from the terrific "twists" which the mass conversion of the economy to war purposes created. The accumulated shortages will intensify the replacement cycle. This will be true not only of consumers' durable goods, but also of machinery, equipment and fixed plant, and, in a still longer cycle, housing. The war has caused a violent distortion in the age distribution of automobiles, for example, and to some extent the same is true of business equipment. Thus, bulges of investment caused by the replacement cycle are likely for some time to be intensified.

In the housing field this may be very serious. After some years of feverish building the market will be largely saturated. Without a thoroughly planned urban redevelopment and housing program, violent replacement cycles will be inevitable.

But this is not all. Investment bulges spring basically from technological developments. These come typically by fits and starts and not in a smooth development of small increments of changes in technique. Often great technological innovations cause a bunching of investment. Technological developments often create vast new industries, cause relocation of population and industry, with induced effects upon investments in transportation and housing. Fundamental technological changes cause forward thrusts into new frontiers, with an attendant bunching of new investments and fixed capital. Basically, the bunching of pioneering investment is a product of intermittent surges in technology.

Thus, it is not merely the impending saturation, when the backlog of war-created demands has been satisfied, that confronts us. That, indeed, will be the basis for the first major postwar depression. To be sure, the forces making for the cycle are based partly on past bulges—the replacement cycle—but in a more fundamental way upon the process of technological change coming, as it does, in fits and starts.

It, accordingly, will not do to be complacent about the prospect of eliminating the cycle by making desirable corrections in the structure of our economy; and it is not true that the correction of structural imbalances will prevent the onward march of the business cycle.

The tendency to discuss the problem of mass unemployment in terms of structural imbalances is, in fact, the current counterpart of the new-era talk of the 1920's. Disillusionment from this point of view will follow just as surely now as then.

The Danger of Forgetting the Business Cycle   It is true that it is not sufficient to "iron out the cycle." That might result only in stabilized stagnation and unemployment. A long-range program of expansion, structural changes in wage-profits relationship and in the distribution of income are necessary. What I wish to emphasize here, however, is the danger of forgetting about the business cycle altogether. We shall quickly discover in the postwar world that our modern economy is a very fast moving one. A depression, once it has started, can cumulate under current conditions with terrific speed. For this situation, long-run adjustment programs by themselves alone are not suitable. What is needed is a cycle policy. This means a program which can quickly be put into motion, highly flexible and subject to quick adjustment and change. It is this area that we are in danger currently of neglecting.

The President in his Economic Report transmitted to Congress on January 8, 1947, referred to the possibility of an impending recession and stated that the "government will watch this situation and be prepared for action if needed." This statement by the President is heartily to be welcomed and it is not altogether true that he was simply "whistling in the dark." We are, in fact, far better prepared to act now than we were in 1929. Nevertheless, it is a fact that in no small measure the President *was* "whistling in the dark." We do not have a program that can quickly be put into action to stem a rapidly cumulating depression. That we will not let it run on as we did in 1929–1932, I am convinced, but we will act tardily and ineffectively because we have, in fact, nothing approaching an adequate program.

This is, indeed, a serious indictment, but all the world knows it is true; and this is the basic cause of current uneasiness with respect to the United States and its role in the world economy.

Need for a Long-Range Program   An adequate cycle program is impossible without a long-range program involving plans and preparations with respect to improvement and development projects, and public works—federal, state, and local. In one exceedingly important area a modest beginning in such a program is contained in the Taft-Ellender-Wagner Urban Redevelopment and Housing bill. But, while it once passed the Senate, there seems no prospect that it will pass the House. And it is only a beginning. Under the slum-clearance provisions of this bill, it would require fifty years to purchase and redevelop the slum and blighted areas and to provide reasonably satisfactory houses for the mass of the population. That a country with the prodigious productive capacity demonstrated in the war can seriously consider taking half a century to improve basically its great urban communities, remove the slum and blight, and modernize urban transportation is a striking proof of the lag of social adjustment to technological change.

There has been a disposition of late to minimize the anticyclical possibilities in a public-investment program. There are, indeed, great difficulties which have often been slurred over. But the pendulum has gone too far. We need to re-examine the possibilities of flexible adjustment inherent in a large and varied long-range public construction, improvement, and development program. Unless this is done, we shall, in fact, engage in wasteful expenditures, once a serious depression is upon us, for we shall discover that it is not possible to meet the onrush of depression without a large expansion of public outlays. Such outlays can be wisely implemented, not merely in public works, improvements, and development projects, but also in low-cost housing and, indeed, in other kinds of durable consumers' goods. The last item in particular has been explored at some length in the postwar programs in Western European democracies, notably, the British Empire countries and the Scandinavian countries.

Need for a Flexible Tax System   Urgently necessary, if we are going to implement a really effective anti-cyclical program, is a flexible tax system. Nothing is more immediately important than public education on this important issue. With a vast federal budget somewhere in the neighborhood of 40 billion dollars, the anti-cyclical possibilities inherent in a flexible tax system are enormous. It is not possible to run the modern fast-moving economy, with its tendency toward violent fluctuations, on the basis of an immovable tax structure fixed for two or more years.

Recently the whole country debated the question of the new tax bill. It is extremely interesting to note that it was debated in terms of depression and inflation. These are short-run business cycle matters, and if the rates are to be counter-cyclically effective, they must be timed. But timing is obviously impossible under the system now in vogue. While the discussion was going on in Congress, the country was under strong inflationary pressures. This indicated the maintenance, if, indeed, not the increase in tax rates. On the other hand, there was looming the danger of impending depression. This situation would indicate a sharp reduction in tax rates. But no one could pretend to say with any accuracy when inflationary forces would subside and deflationary forces take hold.

Thus, while the debate shows that the country is quite aware that taxes are important for the control of both inflation and deflation, it is apparent that the instrument is not now at hand to effect appropriate timing in an anti-cyclical program. Since this is true, it is apparent that we have not yet reached a stage of sufficient economic and political maturity to manage the tax program in a manner required to insure a well-functioning and balanced economy.

Just as Congress has, within limits established by law, empowered the executive to make adjustments in tariff rates, and just as Congress in the Federal Reserve Act has allocated to the monetary authority, within limits established by legislation, the power to raise and lower reserve ratios, so also it now becomes highly important, and, indeed, essential to permit executive adjustment of the basic income-tax rate within limits imposed by Congress. Only in this manner is it possible to get quick timing and an adequate flexibility in our tax structure. The president should periodically report to the Congress, annually in his Economic Report, and probably quarterly, on action which he may or may not have taken, together with reasons for his action. In the final analysis, the power would always reside in Congress not only to lay down the basic pattern within which the executive operates, but also to intervene if it so chooses. Thus, Congress would in no sense abdicate its power but would only make possible an implementation of the tax system as an effective anti-cyclical device.

The Role of the State in a Mixed System   There is general agreement that we stand in danger, sooner or later, of serious depression and mass unemployment, and that this is a definite menace to the very existence of democratic government, to the system of free enterprise, and to the market economy operating mainly under the price system and private enterprise with the state playing an important regulatory (and in some areas a state-enterprise) role—in short, the so-called mixed system which characterizes all Western democratic countries, even the United States. But despite the general agreement about the danger of depression and mass unemployment, it is a tragic fact that there is little agreement about how to meet the danger. There is a disposition to take a chance, to hope for the best, to let well enough alone.

The fact is that we have not been able to resolve the basic

problem of the role of government in our modern world. Particularly, we have not learned how to make government an effective, flexible, and responsive instrument in a varied and highly complex society. This society embraces activities and institutions that are voluntary and noncoercive—a society functioning mainly through private enterprise, co-operative action, and numerous private institutional arrangements, yet a society in which the state functions not only as a balance wheel offsetting fluctuations in the private sector, but also as a provider for ever-growing community services and for basic development projects which underlie and support private industry.

CHAPTER XVIII

Why Demand Must Be Kept High

by Lorie Tarshis

We enjoy prosperity when the national income is high. Since the national income is high when firms sell a lot and have high receipts, it is clear that the key to prosperity is to ensure that their receipts remain high. This, of course, means that buyers must spend freely. Though we do most of the economy's buying in our consumer role, consumers' purchases never equal the whole of our income: hence a large volume of non-consumer purchases are also needed for prosperity. Indeed, the greater the prosperity we hope to secure, the higher must be the expenditures of non-consumers (of firms, government, and foreigners), unless consumers' buying habits can be altered. In any case, if we are to have prosperity a sufficient level of demand must be forthcoming from some combination of sources.

Why Demand Must Be Kept High   At the end of 1947 we were enjoying the highest peak of the greatest boom in our history. In spite of minor though annoying shortages in this country, we were consuming more goods and services than ever before, and at the same time we were building new factories and homes, and installing machinery in industrial plants at an unprecedented rate. And yet the picture is not all cheerful. Not to mention the hunger and poverty of most other countries, we cannot help feeling concern over the danger that our boom will not last; that we shall once again know crowded employment offices rather than crowded department stores.

The danger that our boom will give way to slump compels us to enquire into the conditions for prosperity. What factors must operate so that we are able to keep unemployment at a minimum? And where can we look for aid, if a depression occurs and we seek to restore prosperity?

The National Income and Prosperity We have learned to measure the prosperity of the economy by the size of the national income—though it is generally agreed that such a measure is not sufficient by itself. When income is very high, we have prosperity; for instance today it is about 200 billion dollars a year. When it is low, we have depression; in 1932 it stood at only 42 billion dollars.[1] Thus the task of maintaining prosperity becomes the task of maintaining the national income. And this, as we shall find, amounts essentially to the task of maintaining demand for the goods and services of our economy.

The link between the national income and demand can be most readily seen by an analysis of the national income as directed by two questions. The first question is: "Where does it come from? What generates the national income?" The other is: "What do we do with it? How do we dispose of our income?" The answers to these questions deserve very careful attention.

The Source of Income First, where does our income come from? The immediate answer is obvious, indeed too obvious: from wages and salaries; from rents, if for example we own a building; from interest if we lend money; and from profits. That is a complete catalogue of the sources (by function, to use the economist's term) of the national income. To illustrate, when, as was roughly true in 1946, wages and salaries come to 117 billion dollars, rents amount to 7 billion dollars, interest to 3 billion, and profits to 51 billion,[2] then the national income is the sum of these components, or 178 billion dollars.

But that is not, of course, a complete answer to the question

---

[1] Since this comparison takes no account of price changes, it exaggerates the increase in our *real* income.

[2] This figure includes earnings from unincorporated enterprises, including farms, and in addition corporation profits before subtracting corporate taxes. Thus it is much higher than the figure for shareholders' earnings.

—where does the national income come from? It is inadequate because it leaves unexplained an equally puzzling problem, namely, the sources of the wage and salary payments, and of the flows of rent, interest, and profits. Where then do these payments come from?

In the most immediate sense, we may say that most of them in our economy come from business concerns. For example, 300,000 employees of the General Motors Corporation in 1946 earned 870 million dollars in wages and salaries—obviously paid by General Motors. Holders of about 81 million dollars in bonds of the United States Steel Corporation received interest payments of about 4.8 million dollars—paid, of course, by the corporation. And the shareholders of the General Electric Company received dividends and added to their equity in that concern a total of 43 million dollars in 1946. Firms disburse and generate income in all these ways. A complicating factor which we shall have to overlook at this stage is that the government—federal, state, and local— also disburses income. That fact does not in any way require a modification of the conclusions to be derived from this analysis; but were it to be taken into account, the statement would become unnecessarily complicated, so we shall overlook it.

Firms then are the source of wage and salary payments, and of rent and interest income, and their profits or losses comprise the income of their owners. But this does not answer the main question because we have not yet seen where firms get the funds with which they meet payrolls, interest charges, and rentals, and buy raw materials. In other words we have not yet discovered the factors that determine the size of the income-constituting payments of firms.

The National Income and Business Receipts The answer is clear. The accountant's Statement of Income or Profit gives it directly. An examination of such a statement shows us that the sum of wages, salaries, rents, interest, raw-material charges, and profits is equal to the firm's receipts.[3]

---

[3] We have deliberately excluded allowances for depreciation and certain business taxes. To introduce them would compel us to distinguish certain national-income and gross national-product concepts and this would take us too far afield.

In fact this equality necessarily holds, by virtue of the definition of profits. It should be obvious then that a firm's receipts equal the sum of its payrolls, rents, interest payments, and profits (these are the income-constituting payments), together with its expenditures on raw materials.

The source of income payments then consists in the firm's receipts. When our problem is not the flow of funds from one firm but rather the national income, or the flow of funds from all firms, the equality still holds, though in a still simpler form. The added simplicity comes about because the expenditures of one firm on raw materials constitute the receipts of another. Hence it follows that the total receipts of all firms (omitting what they get from selling materials to one another) equal the sum of their payrolls, interest and rent payments, and earnings; or in other words, the national income.

This conclusion, that the national income equals the sum of the receipts of business concerns (with qualifications about raw materials) marks the first important step in the analysis. The next one, which is still concerned with the source of income, is easier.

Business Receipts and Volume of Purchases   Instead of regarding the flow of funds as firms' receipts, we can equally well regard it as composed of the payments made by various kinds of buyers. If you buy a vacuum cleaner for $50 (cash or credit, no matter), the firm receives $50. No money disappears in the course of the transaction. What the firm receives, someone spends. So, instead of equating the national income to firms' receipts we can express it as equal to the sums spent by buyers (except for purchases of raw materials used up in production). The size of the national income depends then upon the amounts buyers spend.

As an illustration: in 1940 buyers purchased 100 billion dollars worth of goods and services and the national income (before subtracting business taxes and depreciation allowances) stood at the same figure—100 billion dollars.

A high national income means prosperity, high employment, and a large output of the things that we want. And as we now should see, it is high when buyers spend large amounts. The key to prosperity, then, is a great volume of spending.

Source of Spending   Where does the spending come from? In other words, who spends? The spenders can be classified into four groups: first in importance are consumers—you and I when we buy food at the grocery, clothing, a ticket to the movies, or a haircut; next, business firms purchasing new plant and equipment (and adding to inventories); next, the government—as purchaser of, say a highway, aircraft, a school building, and the services of school-teachers, policemen, and so on; and finally foreigners.

It is instructive to check briefly the statistical data bearing on this. In 1933 when the gross national income stood at 55.8 billion dollars,

Consumers spent	$46.3 billion	
Business firms spent	1.3 billion	(on plant, equipment, and additions to inventory)
Foreigners spent (net)	.2 billion	
Government spent	8.0 billion	(on goods and services)
Total	$55.8 billion	

In the first half of 1947 when the national income was running at an annual rate of 225 billion dollars,

Consumers spent	$158.0 billion
Business spent	29.5 billion
Foreigners spent (net)	10.0 billion
Government spent	27.5 billion
Total	$225.0 billion

A tentative summary: the national income equals the sum of the expenditures of consumers, firms (on plant, equipment, and additions to inventory), foreigners, and government. When these spendings are high, the national income is high and we enjoy prosperity; when they are low and demand is deficient, the national income is low and we have depression and heavy unemployment. It is apparent that in order to maintain prosperity we have to maintain total spending at a high level. How can this be done?

Consumers' Spending   An analysis of the national income, this time from a different point of view, will prove helpful. Instead of asking, how is the national income earned, let us ask this time, how do we dispose of our income? The answer to this question will throw some light on the problems involved in maintaining total expenditures or demand at a figure sufficiently high to secure full prosperity.

Again, examination of the data is fruitful. In the following table we show for various years, ranging from deep depression (1932) to peak prosperity (1947), national income, and the amounts spent by consumers.

TABLE 2

INCOME AND CONSUMERS' EXPENDITURES

Year	Income (Gross)	Consumers' Expenditures
	(in Billions of Dollars)	
1929	103.9	78.8
1932	58.3	49.2
1935	72.2	56.2
1937	80.2	67.1
1941	125.3	82.3
1947 (Jan.–June)	225.0	158.0

Two things about these figures are particularly worth noting. First, notice that consumers do not spend all their income; even in 1932 when their income was only 58.3 billion dollars, they spent only 49.2 billion. Second, notice that when their income changed, consumers did not change their consumption by as much: for instance, their income fell by 45.6 billion dollars between 1929 and 1932 and their consumption fell by 29.6 billion dollars or by 65 per cent as much. Between 1932 and 1937 when income rose by 31.5 billion dollars, consumers' expenditures rose by only 17.9 billion. Taking the whole period, for every change of one billion dollars in the national income, consumers' expenditures changed on the average by 650 million dollars. The fact that consumers do not change their expenditures by as much as any change in their income is a most significant one, as we shall see.

Dependence of Income on Non-Consumer Spending We have already observed that a high national income is realized only when buyers (consumers, firms, government, and foreigners) spend freely. To this must be added the fact that consumers do not spend all their income. Or to put it in numbers, we have observed that a 200-billion-dollar national income is achieved only when buyers spend 200 billion dollars a year. And consumers, when their income—that is, the national income—is 200 billion dollars, spend only a part of it, say 140 billion dollars. It follows then that for the national income to be at a prosperity level, other buyers (firms, government, and foreigners) must purchase large amounts of goods and services too—in this case 60 billion dollars worth a year. That is the arithmetic of the problem.

In other words, prosperity is secured when the demand for goods is high [4] but we cannot expect consumers alone to create the whole of the demand. The rest, which may be as much as 30 per cent of the total, has to come from business, government, and foreigners. That is one reason why economists pay so much attention to the spending plans of business concerns and of the federal, state, and local governments; and that too is why they are so concerned to enable foreigners to buy our products. For if the flow of expenditures from these other sources should slacken too markedly, we should have depression: consumers simply do not spend a great deal when their incomes are low. [5]

Changes in Income and Non-Consumer Spending　But this is not all that can be learned from a consideration of consumers' spending habits. We have seen that when there is a change in the national income, say from 150 billion dollars to 200 billion, consumers increase their spending, though by a smaller amount; for example from 118 billion dollars to 140 billion. It follows—and this is a very important step—that for a 150-billion-dollar national income it is necessary to have non-consumer demand equal to 32 billion dollars (the difference between 150 billion and 118 billion) and for a 200-billion-dollar national income, non-consumer demand must be still higher, in this case 60 billion dollars (the difference between 200 billion and 140 billion). In other words, given the spending habits of consumers, an increase in the

---

[4] While a high demand is a necessary condition for prosperity it is not enough. If it were, the countries of Europe would be prosperous today, for the demand is there. But more is needed—most important, a labor force and stocks of capital goods that will be used to produce a large output when demand is high.

[5] Though to some extent this characteristic can be modified by changes in taxes and in other ways.

national income can be secured *only* by an increase in non-consumer spending.

In short, in order to turn depression into prosperity, we must somehow get an increase in total spending or total demand. Perhaps we can operate directly on consumers' spending; if so, well and good. But if not, we must contrive to increase non-consumer demand—the total spending of firms, governments, and foreigners. Failing in that effort, depression continues.

Prosperity: Summary   The importance of building up and maintaining the demand for our products cannot be overemphasized. So long as total demand is high, we enjoy prosperity; if it falls, unemployment grows and depression deepens. But the task (or should it not be "the pleasant office"?) of maintaining demand is not the consumers' alone. Business concerns and government must also do their part, for, as we have seen, they contribute an important and indeed vital section of the effective demand.

CHAPTER XIX

Demand and Jobs

by George Soule

There is a close parallel between the total national demand for goods and services and the number of persons employed. When demand has been low, large unemployment has existed; when it has been high, unemployment has virtually disappeared.

Demand, in the economic sense, is not the desire to buy, but the dollars people have and are willing to spend. For the nation as a whole, demand is roughly measured by the figure known as the gross national product—the sum of dollars spent during a year for goods and services. It includes expenditures for personal consumption, new investment in private business in the United States, new foreign investment, and government purchases of goods and services. There is no other source of demand.

Some say that employment results from demand; others put it that demand results from employment. Both statements are correct; whether an increase of demand enlarges employment or an increase of employment enlarges demand depends upon where one looks first at the flow of purchasing power about the system. It should be noted, however, that the initiative which causes changes in both demand and employment does not rest to any great extent with the individual action of those who work for wages and small salaries or are looking for such work. Few of them stop working voluntarily when they have jobs, or are able to create jobs for themselves when they are idle. Most of them customarily spend almost all they earn. Decisions by business about production and prices, and by government about spending and taxing are more effective in changing demand.

The Record of the War In 1940 the gross national product was 100 billion dollars, and the number employed 47,520,000. Though war preparation had begun to enlarge the demand for labor, there were still 8,120,000 unemployed. Thereafter, as the gross national product grew, employment increased until in 1943 the product had become 192.6 billion dollars and the number employed 53,960,000.

It will be remarked that while the gross product, as measured in dollars, almost doubled between 1940 and 1943, the number employed increased only about 15 per cent. The two totals went in the same direction, but not at the same rate. That was mainly because a dollar could not buy so many goods or so much labor time in 1943 as in 1940. Wholesale prices went up about 33 per cent in this period and hourly wages in manufacturing rose about 50 per cent.

But even when prices remain stable, an increase in demand will not lead to an equal increase in the number employed if the output per worker grows. This occurred in manufacturing, for instance, during the 1920's. In spite of a much larger product in 1929 than in 1919, the number employed in factories barely grew. Productivity probably did not increase during the recent war, though no one can be certain about it.

In 1944, the gross product became 213 billion dollars, but since prices rose more above 1943 than the number of dollars spent, employment dropped slightly, to 53,900,000. Unemployment, however, was the smallest on record, being only 670,000. The reason unemployment shrank, even though fewer were employed, was that the civilian labor force was diminished by the requirements of the armed services.

The same elements can be traced through the figures of demand, employment, and unemployment in subsequent years.

Matching Demand and Jobs The general principles illustrated by the record of the war years may be stated as follows:

(1) The demand for goods and services may be measured

by the gross national product, after allowance is made for any change in prices from year to year.

(2) An increase in real demand for goods and services will correspondingly increase the number employed, provided there is no change in the average output per worker. If the output per worker increases, a correspondingly larger demand will be required to provide jobs for a given number of workers.

(3) The number unemployed at any given time will be the difference between the civilian labor force and the number employed.

It would be possible to predict how large a demand would be needed at any future time in order to maintain full employment if one could be certain what would happen to productivity and to the size of the labor force. Those who have made such forecasts have usually built them up step by step. First the size of the labor force is estimated for some future year. On the basis of past experience it is known how large a demand would be required to employ the estimated number of job seekers, provided there were no change in productivity or prices. This total can then be modified by making it larger for any increase in output per worker which is expected. It provides a target to shoot at, bearing in mind that if we overshoot the mark by creating too much demand, prices will go up.

Population figures offer a fairly good basis for predicting the size of the labor force. Past growth of productivity may be used to forecast what may be expected in that regard. Price changes are more difficult to guess in advance, but it is useful to have an estimate of the required demand on the assumption that prices will remain the same, and then alter the total as the price trend becomes more clear.

One thing is certain: none of the other factors directly affects the number of jobs so much or so swiftly as changes in the amount of total demand. Neither productivity nor the size of the labor force is normally subject to such wide and violent fluctuations as is demand. It follows that if demand can be controlled, we can come much closer than in the past to maintaining any level of employment which is desired.

Policies can also be adopted which will increase or decrease the size of the labor force. Some such policies may have as an object the expansion of the national product; some may be designed to decrease unemployment; still others may have purposes thought valuable regardless of their effect on production and employment. During a war or a national emergency such as that which has engaged the British since the war, the labor force is enlarged by hiring women who have not previously been wage earners or employing retired persons. The labor force may be decreased by prolonging the years of education, or adopting an earlier age for retirement. Expansion of military service will of course diminish the civilian labor force.

In time of peace and in a nation as fortunately situated as the United States it seems undesirable either to expand the labor force simply to increase an already high level of production, or to contract it simply to avoid unemployment provided measures to alter demand are available. Educational policy should determine the number of young persons in school or college and the ages at which they go to work; military policy should determine the number in the armed services; whether or not women work for compensation should be determined by personal need or preference, as should the age of retirement.

The size of the effective labor force may be greatly altered in the long run by health measures which decrease incapacity due to illness and accident, as well as by changes in life expectancy and birth rates which alter the proportion of the population which is of working age.

Demand Greater than Supply   Since employment rises with demand, those interested in making sure that there are enough jobs may assume that the more demand there is, the better. This reasoning is particularly likely to appeal to workers when wage increases are being sought. A demand for labor which is greater than the supply may also be thought desirable because it enhances the bargaining power of employees and widens their choice among opportunities. Unfortunately, however, an excess of demand also has a tendency to increase prices, and usually increases them faster than average wages can be raised, unless effective price control is in force. Such an excess of dollars existed during the war and was barely held in check by rationing, price control, and other measures. The disturbing effects of too much demand quickly became apparent when controls were abandoned after the war.

Aside from the discomforts of price inflation itself, excess demand is likely so to upset the balance of a system of private enterprise that it soon plunges into depression and unemployment. Those at the lower levels of income become unable to buy their accustomed share of what is produced for personal consumption, and so factories lay off men. Even if demand should keep on expanding faster than production, and prices should keep on going up, those whose incomes could not keep up with the procession would soon be almost as unfortunate as if there were no work for them at all. Speculators and the owners of industry and farms gain most by inflation, but their gains have usually been temporary and illusory. National policy should therefore aim not only to keep demand just high enough to offer ample job opportunities, but when it has attained that level, to prevent it from growing more rapidly than the supply of goods and services.

Even a demand which is just large enough to employ everybody except those shifting from one job to another or those laid off for seasonal or other temporary reasons is likely to cause trouble unless it is accompanied by other measures. There may be no general inflation in the sense of an expansion of spending at a faster rate than the growth of production, yet when ample purchasing power exists and it is hard to find workers to fill jobs, those who are in strategic bargaining positions can raise their prices or their wages, as the case may be, at the expense of others who have less bargaining power. Such a development is just as uncomfortable for the victims as inflation itself. General measures to adjust demand, such as governmental fiscal policy and credit policy, therefore need to be supplemented either by a high degree of self-discipline and intelligence on the part of business, organized labor, and other occupational groups, or by governmental controls. In either case, careful planning of the interrelationships of prices, incomes, and production among the various industries is required. This planning ought to be organized democratically, that is, it should enlist the co-operation of the organizations concerned, rather than merely being imposed by government.

Influencing Demand   Other chapters of this book deal with various means of influencing demand. Measures that may be taken by government and banking authorities receive due emphasis.[1] In a regime in which private employment and production comprises so large a share of the total as in the United States, it would be better if business stability could be so nearly achieved without compensatory action by government as to reduce such offsetting measures to a minimum. It is difficult to alternate government spending and retrenchment rapidly enough or widely enough, or to make tax policies flexible enough, to compensate for marked swings in business conditions. It would be preferable to plan government spending according to the needs of the people for the services or goods to be produced, and to embark on long-range programs budgeted years in advance, rather than to have to vary governmental activities over short periods in order to compensate for instability in private employment. There are immense needs for governmental production, which ought to be satisfied without the disturbance bound to be caused by attempts to increase or decrease it temporarily for purposes only distantly related to the value of the product itself.

Planning and control of policies by business management, labor, and agriculture in such a way as to serve the common interest in maintaining stabilized expansion is indeed complex and difficult, but, given sufficient understanding and good will, it ought not to be completely impossible in a regime which has come to be dominated to such a high degree by administrative decisions rather than by blind and impersonal forces of the market. The collapse of demand which began in 1929 was due almost entirely to dislocations in the private sector of the economy, and was not preceded by price inflation or any other disturbance for which government might be held responsible. While space is insufficient here to analyze

[1] See Chapter 20.

the mistakes which led to the calamity, it seems possible that different decisions about prices, production, wages, invest- ment, and credit—decisions which would have been within the competence of leading business and financial organiza- tions—might have led to a more fortunate result.

Finally, it is well to bear in mind that necessary though employment opportunity is, it is a means to other ends rather than an end in itself. Without it, our society falters in every other respect, but even with it, much more may be desired. The conditions of employment, the quality and sufficiency of the product, the satisfactions to be achieved from both work and leisure are all superior to the bare opportunity to work for wages.

Summary The volume of employment depends on the total demand. Demand is the money spent for goods and services. Known in economic terminology as the gross national product, demand is composed of (1) purchases for personal consumption, (2) new business investment, (3) net foreign investment,[2] (4) government purchases of goods and services. Changes in prices must be taken into account in calculating the effect on employment of changes in the gross national product. Changes in output per worker will affect the volume of employment at a given level of demand. The amount of unemployment is the difference between the labor force and the number employed. While the size of the labor force may be deliberately altered, it is better to do so in pursuit of edu- cational and other social objectives rather than merely in order to minimize unemployment, so long as it is possible to obtain full employment by adjusting demand.

Once full employment is attained, it is not desirable to allow demand to increase without corresponding increases in the supply of goods and services. Even with demand and supply in balance at a high level of employment, the balance is not likely to be long retained under a system of private enter- prise unless all concerned are well informed as to the neces- sary policies and exercise self-restraint and co-operation. In planning to maintain demand at a level which will ensure ample job opportunities it is necessary to pay attention not

[2] Cf., however, Chapter 18, pp. 227, 230.

merely to governmental fiscal policy, but also to policies of business, labor, and agriculture which affect both consumers' demand and new private investment. Government may exercise a compensatory influence, but stabilization should extend throughout the whole system.

CHAPTER XX

Monetary Policy

by Lester V. Chandler

Monetary management must be included as an essential part of any successful economic program for a liberal America, that is, of a program that will enable us, without close government controls over the detailed operations of business firms, to achieve and maintain high and relatively stable levels of employment and production without marked inflations or deflations. This statement would not have been widely accepted forty years ago. Though the Constitution gave the federal government the power "to coin money and regulate the value thereof," few people believed prior to 1914 that the government should engage in active, continuous, day-to-day, monetary management. In those days it was widely believed that the government not only should but actually did limit its control of money to the definition of the monetary unit and the enactment of legislation embodying the "rules of the game," and that the system thereafter ran itself "automatically"; it was "managed" by the competition of private firms within the limits set by the broad "rules of the game."

We now know that this description of even the pre-1914 system was naive; the influence of the government was far greater and the "automatic" character of the system far less pronounced than was then believed. No informed person can contend that the present-day monetary system is largely "automatic," that its functioning is not greatly influenced by government actions, or that "laissez faire" in the sphere of money will necessarily produce an appropriate behavior of spendings. These beliefs have been washed away by the tides of two world wars, two serious depressions, the establishment of the Federal Reserve System and the evolution of its management activities, the increase of government budgets, and the enhanced understanding of monetary phenomena.

The government inevitably possesses and exercises a strong influence on the functioning of the monetary system. This is true whether it takes positive actions with its objectives clearly in view or whether it passively drifts along without clearly defined objectives. It cannot escape responsibility for monetary developments. Since the government cannot be neutral, it should use its influence for desirable rather than undesirable results and it should have a "monetary policy," that is, it should select its objectives rationally and use its powers in a co-ordinated way to attain those objectives.

Objectives of Monetary Policy The wide swings of business activity and prices since 1914 have taught us much about the appropriate objectives of monetary policy. Prior to 1914 many believed that the one objective of monetary policy that should take precedence over all others, and that was by itself a sufficient objective, was to keep the value of the dollar constant in terms of gold. We now know that this objective is almost always an inadequate guide to policy even when it is not actually misleading. Though the dollar price of gold remained stable throughout the period, we suffered the inflationary boom of 1919–20, the sharp deflation and unemployment of 1920–22, minor depressions in 1924 and 1927, and the deflationary breakdown of 1929–early 1933. And then with the price of gold again stable, we suffered a serious inflation during and following World War II. These experiences drive home the fact that mere adherence to a gold standard does not assure stable prices, or full production, or full employment. The maintenance of a gold standard is at best an inadequate guide to policy, and on occasion it can make more difficult the attainment of other objectives. Can there be any doubt as to the proper choice when the maintenance of a stable price of gold would conflict with the achievement and maintenance of full production and employment and stable prices for goods and services in general?

It seems likely, however, that we can, if we wish, continue to stabilize the price of gold without sacrificing more basic objectives of monetary policy. With more than 22 billion dollars of monetary gold in our system and with the prospect of adding to it instead of losing it, no fear of a gold shortage should deter us from an expansionary policy if and when such a policy should become appropriate. The greater danger is that continued gold inflows will inject inflationary pressures as foreign governments permit their gold producers to sell here rather than elsewhere or deliberately unload here a part of their accumulated gold stocks to alleviate their shortage of dollars. These pressures can be offset, however, by appropriate actions on the part of the Federal Reserve and the Treasury. It would be folly to allow inflation here to be aggravated by the gold policies of other countries even if we decide that gold purchases abroad constitute the most desirable method of extending relief to other countries.

What, then, should be the basic and dominating objective of our monetary policy? It should be to insure a rate of spending for output that will produce a high and secularly rising level of production and employment without either deflation or inflation of price levels. Refinements of this statement are, of course, possible, but they are probably not worth while at this stage. This objective is in line with the purposes of the Employment Act of 1946, and it states in simple terms the things that our people expect from our economic system. It says, in effect, that we should utilize monetary policy to avoid both deflationary, under-employment, under-production periods such as that following 1929 and inflation of the type that we have had in the recent period.

This objective can be stated more fully by analyzing spending for output. As has been noted by others in this volume, these are composed of (1) consumer spending for goods and services, (2) private investment expenditures by individuals and business firms for new construction, producers' durable equipment, and business inventories, (3) net foreign investment—the excess of foreign spending for our goods and services over our spending abroad, and (4) government spending for goods and services. These constitute the effective money demand for the output of our economy, and it is with reference to the size of this effective demand that business determines the size of its output, the amount of employment that it offers, and the height of its prices.

Why has private spending for output fluctuated so widely? Economists are now generally agreed that the primary source of fluctuations is to be found in the gyrations of private spending for investment—spending for new construction, for producers' durable equipment, for inventories, and for investment abroad. Instead of adding to their stocks of capital goods at a constant rate from month to month and from year to year, business firms and individuals spend feverishly for these purposes at some times and then virtually cease these spendings at other times. The fluctuations originating in investment spending are then magnified and spread throughout the entire economy through their induced effects on consumption. For example, decreased spending for investment goods decreases the incomes of the investment goods industries, which decreases the ability of the members of those industries to spend for consumption goods, which decreases the incomes of those in the consumption-goods industries, which decreases their spending for consumption, which lowers incomes still further, and so on. By this process an original decline of investment spending brings about a magnified or multiplied decline of spending for output, a large part of the decline consisting of the induced fall of consumption.

In a comparable way an initial rise of investment spending can bring about a multiplied or magnified rise of the national income. The increase of investment spending raises the income of those in the investment-goods industries, which increases their ability to spend for consumption, which increases the incomes of those in the consumption goods industries, which increases their ability to spend for consumption, which increases incomes still further, and so on.

There can be no doubt that the rate of investment spending (public and private) occupies a key position in the problem of maintaining economic stability at a high level. In fact, we can restate the primary objective of monetary policy in these terms: it should be to maintain investment spending for output at that level which will absorb all the savings that the community elects to make out of its income under conditions of full employment and full production. Public policy can affect both the level of investment spending (public and private) and the level of savings out of a full-employment national income. There is certainly no presumption in favor of government investment spending as against such spending by private enterprise; in fact, most liberals would be pleased if private enterprise would absorb and spend all the national savings out of a full-employment income that were not needed for "essential" public works.[1] To this end they support measures, both public and private, that will maintain private investment at a high and stable level. But they also insist that government investment policy cannot be neutral in its effects on general economic conditions, and that government spending, as well as taxation, is a legitimate and potent force that may properly be used as a part of a full-employment, stable-price program.

Instruments of Monetary Policy   Our experience since 1914 has also taught us that the term "monetary policy" must not be construed too narrowly. For some time after the establishment of the Federal Reserve System there was a tendency to believe that "monetary policy" was synonymous with Federal Reserve policy, and that the only instruments of monetary policy were those Federal Reserve measures that affected the volume of commercial bank reserves, thereby influencing the ability of the banking system to lend and create checking deposits. This narrow view of monetary policy has been outmoded by at least two developments. The first is recognition of the fact that orthodox Federal Reserve measures alone cannot maintain stability, and that by themselves they are particularly ineffective in halting a decline. Though the banks may be flooded with excess reserves, they are unlikely to lower interest rates enough, especially long-term rates, to raise borrowings and actual spending for investment to full-employment levels. In fact, no decline of interest rates, so long as these are above the zero level, may be able

[1] Other contributors in this volume might define "essential" rather broadly.—Ed.

to raise investment spending sufficiently in periods when enterprisers have gloomy expectations as to future profits. This does not mean, however, that an easy-money policy by the Federal Reserve is not an essential part of a recovery program.

A second development outmoding the narrower view of monetary policy is our increased understanding of the fact that many governmental activities other than those of the Federal Reserve exert a powerful influence on the quantity of money, the speed with which money is spent for consumption or investment, and the level of interest rates. If not properly integrated, these activities may greatly reduce the effectiveness of Federal Reserve measures and even offset them completely. But if these other activities are properly coordinated with Federal Reserve measures and all are attuned to a rationally selected objective, their effectiveness can be greatly enhanced. We should include in "monetary policy," therefore, all those measures that bear upon the rate of spending for output. Of these numerous measures we can examine only a few of the most important.

Among the most important classes of government activities making up monetary policy in the broad sense are the following: (1) Federal Reserve and Treasury policies of the traditional types—those affecting the reserve position of the banking system; (2) Treasury fiscal policy—spending, taxing, and borrowing or debt retirement; (3) policies of other governmental financial institutions that insure loans and make loans.

The Federal Reserve System and the Treasury We are all familiar with the principal instruments of Federal Reserve policy. It can curb an overexpansion of credit and investment spending by tightening the reserve position of the banking system. It can decrease the banks' excess reserves or actually make their reserves deficient by decreasing its own loans to banks, by selling its security holdings in the open market, and by increasing the legal reserve requirements of banks. In these ways it can limit the banks' lending power and force them to limit their credit by raising interest rates, or by rationing, or by both methods. On the other hand, the Federal Reserve can supply banks with large excess reserves by purchases of securities in the open market and by lowering the banks' legal reserve requirements. It can also encourage banks to borrow from it. With large excess reserves the banks bid down interest rates, especially short-term rates in the open market, though long-term rates and rates to small customers of banks fall less rapidly. We now have ample evidence, however, that flooding the banks with excess reserves does not insure that either the money supply or spending for output will rise automatically.

The Treasury has central-banking powers over bank reserves comparable to those of the Federal Reserve. These are exercised primarily, though not exclusively, through its control over the amount of money held in its vaults and the amount of its deposits at the Federal Reserve.[2] It can reduce bank reserves by borrowing or taxing money from the banks or the public and in effect locking it up in its own vaults or depositing it at the Federal Reserve. And this is precisely what it should do if, through gold imports or otherwise, bank reserves are raised to dangerously high levels and the Federal Reserve cannot cope with the situation. It should certainly not be deterred from this course by the fact that it might have to pay interest on bonds issued for the purpose. On the other hand, the Treasury can add to bank reserves by paying out balances previously accumulated in its own vaults or as deposits at the Federal Reserve.

Government fiscal policy exerts such an important effect on the rate of spending for output that it must be included as a part, and an essential part, of monetary policy. Fiscal policy inevitably exerts its strong influence whether the government attempts to balance its budget during each period required for the earth to complete its journey around the sun or whether policy is based primarily on economic rather than astronomical criteria. Let us look at government taxing and spending separately.

Government Taxing and Spending   Taxation *taken by itself* tends to reduce private spending and is anti-inflationary or deflationary. It is a method by which the government

---

[2] It can also affect the size of member bank reserves through its issue of silver-based money and paper money.

takes away a part of the money incomes of persons and business firms and leaves them with a smaller ability to spend for consumption or to provide funds for investment. Taxation is therefore an instrument of monetary policy that can be used to influence, though perhaps not to control accurately, the rate of private spending. An increase of taxation can be used to withdraw more funds from the public and reduce private spending power; a reduction of taxes can be used to leave the private sectors of the economy with more spending power. The effects on the various types of private spending depend, of course, on the types of taxes used. A tax system bearing very heavily on the lower-income groups that ordinarily save but little will reduce consumption spending relatively more than saving, whereas one that places a heavier burden on high incomes will have a greater effect on saving and less on consumption.

Though taxation taken by itself is anti-inflationary or deflationary, government spending for output *taken by itself* is anti-deflationary or inflationary. Government spending for output is a part of the effective money demand for output; it contributes to the national money income. By increasing its spending for output the government can increase its contributions to national money income and by decreasing its spending it can tend to reduce the national money income.

Since taxation by itself is deflationary (or anti-inflationary) and government spending by itself is inflationary (or anti-deflationary), it follows that the net effect on the level of the national money income depends on the relation between the two. By taxing away from persons and business firms more money income than it is currently spending, the government can exert a net deflationary or anti-inflationary effect. Thus, to strive for a surplus of revenues over expenditures is an appropriate government policy in the face of inflationary dangers. But by spending more than it is currently collecting from the public in taxes the government can exert a net anti-deflationary or inflationary effect. Such a policy is appropriate in the face of threatening deflation and unemployment.

The economic effects of a government surplus or deficit depend to some extent on how they are handled. Let us look first at the case in which the government is running a surplus by taxing more than it is spending. These excess funds might be used to pay off a part of the government debt held by individuals or banks. If these do not go into private investment spending the net effect is deflationary. This is likely to happen in a depressed period. But if they flow into private investment spending, as they would be likely to do in an optimistic period such as that following the war, there may be no net anti-inflationary effect, or at most only a limited anti-inflationary effect. If, therefore, the government wants its surplus to exert an anti-inflationary effect in such a period, it should lock up a part of it as cash in its own vaults, or hold it as an increased deposit at the Federal Reserve, or have the Federal Reserve decrease the lending power of the banks to the desired extent.

The economic effects of a government deficit depend on the method of finance used. If the government borrows the funds from individuals, or if it borrows the funds from banks at the expense of bank loans to others, the anti-deflationary effects of government spending may be at least partially offset by decreased private investment. To insure that deficit financing will exert its maximum anti-deflationary effects, the government should finance its deficit by (a) drawing on any accumulated cash in its vaults or any accumulated deposits at the Federal Reserve, or (b) by borrowing from the Federal Reserve, or (c) by borrowing from the banks and having the Federal Reserve supply the banks so liberally with excess reserves that no rise of interest rates will occur and government borrowing will not be at the expense of private borrowing and investment, or (d) a combination of the above methods. Our experience after 1932 has shown clearly that, given a liberal Federal Reserve credit policy, the government can borrow large amounts without raising interest rates and without reducing the availability of credit to private borrowers. This is not to argue that Federal Reserve credit policy should be used to maintain low interest rates simply to make it cheaper for the Treasury to borrow. It should not. In fact, the cost of Treasury borrowing is relatively unimportant compared with the maintenance of full employment and stable price levels. Federal Reserve policy, as well as other components of monetary policy, should be attuned to this basic objective. The point is that Treasury deficits should occur only when unemployment and deflation exist or threaten and that at such times low interest rates and easy credit are necessary to encourage private borrowing and investment.

We shall not examine in detail the policies of the numerous other government financial institutions. These provide full credit facilities to agriculture and agricultural co-operatives, and some of them lend to other types of business. In addition, the FHA, the RFC, and others guarantee large amounts of loans made by private lenders. Through both their own operations and their effects on private lenders these government institutions exert a great influence on the amount, types, and terms of loans and investment spendings. In the past the activities of these institutions have not been properly integrated with other parts of our monetary policy, and they have at times militated against the success of other measures. The role of these institutions should be studied carefully and their activities integrated into a broad and consistent monetary policy. In 1946–47, for example, the Federal Housing Administration was responsible for a liberal mortgage credit program which aggravated the difficulties confronting the Monetary Authority.

One of our major theses up to this point is that all government powers over the rate of spending for output should be integrated into a co-ordinated monetary policy. Another major thesis is that the measures taken should be flexible, prompt, and sufficiently strong to achieve their objective. The dominant objective of monetary policy should be constant—the attainment and maintenance of stable full employment and stable price levels. But the actions taken must change and change quickly as the outlook changes. Inflation calls for one set of actions; deflation and unemployment call for quite a different set. Is one to be called inconsistent because he turns on the furnace in the winter and the cooling system in the summer?

Monetary Policy in Inflation Inflation has been our problem since soon after our entrance into World War II. It has been aggravated by inadequate taxation during the war, by an inadequate system for increasing individual savings and bond-buying out of swollen war-time incomes, by an unjustified reduction of taxes, and by a premature relaxation of direct controls that might have prevented much of the inflationary damage since 1945. But what is the appropriate monetary policy for the remainder of the inflationary period? First and foremost, tax collections must exceed government spending. Should government spending be reduced? In this period every government expenditure must be justified by the social usefulness of the thing purchased with it. Recognizing that goods and services used by the government are in this period taken from other uses to which they would otherwise be put, we must ask in each case whether the social usefulness of the government project is as great as the usefulness of the alternative things we might have. Only this principle, not a dogged maintenance of the status quo or an arbitrary across-the-board cut, can give us a rational government-spending policy. But in any case tax collections in this period must be at least great enough to cover government spending and they should yield a surplus, the size of the surplus to depend on the best expert judgment as to the future outlook. The government will be taking a part of our output and productive capacity to carry on its own functions and, as is clear, to aid in the reconstruction of Europe. To take a part of our real output and not to extract from us, via taxes, a corresponding part of our money incomes is certainly to enhance inflationary pressures.

The Federal Reserve should also maintain a credit policy restrictive enough, in the judgment of its officials and in view of the other parts of our monetary policy, to prevent an excessive expansion of credit and investment spending. It appears that our own gold production plus sales of gold here by other countries suffering a shortage of dollars may inject an unwanted inflationary pressure into our economy. One may seriously question whether this is the best form of extending aid to dollar-hungry countries. But if we do buy the gold, we should not let it endanger our monetary policy. The Federal Reserve, by selling securities in the open market, or the Treasury, by taxing or borrowing to buy the gold and then locking it up, should "sterilize" the gold imports and prevent them from inflating the monetary base.

The other government financial institutions which lend or guarantee loans to private borrowers should re-examine their policies and bring them into line with the objective of stopping the inflationary rise of spendings.

Monetary Policy in Deflation   Sooner or later the present inflation will come to an end. We all hope that it will be followed by a period of stable high employment without deflation and with only the necessary readjustments of the price structure. But there is the possibility and even a probability that it will give way to a period of falling spending for output and unemployment. If and when this begins, our monetary policy should immediately be adjusted to the situation. The Federal Reserve and the Treasury should promptly supply the banks with sufficient excess reserves to keep interest rates at low levels and to insure the availability of credit for private investment. This policy, though favorable to private investment, is likely to be inadequate to keep private investment spending at a high enough level to support full employment. Complementary measures should be employed. The government financial institutions that lend and insure loans by private lenders should liberalize their policies to make investment more attractive.

In the face of an existing or incipient deflation, tax collections should certainly not exceed government spendings; the government should not shy away from deficits in such a period. Tax collections will automatically fall, of course, with a decline of the national income even if existing tax rates are maintained, but some of these rates should be reduced. Reductions should be concentrated on those taxes that bear heavily on consumption spending. The numerous and burdensome excise taxes should be cut drastically and some of them entirely eliminated. The lower-income groups should also have their income-tax burden reduced, probably by a rise of exemptions. The reduction of taxes will leave the private sector of the economy with greater spending power.

Along with reduction of taxes the government should increase its spending, that is, its contribution to the creation of national money income. Since the subject is treated in detail in other chapters of this book we need not expand our treatment of government-spending policy here. The principle to be emphasized is that in a period of unemployment induced by insufficient spending for output the government should not reduce its contribution to effective demand but should increase it.

International Monetary Policy   We are now a member of the Bretton Woods institutions—the International Monetary Fund and the World Bank. Because of our great voting power, our great economic strength, and the key position of the dollar in international finance we are by far the most influential member of those institutions. We should not only co-operate with them fully, but should also take the lead in developing sound and effective policies in the field of international monetary relationships. And above all we must remember that these institutions cannot succeed if the member nations, including our own, do not have sound domestic monetary policies.

Summary   I have not attempted in this chapter to lay down precise specifications for the monetary policies to be followed at each point of time. By its very nature monetary management is a job for experts who are in a position to study continuously the current situation, changes in the recent past, and prospective changes in the future. A policy that is appropriate this month may require alteration in the near future. I have therefore concentrated on the guiding principles. With its great economic power the government cannot be neutral in our economy; it is inevitably a powerful stabilizing or unstabilizing influence. It should therefore co-ordinate its activities into an integrated monetary policy directed to the basic peacetime objective of our economy—the attainment and maintenance of full employment and production and a stable purchasing power for the dollar. To be effective, monetary policy must be construed in the broad sense of including all the government activities that bear on the rate of spending for output. These measures should be employed in a co-ordinated way and they should be changed promptly as economic conditions change. Passivity in the face of changes in economic conditions is perhaps the worst monetary policy that a nation can have; it is usually not neutrality but an encouragement to instability.

CHAPTER XXI

The Inflation Problem

by Seymour E. Harris

Danger of Excess Demand   In order to keep our economy on an even keel, it is necessary not only to assure sufficient demand but also to exclude excess demand. To blow up a large balloon, we need to use a good deal of energy; but we can also use too much, with unfortunate results. In blowing up our economy through pumping in demand, we have to be on guard against providing too much purchasing power and demand. Those of us who, in the thirties, supported a full-employment program, an economy with more jobs than workers, were to find that a full-employment economy operating on all cylinders raised more serious problems than many of us had anticipated. Capitalism may flounder in the quagmire of deflation; but it may also, with disastrous consequences, welter in inflation.

Inflation and Rising Output   Inflation is a barometer of shortages of goods and services relative to demand. As output advanced from the low point of the early thirties to the peaks of 1947–48, prices gradually rose. Paradoxically enough, the inflationary threat appears not, as businessmen seem to believe, in periods of curtailed output but rather in periods of high output. Compare the direction of price movements in 1932 with those of 1947 when output was almost three times that of 1932. As output expands, inflationary pressures multiply because, among other reasons, workers and farmers seek higher returns per unit of output, because bottlenecks develop, because in a high-employment economy, each group, strategically placed, can exploit the others. Thus with labor fully employed (Chart 5) the pressure for an inflationary wage policy increases. In such periods, moreover, there is a tendency to produce for war or for investment, with the result that income earned and available for expenditures for consumption is much in excess of the consumer goods made available at stable prices. When the country produces 200

THE LABOR FORCE

Civilian employment was at record levels in 1947.

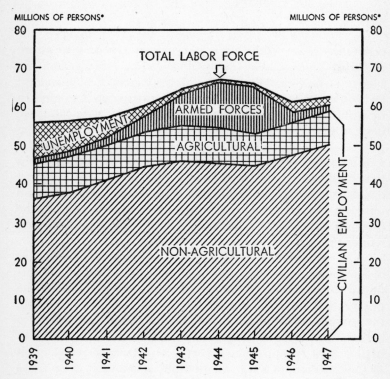

MILLIONS OF PERSONS*

MILLIONS OF PERSONS*

*14 years of age and over

SOURCE: U. S. DEPARTMENT OF LABOR (1939) AND DEPARTMENT OF COMMERCE (1940-1947).

CHART 5

billion dollars worth of goods and 100 billion dollars go to war expenditures, the obvious result is a large excess of demand. Control and other wartime measures will contain the pressures temporarily.

Excess of Demand   In the course of the war and early postwar years, this country accumulated about 200 billion dollars of cash, bank deposits, and government securities convertible into cash, thus increasing the volume of liquid assets by about 200 per cent. During the same period, purchases of consumers' durable goods, as well as maintenance and extension of capital goods, had to be postponed. With unusual demands emanating from the accumulation of liquid assets, high current incomes, and shortages both at home and abroad, inflationary pressures were bound to increase.

An obvious way out is to adopt policies which would result in contracting demand as much as possible in the current condition of excess demand, and in postponing demand as much as possible to later periods of anticipated shortages of demand. Simple as this principle is, Congress does not seem to have understood it.

Unwise Fiscal Policies   It is a cardinal principle, now generally accepted by economists, that when there is too much demand government has the responsibility of reducing it by curtailing expenditures and increasing taxes; and when there is too little demand, to expand it by increasing expenditures and reducing taxes. Yet in 1945, the Administration, influenced perhaps by unfortunate but understandable errors in forecasting, made a serious blunder in cutting taxes; and in 1947–48 the Republican majority in Congress was determined to reduce taxes further. (The Democrats also seemed to be intent upon trading votes for taxes.)

Perhaps we should not expect too much of the Republican party in its economic-stabilization policies. Ever since the Civil War, that party has shown a perversity and obtuseness in fiscal policy which is beyond the comprehension of the writer. In the years between the Civil War and World War I, the Republicans had imposed upon the country a currency system and debt policy which, despite the country's rapid growth, tended to starve the currency. In the second half of the 1920's, they suddenly reduced taxes and the rate of debt repayment, thus further kindling the inflationary conflagration of that period. And now they deal with inflation by cutting taxes further.

In their determination to cut expenditures, to be sure, they are acting wisely; but they should use the scalpel, not the axe: government responsibilities may be even more important than fiscal policy, for example, defense; and cutting appropriations for enforcement of tax laws may cost many times what is saved. It is indeed difficult to understand the apostles of Gladstonian finance (for example, Senators Byrd and Taft, and the NAM), who also generally are most fearful of Socialism and Communism. They are in the van in the movement to cut defense expenditures, yet in their determination to keep public expenditure down they are prepared to expose us to the dangers of unpreparedness, and Russian control of the world.

Money Not Necessarily Excessive   Many have become fatalistic concerning the inflation problem. The supply of money is three times that of 1939; in their view, we may just as well accept the inevitable, a rise of prices of 200 per cent. I do not agree. In the years 1800 to 1940, the amount of money and deposits rose by 1,750 times, the national income by but 110 times, and prices actually fell. In other words, the country can grow up to rising supplies of money as income increases, particularly since with higher incomes, the demand for cash and bank deposits increases even more. But the rise in prices will not thus be kept in check so long as our government pursues wrong policies. Unless strong measures are taken to assure the public that the value of their money will not be frittered away in rising prices, the flight from cash to goods will become more rapid.

Essentials of an Anti-Inflation Policy   What then would be the essence of a vigorous anti-inflationary policy? Above all, it will be necessary to keep demand down and make more goods available for consumers.

(1) Fiscal policy. Keep taxes at their present level and, if politically possible, raise the income-tax rate for all but low incomes; and increase excise taxes on luxuries. Protect the

country against a perverse fiscal policy, should a decline follow in the near future, by delegating to the executive discretionary authority to change rates every three months on the basis of results provided by the best forecasting techniques available. (Forecasting is absolutely necessary. No action can be taken without assumptions concerning future conditions. We must, however, recognize the possibility of error, and we should be prepared to adapt policy to the changing prospects.) Clearly, wise fiscal policy is not to be achieved if there is a lag of three years between the changing economic situation and changes in tax rates and public spending.

(2) Reduce credit—but cautiously. Keep down spending by stimulating savings and discouraging extensions of credit to consumers and business. Surely with present high levels of income and liquid assets held by both business and consumers, there is little excuse for the rapid expansion of bank credit in recent years. In the two and a half years ending June 30, 1947, loans of American insured commercial banks had grown from 21.3 to 33.3 billion dollars. In these two and a half years, the rise of loans exceeded in absolute and relative amounts the expansion in the highly inflationary period, 1922 to 1929. For 1947, the rise was 7 billion. Clearly, the banks have to be checked. I see no practical way of restraining them other than along the lines proposed by Mr. Eccles: a rise in reserve requirements accompanied by measures which will prevent the banks from dumping government securities on the market. (In the year ending June 30, 1948, the reserve banks succeeded to some extent in restraining banks.)

Monetary authorities should take the required action in a manner to preclude a *large* increase in the rate of interest. In an inflationary economy, it is indeed necessary to discourage investment; and investments running at an annual rate of 30 billion dollars for two years are altogether too high. But the economy is very vulnerable; and the federal government, with a debt of 260 billion dollars and large obligations to the nation, cannot countenance a substantial rise of rates. A general hardening of rates should then be accompanied by special measures to protect public issues (for example, support by the Reserve banks or compulsory immobilization of government securities by banks). A large rise in interest rates may not only discourage investment but it may ultimately depress our economy. At this juncture, we prefer specific to general attacks, precision bombing to saturation bombing. For this reason, it will be well to discourage excessive investments through the use of an allocation system; and in so far as this specific attack is used, less reliance will have to be placed upon a general rise in rates.

(3) Proper use of controls. We must depend more on controls until the situation once again becomes normal. Had the country listened to Bowles in 1945–46, we would have had far less inflation, and with the containment of inflation, a better distribution of goods. Chart 6 indicates the large rise of prices after controls were lifted. Now the country requires export controls and allocations which will achieve a proper distribution between goods for domestic and foreign use; the most effective division of exports among countries and classes of commodities; the appropriate distribution of scarce items (for example, iron, coal, power, grains, housing materials) according to essentiality: grain for food, not for alcohol; wood for veterans' homes, not for luxurious summer hotels; oil for heat, at the expense of excessive pleasure driving. If all these do not suffice, then we should prepare to use limited price control and rationing. Congress should not only provide the necessary powers to make possible the use of these controls but also should make them effective. They have failed to do this so often in the past by neglecting to appropriate adequate funds for financing a staff to promulgate sound regulations and enforce them.

(4) Voluntary restraints. Finally, as Keyserling, Soule, Gilbert, and Fainsod contend, we should expect co-operation and restraint on the part of large group interests. It would be helpful indeed if capital, labor, and agriculture would agree to a holiday on price and wage increases except as justified by changes in productivity. With the present dynamic labor movement, high profits are bound to be a signal for starting the inflation spiral. From 1945 to the first half of 1947 employee compensation had risen by but 2 per cent, consumers' prices by 22 per cent, corporate profits before taxes by 44 per

WHOLESALE PRICES

*Wholesale prices, after leveling off in the second quarter of 1947,
resumed their sharp rise in the second half of the year.*

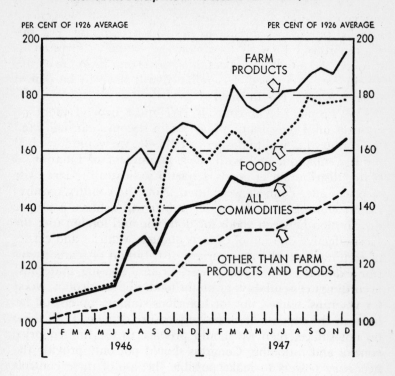

PER CENT OF 1926 AVERAGE

PER CENT OF 1926 AVERAGE

PERCENTAGE INCREASE SINCE JUNE 1946

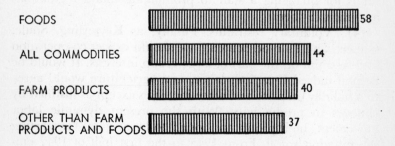

FOODS — 58

ALL COMMODITIES — 44

FARM PRODUCTS — 40

OTHER THAN FARM PRODUCTS AND FOODS — 37

SOURCE: U. S. DEPARTMENT OF LABOR.

CHART 6

cent and after taxes by 96 per cent, property and rental income by 26 per cent. Labor leaders are therefore reluctant to agree to a holiday on wage increases. An excess-profits tax may make labor leaders more tractable. Once productivity resumes its prewar advance (in 1946, 22 industries, largely non-consumer, raised their man-hour output by 6+ per cent on the average), then it will be possible both to raise wage rates and reduce prices.

In summary, a correct price policy should bring about a reduction of demand and a rise of supply. But concentration on raising supplies will not solve the inflation problem; and in fact may aggravate it.[1]

[1] Cf. Concluding chapter, pp. 370–1.

CHAPTER XXII

The Farm Problem

by Seymour E. Harris

What Is the Farm Problem?   One of the contributors to this volume expressed surprise that there was to be no essay on the farm problem. I proposed at first to deal with the problem in the introductory essay; but I have been convinced this would be a mistake. Hence this brief chapter. No one would deny the important contributions farmers make to our national life, nor their disproportionate political influence. In 1946, however, farm income was not of outstanding importance: it was approximately 19 billion dollars, or 11 per cent of the nation's product.

It is not easy to fit this essay into any one part of the book, and it might have been a separate part by itself. A discussion of the farm problem might also fit into Part III (Resources and Their Development) or Part IV (Planning and Controls), or the present part which deals with stabilization of demand. That a large part of the farm problem is related to that of stabilizing demand is the reason for including it here.

The farm problem is essentially one of prices and incomes: farm prices are much more flexible than prices of industrial products, and the response of supplies to price changes is much smaller and slower than for industry. In periods of prosperity, farm prices and incomes tend to rise much more than other prices and incomes generally; and in periods of depression they fall much more. Thus, from 1929 to 1933, agricultural output declined by but 6 per cent, while wholesale prices of agricultural products dropped by 63 per cent.

Iron and steel output, however, declined by 85 per cent, and prices but 20 per cent. Chart 7 shows the larger movements of agricultural prices relative to industrial prices, and of industrial production relative to farm output.

Excessive Supplies   Agriculture's problem over the years has been large supplies relative to demand, a relationship induced by substantial gains of productivity, sluggishness of population movement from farms to cities in response to higher economic rewards, and a deterioration in exchange terms for farmers, accentuated in depression periods when city incomes fall.

Large gains in productivity are evidenced in the rise of farm production by 10 per cent in World War I, and by 10 per cent additional before World War II. By 1946 output was 36 per cent above that of 1939, a total rise of 65 per cent since 1914. This large increase in output occurred despite the fact that the amount of land in use for farming had remained relatively stable since World War I and despite a decline in the farm population from 30 millions in 1940 to 25 millions in 1945. Mechanization and improved soil use largely account for the gains.

Collapse of Demand   In the early thirties, the serious downturn of economic conditions, together with the high levels of farm output and growing barriers to trade, brought a serious crisis in agriculture. With gross farm income down from 5.7 billion dollars in 1929 to 1.7 billion dollars in 1932, drastic action was required. The government relied primarily upon measures which would tend to restrict output and raise prices and incomes, and to some extent upon artificial means of stimulating demand. Government payments made on the condition that farmers restrict output or adapt production to the changing pattern of demand became an important part of farm income. By 1939, cash receipts from marketings had risen to 8 billion dollars, and government payments to 807 million additional. In 1932, cash receipts (not, as above, gross income) had fallen to 4.8 billion dollars.

Mistaken Farm Policy   Public policy in the depression aroused much opposition, particularly among those who were critical of restrictive measures in a world with much

AGRICULTURAL AND INDUSTRIAL PRODUCTION, AND PRICES, IN THE UNITED STATES, 1913-1947

Index Numbers (1935-39 = 100)

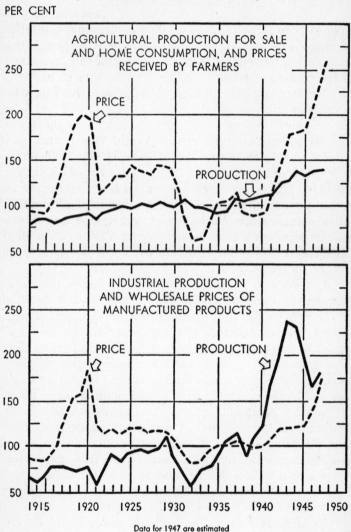

SOURCE: U. S. DEPARTMENT OF AGRICULTURE, BUREAU OF AGRICULTURAL ECONOMICS.

CHART 7

poverty. The policy was vulnerable on other grounds also. First, partly as a result of the new farm policies, United States farm prices tended to rise greatly above world levels, thus choking off an important part of the farmers' normal market and making necessary either the discovery of alternative markets or an intensification of curtailment policies, with its accompanying regimentation of farmers and its drains on the federal budget. Second, farm policies imposed in no small part by well-organized farm lobby groups favored the relatively well-to-do elements in the farm population, that is, the farm owner against the less fortunate groups, farm tenants and farm labor. It is a reflection on the farmers and their representatives in and out of Congress that in the thirties the authorities showed little interest in the farm tenant and managed to exclude farm labor from the benefits of social-security and minimum-wage legislation.[1]

Improvement in War   In the war and early postwar period, favorable demand conditions and rising productivity and output further improved the position of the farm population. Despite long habituation to restrictionist policies, the incentive offered by rising demand and guaranteed minimum prices elicited a record level of output. As a result of rising prices, an improvement in the ratio of price received to price paid, and increased output, the assets of farmers rose from 53.8 billion dollars in 1940 to 111.2 billion in 1947, and their equity from 43.8 billion dollars to 102.8 billion. Their liabilities were down by 1.6 billion dollars. Net income rose from 6.4 billion dollars in 1940 to 18.2 billion in 1946.

Proposed Farm Policy: Emphasis on Rise of Demand   It is now time to assess the farm policy of the future. So far government commitments to maintain prices at close to parity have not been costly; for unusual and unexpectedly long continued high demand substantially explain the improvement in prices and incomes obtained. But once demand returns to normal, it is not likely that short of imposing a highly regimented regime upon the farm population, the government will be able to enforce a policy which will yield prices equal to around 90 per cent of parity.

[1] Cf. Chapter 3, p. 52.

On the basis of the experience and mistakes since 1933, the following lines of action seem appropriate.

(1)   An increased dependence on improvement of demand rather than curtailment of supply: That means, above all, the management of our economy in a manner which will provide high and stable incomes for the non-farm population, and thus enable them to spend adequately on farm products. It also includes a guarantee of markets in so far as other measures suggested below fail to provide a reasonable standard of living for the farmer. Stamp plans, school lunches, and other ways of using output seem far better than the medicine of cutting production.

(2)   Improved education on nutrition and a sane policy in the international field: These measures will also increase expenditures on farm products. International policy should reduce emphasis on high domestic prices relative to international prices of farm products, and contribute to the reduction of trade barriers everywhere.

(3)   The farmer's share of the consumer's dollar: Despite the more rapid rise in prices at the farm than that in prices of farm products for the consumer, a result in no small part of controls and rising prices, the farmer still receives too small a part of the consumer's dollar.

(4)   Allocation of resources: It is not necessary, and would be most unwise, to allow market prices undisturbed by policy to determine the allocation of resources. Much progress has already been made in conserving soil, in restoring farm lands, and in offering incentives to adjust production to the variations of demand and in accordance with the quality of the soil. Government should continue to make incentive payments to accelerate desired redistribution of resources and changes in land use, including movements from farms to cities. But this is not a proposal to use government funds to cut output generally—not so long as consumption of farm products both in this country and elsewhere is far below what it should be.[2]

(5)   Storage, subsidies, crop insurance: Should the government in co-operation with private enterprise succeed in stabilizing income at a high level, the problems of the farmer

[2] See introduction to Part III where this issue is discussed more fully.

would largely be solved. (I would subscribe to that position even though farmers have had their difficulties even in periods of relatively high employment.) But we cannot count on full employment and stability. We shall then have to depend to some extent on storage of farm products, on subsidizing consumers of farm products, on improved techniques for offsetting cyclical fluctuation through measures taken by the individual farmer, and on crop insurance (largely to deal with uncertainties of weather).

(6) Income support: Should these prove insufficient, it would be well to rely not primarily on price guarantees but on income support.[3] The latter is to be preferred to price guarantees which tend to interfere with adjustment of output to demand, and which may be used to restrict output. Clearly, there is no sense to the income-parity concept which farm groups are now pushing. What is wanted is an adequate income to assure minimum standards and adequate output, but not a standard so high as to discourage the movement of resources out of farming in response to curtailed demand and continued gains in productivity.

(7) Higher wages and social security: Finally, we emphasize the importance of giving the submerged population the advantages which the relatively prosperous farm owners have denied them. Farm wages are at a record level, but depression will find farm wages once more unsatisfactory, and without the support of a social-security program.

[3] Cf. Bowles in this volume, and Theodore W. Schultz, *Agriculture in an Unstable Economy* (New York, 1945).

PART SIX

International Economic
Relations

Introduction

by Seymour E. Harris

Expansion of foreign loans or gifts with its accompanying substantial rise of exports increases demand; and for that reason it might have been a subject for consideration under Part V. Unfortunately, in a full-employment economy, the stimulus provided by large exports contributes to inflation rather than to an expansion of output: foreign claims on goods are made effective by bidding them away from domestic buyers through price competition. In 1947, for example, when consumption expenditures were well over 160 billion dollars and domestic investment was at 30 billion dollars, net foreign investment of around 10 billion dollars further increased demand for the goods produced by a full-employment economy. This large quantity of exports made possible by foreign investment (including grants) may well contribute to the support of demand and employment, once the demand for consumption and domestic investment falls substantially. But until a deficiency of demand develops, large foreign loans and gifts will add to inflation. As we shall see, it is possible to stave off inflation if appropriate control measures are taken to reduce demand in domestic markets, as an offset to the rise of foreign demand.

Since this country exported but 5 per cent of its national output in the interwar period, it might be assumed that international economic relations are of secondary or lesser importance; but nothing could be further from the truth. In response to the growth of bilateralism in trade and the

273

deepening of the depression in the thirties, United States trade dropped not only absolutely but as a percentage of United States income and world trade. The decline contributed substantially to the deterioration of economic conditions in this country, particularly since, as exports were reduced, the effects on total income were multiplied. The ensuing losses were not evenly divided but were felt especially by particular groups. The politically powerful farmers incurred a large part of the losses, with the rest of the country in turn being compelled to share them, since the farmers, through Congressional legislation, forced a redistribution of losses.

As Lerner shows, the problems are mainly political; they are economic only in so far as unfavorable political relations bring economic and political warfare. Our economic strength should be used to bolster the economies of Western Europe, thus making them less vulnerable to Russian pressure. Lerner states the correct lines of American policy: the choice is between liberty and totalitarianism, not between capitalism and socialism; the system of enterprise chosen should meet the test of efficiency; the manner of help should be loans at going rates of interest, and reduction of tariff barriers in the United States, the latter to assure favorable conditions of trade; the conditions of loans should be guarantee of use of the proceeds for productive purposes, and readiness to adjust exchange rates at levels which will help yield an equilibrium in the balance of payments. In the state of the world in the late forties, it will be necessary also to make large grants as well as loans; and too much should not be expected of adjustments in exchange rates.[1]

[1] Cf. Lerner's essay.

CHAPTER XXIII

Foreign Economic Relations of the United States

by Abba P. Lerner

The Political Problem—Russia   The importance of foreign economic relations for the United States is primarily political. The purely economic considerations are not so important as the political. If the rest of the world simply disappeared it would still be possible for our economy to prosper and to grow. But we cannot ignore the rest of the world because the stability of our own society, its prosperity, and its freedom depend on there being stability, prosperity, and freedom in the rest of the world. It is no mere rhetorical phrase which tells us that our shrunken world cannot persist "half slave and half free." It is the hard fact of the existence of a powerful empire, expanding and ambitious, its rulers fanatically believing that a deity called History has charged them with the task of extending their rule over our whole planet in the name of the Dictatorship of the Proletariat. They are convinced that it is their right, even their duty, to use force and chicanery and to be undeterred by human suffering if these should be in any way deemed to further the accomplishment of this end. The Russian Empire, if not checked in its ambitions or changed in its nature, will expand until it has isolated the United States. It will then try to blackmail us and weaken us until we can be captured and incorporated in the Russian slave society. The primary importance of our foreign economic relations is that they can play an essential part in a policy for preventing the extension of Russian conquests and in maximizing the chance of avoiding an atomic war.

Economic Breakdown in Russia's Plan   For all its fanaticism and ruthlessness, the Russian system is less efficient than ours for producing goods and services with which to raise the living standards of the population. It is unable to win significant support wherever people enjoy some economic security and personal freedom and have some knowledge of what life is like for the common man in Russia, either in or out of the labor camps. For some time to come the Russian Empire will not be strong enough to push its conquests much further by purely military means, so that for the present it must rely on the seizure of power in various countries by the local Communists. This process depends on a combination of the suffering, insecurity, fear, and despair caused by economic breakdown with an ignorance of what lies behind the "Iron Curtain." This combination may induce an apathy which would permit the Communists, with Russian help, to install a secret police responsible only to Moscow, to deport or murder all potential opponents, and to celebrate the completion of the conquest with a mock plebiscite.

An essential part of this process is the persistence of economic failure and economic insecurity. Our foreign economic policy can bring about the rehabilitation of the countries outside the "Iron Curtain" and provide economic success and economic security. This would spoil the Russians' design. That is why they are so enraged by the Marshall Plan. It may remove the misery essential to their scheme.

Giving, Lending, and Trading   The rehabilitation of Europe and Asia means in the first place the building up of their productive equipment. The United States can help either directly, by providing some of the equipment, or indirectly, by providing food and other consumption goods which would make it possible for more of the local resources to be diverted to the provision of productive capital equipment.

Some of this help may take the form of a simple gift. For this there is the further justification, if human need and our own security are insufficient justification, that our allies made much greater sacrifices in the war than we did. They emerged from the war impoverished, while we emerged richer than ever. Surely it is such help that must have been meant by our so easily forgotten slogan of "equal sacrifice" in the war. The Russians, who suffered more from the Nazis than any people except the Jews, should come high on the list if only there were some assurance that the help would be used for raising the living conditions of the Russian people and not for warming up the Cold War on the West.

Far more important than such gifts, because they can be much greater, are the opportunities for loans for productive investment in the devastated and undeveloped parts of the world. If loans are not to become unintended gifts, they must be made only where there is a reasonable expectation of their being repaid and with interest high enough to cover the risk of default. In the poor and devastated countries additional productive equipment would increase annual output by 20 per cent of the capital or more. The borrowers would therefore gain the difference between this and the 3 or 4 per cent interest. We on our side would gain by earning more on these foreign investments than we could earn on domestic investment. Such foreign loans have the further benefit that they establish a direct interest on our part in the continued prosperity of the countries in which our money is invested so that we are less likely to be suspected of harboring evil intentions toward them.[1]

It is obviously essential for such a plan of lending that we should make it possible for the borrowing countries to get from us the American dollars necessary for their interest payments and capital repayments. This means that as soon as the repayments and interest payments come to more than new loans, we will have to buy more than we sell abroad by reducing and perhaps removing our import restrictions.

Even more important than the foreign loans are the benefits which these countries would obtain from being able to

[1] This would be particularly valuable for loans to Russia, with adequate guarantees that they would be used for peaceful purposes. See "The President Addresses the World," *Bulletin of the Atomic Scientists* (April 1947).

trade goods and services with us. This would increase their productivity by permitting them to specialize in those activities where their efficiency is greatest (or their inefficiency least). We too would gain in the same way, but while for us the gain would merely mean a further increase in our high standard of living, for the poor countries it can make all the difference between (1) a vicious circle in which they cannot work properly because they have not enough to eat, and they do not have enough to eat because they cannot work properly, and (2) the beneficent spiral of increasing production and efficiency toward prosperity and wealth. For this too we must remove the restrictions on our foreign trade.

By our gifts, our loans, and our trade we can help to provide the economic prosperity needed for a free society. The gifts will of course mean an economic sacrifice and the lending will mean a temporary reduction in our own level of consumption or in the tempo of our own further industrial development. But these economic sacrifices will be more than offset in the long run by economic benefits. Greater trading opportunities will be provided by a richer world. And in time we will be receiving the interest and the capital repayments of our loans. These economic gains, however, are merely incidental, if fortunate, accompaniments of the program. The real reason for our undertaking it is that it makes possible the development of free and therefore peaceful societies on whose prosperity our own freedom and security depend.

The Conditions of Aid　　Since the primary purpose of a program of economic help for Europe and Asia is to assure peace and democracy, it is inevitable that some conditions should be attached to the help. It would not do to let it be used in warlike preparation against us, directly or indirectly. Nor would it make sense to permit it to be wasted in bolstering up unnecessary inefficiencies. The help must be utilized to bring about the prosperity and the freedom which justify it.

Yet there is a reluctance to impose any conditions on these loans. Objections are raised by those who are supersensitive to charges that the Marshall Plan is a means of subordinating the rest of the world to the capitalism of the United States, as if it were a kind of imperialism or exploitation to make it a condition of the help that it be used for the achievement of prosperity, freedom, and peace, and not preparation for war upon the helper.

On the other hand there are those who believe that we should insist on the prohibition of any kind of socialism, on the grounds that only a private-enterprise economy can yield economic prosperity, individual freedom, and a basis for peace.

This conflict reflects two attitudes that agree in seeing the struggle between capitalism and socialism as a struggle between good and evil but which differ in their view of which is wholly good and which is wholly evil. Liberals are now beginning to recognize that neither capitalism nor socialism represents either pure goodness or pure wickedness, that private enterprise and public enterprise are both useful *instruments* for serving the public welfare, and that the issue between them is best resolved in each particular instance by the pragmatic economic test of which is able to operate more efficiently. That instrument is better in any situation which can provide better pay for the worker or better conditions of work or result in a bigger or better product. The best way to make this decision is to permit private and public enterprises to compete on equal terms and let that form of enterprise win which is more efficient in the particular circumstances.

The lesson of all this for the liberal, who is primarily interested in the freedom and the dignity of the individual, is that to concentrate on a supposed struggle between capitalism and socialism is to miss the fundamental issue. Freedom has grown and has been destroyed in societies which favored private enterprise, and freedom has also grown and has been destroyed in societies which favored public enterprise. The liberal must recognize that if he wants freedom he must fight not for capitalism and not for socialism but for freedom.

Democratic Functionalism as a Condition The liberal who has completely freed himself from the confusion of individual freedom with either capitalism or socialism can describe his position as Democratic Functionalism. Whether a capitalistic or a socialistic mechanism is to be used should depend on which functions better in the circumstances. It is merely a technical difference between methods and should be decided by technicians or by competition. What the liberal is really interested in is the preservation of the *democratic* civil rights of the individual. Democratic Functionalism thus concentrates on the essence of liberalism freed from the capitalistic or socialistic auras. Democratic Functionalism enables us to say what conditions for help are justifiable and what conditions are not. Democracy, that is, civil liberties, freedom of opinion, and availability of knowledge of the external world, is an essential condition. Without that the people are at the mercy of authorities who can manipulate them by giving them the appropriate imaginary picture of the world that would elicit the desired response. Given democracy all else is secondary. Whether there is private or public enterprise in any industry should ideally be settled by the pragmatic test of efficiency. A country may have aesthetic or other preferences for some particular kind of economic organization, and where the difference in efficiency is not too great it can indulge in such a preference. But the cost of such a deviation from Democratic Functionalism should be known and there would be nothing untoward in the helper demurring if too much of his help is being dissipated in such a luxury.

Democratic Functionalism for the United States   Democratic Functionalism is just as good medicine for the helper as for the helped. We have already applied it in suggesting the removal of the tariffs so that there would be an objective test, by competition, whether it is more efficient for us to import a certain commodity or to make it for ourselves. And where for any reason competition is not applicable the same principle tells us that a country should import any commodity whose marginal cost of production is greater than the import price and that we should export any commodity whose marginal cost is less than the export price. This has been called the principle of non-discrimination. In the same way the maximum benefits from our economic help would be enjoyed if the receiving countries were induced, as a condition of the direct help, to enter into as wide a customs union as possible.

Such a condition of help would probably be of much more assistance in rehabilitation than the direct help itself.

The primary domestic condition for a satisfactory American foreign economic policy is of course the maintenance of full employment and the prevention of severe inflation. The Russian plan seems to be based squarely on the belief that a depression in America will come soon and that this will deliver the rest of the world into Russia's hands. Connected with this belief is the argument that American aid to Europe and Asia is necessary to enable the American economy to maintain its prosperity—as if it would be impossible to find people in the United States who would like to consume more goods or enjoy more leisure or as if it would not be possible to "save" the American economy by dumping such alleged surpluses into the ocean.

The prevention of inflation is associated by many people with the balancing of the budget. It is true that a balanced budget coupled with a refusal to increase the amount of money makes any hyper-inflation impossible. But it does not prevent considerable inflation of the milder variety and it does nothing to prevent very serious deflation and unemployment. More direct measures are necessary to prevent inflation and depression, and this means working directly on the total rate of spending in the economy, keeping it from going too high or too low.[2] The application of Democratic Functionalism to the rate of money spending is nothing other than "functional finance" which is discussed elsewhere in this volume.

It is consequently not very reasonable to impose a balanced budget on the countries helped, as is suggested by some of the "capitalist" liberals. An insistence on a balanced budget is not so much too strict as somewhat beside the point. It is possible and much better to concentrate on the real objectives —the prevention of depression and of inflation by keeping total spending from going either too low or too high.

Dangers of Obsolete Economic Orthodoxies   It is not only the internal finances of countries that are in danger from too uncritical an acceptance of traditional capitalistic

[2] See Chapter 18.

economic principles. An attempt has been made to create a satisfactory framework for the international financial affairs of different countries by the International Monetary Fund. Here the danger comes from those who consider it the primary purpose of the fund to stabilize exchange rates at all costs. Just as those to whom the balancing of the internal budget is an overriding principle hinder rather than help in the really important problem of preventing inflation and depression, so those who are fascinated with the stabilization of exchange rates can cause this fetishism to get in the way of the really important task of freeing foreign trade.

Insistence on maintaining the rates of exchange when there is a "fundamental disequilibrium"[3] which calls for permitting the foreign value of a country's currency to fall has very serious effects. It forces the country to restrict its imports in relation to its exports by means other than the depreciation of its currency. The alternative means are never more satisfactory. They include tariffs, which everyone recognizes to be harmful to international trade; quantitative restrictions on imports by licenses of various sorts, which are agreed to be worse than tariffs; exchange controls, which are about as bad but more irritating; export subsidies, which are even more unpopular (though not with such good reason).

There is one method of adjustment which, when achieved, is not more harmful than permitting the foreign value of the country's exchange to fall. This is to reduce the wage and price level in the country. But this solution, on which the defenders of fixed exchanges always have to fall back, is usually brought about by a long period of extreme depression. And when it is finally achieved the results are in no way better than those obtained by the instantaneous and painless adjustment of the rates of exchange.

The present dollar shortage throughout the world is a reflection of the attempts by almost all countries to keep the values of their currencies higher in terms of the dollar than is consistent with "fundamental equilibrium." Depreciation of such currencies would make it easier for these countries to sell goods abroad and would discourage the purchase of

[3] See Chapter 23, last paragraph, for discussion of equilibrium rate.

some imports, so that there would be less need for the rationing, priorities, and other bureaucratic controls of imports from "hard currency" countries that are now interfering with the rehabilitation of the war-stricken countries.

If we could get over the irrational fears that we have of "competitive currency depreciation" and allow the different currencies to find their values in a free market, the benefits to everybody would be enormous. Democratic Functionalism would call for the use of the price mechanism as the most efficient means for determining who needs the imports most, by seeing who is willing to pay for them. It would thus free enterprise (both public and private) from bureaucratic suffocation. By shifting resources from the industry of running a bureaucracy and from the industry of getting permits from the bureaucracy to the industries producing useful goods and services, and by setting enterprise free from bureaucracy, Democratic Functionalism could lead to an economic revival comparable only to the salvation of the Russian economy by the New Economic Policy in 1921.

Summary   Foreign economic relations are important for the United States not so much for their economic as for their political consequences. Our foreign economic policy can contribute to the rehabilitation and the prosperity of the war-stricken nations. Without such rehabilitation and prosperity they are almost certain to be swallowed by the Russian Empire and mobilized in a war machine against us. A generous and liberal foreign economic policy can prevent this from happening and by spreading democracy up to the borders of Russia and ultimately within its borders we can hope to escape the atomic third world war.

For the most effective carrying out of this program we must recognize that the fundamental issue is not between capitalism and socialism or between private and public enterprise, but whether men are to be slaves or to be free. The guiding principle is Democratic Functionalism. The ultimate objective is freedom and its primary instrument is a democratic form of government. Efficiency is always important and often essential and the maximum of efficiency is achieved by the scientific or pragmatic test of which alternative mechanisms function best. Democratic Functionalism operates for domestic full employment as functional finance. In the international field it permits the price mechanism to determine the foreign-exchange rates and obviates the need for bureaucratic allocation of scarce goods.

The future security of the United States demands generous gifts for rehabilitation now, large development loans (at interest rates greater than can be earned at home), and the removal of all obstacles to trade, by ourselves and by everybody we can influence.

In this way we can remove the rocks on which previous attempts at internationalism have been shattered so that the One World, envisaged by liberals and by socialists in the past, can be built by their joining forces as Democratic Functionalists in the future.

CHAPTER XXIV

Dollar Famine and Trade Policy

by Seymour E. Harris

History Crises in international economic relations in the last generation have sprung largely from dollar shortages, and more recently, dollar famine. Dollar shortage is a generic term used in fact to describe a crisis, outside the United States, in production and in the balance of payments. For thirty years now, this country has been the magnet for the world's outpourings of gold. Though the inflow has been persistent, with total supplies rising from 1.5 billion dollars in 1914 to 22 billion in 1947, and though the United States on government or private account transferred 15 billion dollars on capital account from 1914 to 1919 and 9 billion in the twenties (offset by an inflow of 5 billion dollars in the thirties), the country nevertheless continued to attract vast supplies of gold from abroad.

America's pre-eminence as an industrial nation, its capacity to produce in large quantities and at low unit costs, its ability to provide a variety of goods in response to what was wanted—all of these help explain the great demand for dollars, and the relatively inadequate demand for foreign currencies. Indeed, we were fortunate in our large and rich resources, in the relatively small proportion of population to resources, in the vastness of our free-trade area and therefore in the large scale of output and low unit costs, in the high general level of education, and in the effective system of private enterprise, with its relatively free movements of talent to the top. Europe, on the other hand, suffered from the devastating effects of two all-out wars. Her inadequate productive capacity reflected unsatisfactory political conditions, inability to hold her ground against newly industrialized nations contesting European pre-eminence, and lack of venturesomeness, a sign of industrial decadence.

Recent Dollar Famine and Its Treatment   On top of these sources of decline, a serious crop failure, the slow recovery of Germany, the workshop of Europe, the political unrest, the unavailability of resources from Eastern Europe, the reduced output of coal, and the exhaustion of dollar resources following attempts to accelerate recovery by relying heavily on imports—these brought a new crisis in 1947.

Surely, correct American policy is to provide the aid required under the Marshall Plan. Should the plan require outlays of 20 billion dollars over four years, the risk would be a prudent one and, though the cost would be large, it would be well within our capacity to meet. We need only compare the 350 billion dollars spent by this country for World War II, the rise of national income from 45 billion dollars in 1932 to 203 billion in 1947, the rise of consumption by 115 billion dollars annually over the same period, with annual costs of the Marshall Plan of 5 billion dollars to conclude that the burden will not be a severe one. Against the costs of a new world war, these outlays would be very small. Yet they would contribute towards the maintenance of democratic traditions in Western Europe and, therefore, significantly reduce the chances of war—an argument that should enlist support for the program. These expenditures are consistent with a balanced budget here if taxes are not reduced. They are also compatible with no large additional inflationary pressures if proper measures are taken to economize and allocate scarce items and if supplementary controls, which need not require minute regulations and interference, are imposed.[1]

Encouraging Production in Other Countries   American policy can be improved greatly. In the thirties, this country became a capital borrowing nation, importing 5 billion dollars of capital, a rather unusual position for the richest country

---

[1] Cf. Chapter 21, and S. E. Harris and others, *Foreign Economic Policy for the United States* (Cambridge, Mass., 1948), and S. E. Harris, *European Recovery Program* (Cambridge, Mass., 1948).

in the world. In part, the inflow was not of our doing. But our tariff policy, which shut out goods, intensified the balance-of-payments problems of other countries. And our policy in 1933–34 of reducing the gold value of the dollar by 40 per cent thus making American goods cheaper, a policy introduced to give the farmers a quick shot in the arm, was probably also a mistake; for it gave this country an advantage in foreign markets which was scarcely justified in the light of the long-run excessive strength of the dollar. What was wanted was not more, but less, foreign demand for dollars.

Americans will have to learn that the balance of payments will not be in equilibrium until this country accepts a weakening of her competitive position *vis-à-vis* the rest of the world, and, therefore, a rise in the level of imports relative to exports. The correct approach is a reduction of tariffs here or, failing that, a rise elsewhere; an increase in the value of the dollar or, alternatively, a lowering in the value of foreign currencies (thus encouraging exports from foreign countries as their currencies become cheaper); and a willingness to lend in order to make foreign economies more productive and to strengthen their competitive position. (I am not so sure, however, that a reduction in the foreign value of European currencies|in 1948 will greatly strengthen their position, as American official policy seems to be proposing. France, for example, may get more dollars by selling at high prices, that is by keeping the franc up, because her resources for export markets are restricted and demand for her products is strong.)

Of this we may be sure: we cannot expect to take shipping business away from the British and Scandinavians by a subsidy program, pay export subsidies on cotton to the detriment of India, Brazil, and Egypt, run away with the women's fashion industry at the expense of France, produce synthetic rubber at the expense of Eastern Asia, produce subsidized wool at the expense of Australia, and keep out Swiss watches to support domestic manufactures—and yet import what is required of a creditor nation. Our choice is to use our resources fully at home—not an easy, or a practical, way out, in the present uneasy world; or to export much more than we import in the next ten years and get ready to import much more than we export by the later fifties; or export the excess and, failing to import adequately, give goods away.

General Lines of Policy   First, as has been suggested above, it is necessary to give Europe the aid without which she will not recover in time to withstand pressures from the East. As far as possible, the required goods should be obtained from abroad; for the more they are drained from foreign sources, the less the inflationary pressures in this country. The shortages are serious in this country, particularly in foods, and explain why President Truman suggested in his December 1947 message to Congress on the European Recovery Program (ERP) that this country only provide about 20 per cent (tonnage) of the foods and fertilizer requested of the non-participating countries by the Committee on European Economic Cooperation for the years 1948–51.

Second, in order to carry through this foreign-aid program, it is necessary to pursue correct economic policies at home. They include anti-inflationary measures—maintenance of present tax rates, cautious control of bank credit, allocation of scarce items, export control directed to favoring exports of commodities contributing to European recovery, and, in the few most essential and inadequately provisioned markets, price control and rationing. In an inflationary situation, additional demand equal to but 2 to 3 per cent of the national income might have serious effects, particularly in markets for food, equipment, and raw materials where shortages are serious and the European demands under the ERP upon our output for 1948–51 are substantially in excess of a few per cent of our output. Should the ERP greatly strengthen the inflationary pressures, then not only would great damage be done to our economy, but the ERP would also be jeopardized.

Third, this country should take the lead in support of a program to reduce trade barriers of all kinds: tariffs, restrictions on quantity of exports, exchange control, etc. At London, Geneva, and Havana, Messrs. Will Clayton, Clair Wilcox, and others have made vigorous efforts to provide and perfect an International Trade Organization. It is not easy to reconcile the differences among the participating countries. The first objective is to reduce tariffs; and much has already been accomplished on that score. A second and related objective is to attack quantitative restrictions. Here it is necessary to make all kinds of exceptions, though, as far as possible, where exceptions are made, there should not be discrimination. For example, should quantitative restrictions be necessary, exports from each country should have equal treatment; the same proportion of the total imports should be allowed from each country as in a base year.

Countries intent upon industrialization insist upon special privileges, including quantitative restrictions, in order to advance on the industrial front. Empire countries seek imperial preferences. Agricultural countries are intent upon protecting their markets against foreign competition, and also upon making commodity agreements as a means of restricting output and raising prices of their exports. All countries demand the right to impose restrictions on trade when they are threatened with serious adverse balance of payments. Granted that the resulting document is far from perfect, the ITO marks an advance over the chaos of the last ten years.

In short, objectives of this country's policy should be to reduce trade barriers; to weaken cartels because they try to make profits by restricting output and raising prices; to protect consumers against commodity agreements, which have similar purposes; to restrict the use of exchange control (a weapon used to control payments abroad and for other purposes); to control the use of variations in exchange rates to those required to attain international stability; to stimulate capital movements as a means of furthering rehabilitation and industrialization and, thereby, of raising incomes.

With higher incomes abroad encouraged by these policies, and more trade, the danger of economic warfare and hence political warfare will be reduced. So long as this country has half the world's income and about nine times as much income per capita as the rest of the world, peace is threatened. It is our responsibility to help others improve their position. The Marshall Plan, renewal of private lending, reduction of trade barriers including extension of the Reciprocal Trade Agreements, and success of the ITO will all help; and in the process we shall improve our own position.

PART SEVEN

Labor, Social Security, and Education

Introduction

by Seymour E. Harris

The problem of labor and social security is in part a problem of demand and in part one of social justice. Through collective bargaining, labor achieves increased power in its negotiations with capital, and thus obtains not only better working conditions but also an increased share of the national dividend. In the modern highly productive economy, it is absolutely essential that, in order to assure sales of output at prices allowing a reasonable profit, the masses receive an adequate share of the national income; and it is also necessary that with rising productivity, hours of work be reduced. Wide disparities of income are revealed in Chart 8. Collective bargaining contributes to the solution of the problem of deficient demand by protecting labor's stake in the output of industry, and also by forcing upon industry reductions in hours as a partial offset to rising productivity. Social security, in so far as it is financed out of the general taxes or the payroll tax imposed on employers, instead of the payroll tax imposed on workers, tends also to raise the level of consumption; for the net effect of such transfers is gains by consumers at the expense of potential savers. Social security does much more than raise the propensity to consume; it yields an improved time pattern of spending as it promotes subtraction of purchasing power in prosperity and addition in depression. It also relieves distress caused by unemployment, illness, and old age.

Education is in part a problem of distribution, for it is a

way of spending income. It is also a production problem, for income tends to rise with improved educational standards, that is, extension and improvement of education tends to raise productivity. And since education is an outlet for spendable funds, it might contribute to adequacy of spending and stabilization of demand.

AVERAGE FAMILY INCOME

All groups received more income in 1946 than before the war. Greatest relative increases were in the lower and middle groups.

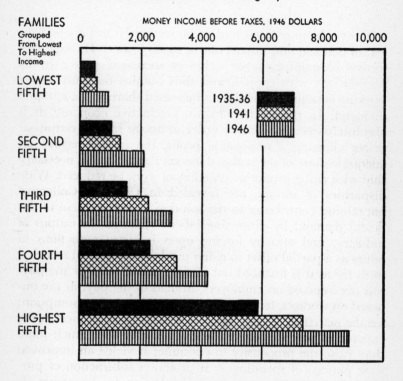

SOURCE: *THE ECONOMIC REPORT OF THE PRESIDENT*, JANUARY 1948.

CHART 8

CHAPTER XXV

A National Labor Policy [1]

by John T. Dunlop

Collective bargaining has been the explicit cornerstone of our national labor policy at least since the enactment of the Wagner Act in 1935. The Taft-Hartley Act professes the same foundation for labor-management relations.[2] In identical language, both acts declare it to be the policy of the United States to encourage ". . . the practice and procedure of collective bargaining . . . by protecting the exercise by workers of full freedom of association, self-organization, and designation of representatives of their own choosing, for the purpose of negotiating the terms and conditions of their employment or other mutual aid or protection."[3] The policy of active encouragement to collective bargaining was a significant factor in the growth of union organization in the last decade.

Extent of Collective Bargaining Today By the end of 1947, 15 million workers were members of labor organizations in the United States. They were organized into more than 60,000 local unions which for the most part were constituent parts of 145 international or national unions affiliated

[1] The term "labor policy" is used here to cover only industrial relations and wage determination. The whole area of social legislation—health insurance and medical care, public housing, the extension of social security, and education—is beyond the scope of this paper. See the programs proposed by President Truman, the 21-point legislative program, September 6, 1945, and the 5-point program in the special message, November 19, 1945.

[2] See the section below on the Taft-Hartley Act (pp. 298–305) for an appraisal of the extent to which the profession is valid.

[3] National Labor Relations Act, Section 1, and Labor Management Relations Act, 1947, Title I, Section 1.

with the American Federation of Labor (AFL) and the Congress of Industrial Organizations (CIO). The ten largest unions, each with a membership over 300,000, comprised 37 per cent of all organized workers. The terms and conditions of employment for these union members were set forth in some 75,000 written agreements negotiated with employers or their associations.

While 42 million workers were employed in non-agricultural pursuits during 1947, collective bargaining was far more decisive for setting the terms of labor bargains than a simple comparison with the 15 million union members might suggest. The percentage of employees organized in various sectors of the economy was as follows:

TABLE 3

NUMBER AND PERCENTAGE OF ORGANIZED EMPLOYEES, AUGUST 1947

	Number of Employees (in Millions) August 1947	*Estimated Percentage under Union Agreement*
Manufacturing	15.5	69
Mining	.9	80–100
Construction	1.9	80–100
Transportation	3.0	80–100
Public Utilities	1.2	40–60
Trade	8.6	Below 20
Finance	1.6	Below 20
Service	4.6	20–40
Government	5.3	Below 20
Agriculture	9.5	Below 20

After collective bargaining has become significant in an industry, it tends to condition all labor bargains, at least within narrow limits. The influence of collective bargaining extends beyond the area of union membership.

Even in years of serious industrial strife, more than 90 per cent of all agreements are renewed or negotiated without stoppage of work. Moreover, the processes of collective bargaining resolve the millions of questions and grievances that arise from day to day in the operation of industry and commerce under agreements. Among the 270,000 employees of

General Motors Corporation under agreement with the UAW-CIO, for example, approximately 35,000 grievances are filed in a year—an average of one grievance during the year for each eight employees.[4] The peaceful resolution of these disputes by the grievance machinery, including the impartial umpire, even in an atmosphere of tense struggle for power, is a testimony to the evolution of industrial jurisprudence.

There is wide variation in the actual content of collective bargaining. Some agreements are narrowly restricted to matters of wages, hours, and working conditions. The scope of the bargaining in other cases has been expanded to include the joint administration of health, welfare, and pension plans; job evaluation and merit-rating schemes; production bonus arrangements and joint efforts to improve product and decrease costs. The scope of collective bargaining is different under each agreement. Most cases will fall between the extremes of the ladies'-garment industry where collective bargaining is concerned with the broadest types of problems and the automobile industry where collective bargaining tends to be narrowly circumscribed and where the efforts of the union to expand the scope of bargaining have been strongly resisted by management. One of the great merits of collective bargaining is its flexibility. Two parties can mold their relationship to meet unique problems; it requires no Procrustean uniformity.

With the growth of organization in the labor market has come a re-examination of the consequences of collective bargaining for the community. Is it true that the public interest in the settlement of disputes is identical with the common interests of labor and management? [5] What is the extent of public interest in the relations between union members and the union as an organization? What are the consequences of collective bargaining for output and employment? How much encouragement should public policy provide to the organiza-

---

[4] Frederick H. Harbison and Robert Dubin, *Patterns of Union-Management Relations* (Chicago, 1947), p. 81.

[5] Jesse Freidin, "The Public Interest in Labor Dispute Settlement," *Law and Contemporary Problems*, XII (1947), pp. 367–88.

tion of wage earners? What form should this encouragement take and what barriers to organization shall be permitted? The Taft-Hartley Act provides different answers to most of these questions than would have been indicated by the Wagner Act.

The Taft-Hartley Act   The enactment of this law, as a political matter, represented the judgment of a large majority of citizens that "labor had gone too far and something should be done." Even labor spokesmen now recognize this fact. "Labor unions are not in good with the public generally, or the N.A.M., and all the reactionary forces couldn't have passed this legislation." [6] Public support and demand for a bill, however, cannot be interpreted as approval of the complex and intricate provisions of the Taft-Hartley Act.

This act is a polyglot of provisions and consequently most difficult to appraise save in great detail.[7] Some sections derive from early real or fancied abuses in the administration of the Wagner Act and do little more than write into law the most recent practice of the NLRB.[8] Other provisions represent long overdue reforms, illustrated by the designation of unfair labor practices on the part of unions, such as jurisdictional disputes and secondary boycotts. Other sections concern the obligations of the union to its members and the rights of members *vis-à-vis* the organization. The main impacts of the Taft-Hartley law on collective bargaining, however, are more general and less obvious. The following constitute some of the most fundamental problems raised by the act.

(1)   The process by which the act was passed has made the framework of labor-management relations narrowly a matter of partisan politics. Organized employers and their spokesmen in supporting the bill have thrown down to the labor

[6] See the forthright speech by George Meany, Secretary-Treasurer, American Federation of Labor, *Proceedings of the Fortieth Annual Convention of the Building and Construction Trades Department of the American Federation of Labor*, October 3, 1947.

[7] For a careful and detailed analysis of the act, see Archibald Cox, "Some Aspects of the Labor Management Relations Act, 1947," *Harvard Law Review*, Vol. LXI, Nos. 1 and 2 (1947).

[8] Such as the provisions on free speech for the employer.

movement the challenge of political action. The framers of the act—both nominal and real—had the endorsement of the spokesmen of organized employers. There were no recommendations of a commission or an independent and moderate body of experts. No nationally prominent independent or moderate expert participated in the framing of the law. Under these circumstances the law appears vindictive and partisan, regardless of the intrinsic merits of the particular provisions. Perhaps the most fundamental issue raised by the act is the method by which changes in the legal setting and status of collective bargaining are to be made in this country.

The act has introduced into labor-management relations the political weapon on a scale never before utilized in this country. It would be a different matter if the framework of collective bargaining were established by law after careful study by recognized experts. It will be difficult for the labor movement to escape the conclusion that the employers have simply resorted to a new weapon—political action. The history of labor movements suggests that political action is a tool more suited to labor organizations than to management over the long run. Employers may well heed the prophet: "They have sown the wind, and they shall reap the whirlwind."

(2) The effect of the act on the process of organizing new employees and new plants must be distinguished from its effect upon the operation of collective bargaining where unions have become well established. The act seems to be most serious in its effects on the extension of collective bargaining to unorganized employees, particularly when the employer chooses to resist the advance of the union.[9] Section 7 of the Wagner Act was rewritten to include in the rights of employees the right ". . . to refrain from any or all of such activities . . ."[10] This seemingly harmless guarantee to an individual worker must be appraised in the context that it is now an unfair labor practice on the part of the union ". . . to

[9] Established unions, however, may be affected by the procedure for removal of certification and by actions of employers where unions have chosen not to qualify for use of the facilities of the NLRB.

[10] Except where an agreement requires membership in a union as a condition of employment as authorized in Section 8 (a) (3) of the act.

restrain or coerce employees in the exercise of the rights
guaranteed in Section 7 . . ." including the right to refrain
from joining a union.

As a practical matter employers could file unfair-labor-
practice charges in most normal organizing drives on the
ground that workers have been coerced into organization, and
thus postpone elections, unless new procedures are adopted
by the board. The act has provided the employer who wishes
to resist organization with a great many new weapons which
can almost indefinitely delay and weaken the growth of a
new union. The act does not greatly change the organizing
situation where the employer wishes to abide by a *bona fide*
expression of the opinion of his employees; but the act has
put new weapons in the hands of the employer who wishes
seriously to resist the organization of his plants. The act
strikes at the growth buds of the labor movement. The
serious nature of these possible limitations on the extension
of organization led Archibald Cox to conclude: "The Taft-
Hartley amendments represent an abandonment of the policy
of encouraging the spread of union organization and collective bargaining."

(3) The act introduces the principle of the public regulation of the contents of labor agreements. This is a new step
of far greater significance than the particular restrictions on
contract provisions contained in the law. The sections which
outlaw the closed shop, specify contract termination procedures, and regulate welfare funds are illustrative of this new
step. What contract provisions merit sufficient public interest to warrant governmental determination? Is the Congress the agency for determining the type of detailed regulation contained in the law? Will the principle be extended to
seniority provisions, arbitration clauses, to all sections of the
agreement? What happens when the parties agree on a provision the government has censored? Is the government likely
to be able to enforce such regulation? The closed shop, for
example, is desired by both sides in many industries. Under
these circumstances is the public policy likely to be accepted?
These questions indicate that the act envisages more revolu-

tionary changes in the status of collective bargaining than is ordinarily understood.

Civil Liberties within Labor Organizations An adequate national labor policy would provide a code of rules to insure basic civil liberties to union members. Logically such guarantees could be established by action of the union itself, by contract with the employer, by the courts, or by an administrative agency created by statute. Although violations have been relatively rare, the unions have failed to provide what most observers would regard as adequate safeguards.[11] There have been some contracts where discharge under a union-shop clause, arising at the request of the union, is subject to review by the impartial umpire.[12] Arbitrary action by the union is subject to the same review as that by management. The courts have in some cases reviewed actions of labor unions in their relations with their members.[13] In most countries with a developed labor movement these essential civil liberties are provided by statute.

The Taft-Hartley Act includes the first attempt in the United States to deal with these questions for the country as a whole.[14] In treating the relation between the union and its members, the act provides that in order to use the facilities of the NLRB a union must: (a) distribute financial reports or make them available to members,[15] and (b) file anti-Communist affidavits for each officer. (c) The act contains a curb

[11] See Philip Taft, "Judicial Procedure in Labor Unions," *Quarterly Journal of Economics*, LIX (1945), pp. 370–85.

[12] For example, the contract between the Selby Shoe Company and the United Shoe Workers of America, CIO, February 11, 1946; Boston Edison Company and United Brotherhood of Edison Workers, Independent.

[13] See Clyde W. Summers, "The Right to Join a Union," *Columbia Law Review*, Vol. 47 (1947), pp. 33–74; Jesse Freidin, "Some New Discharge Problems Under Union Security Covenants," *Wisconsin Law Review* (1946), pp. 440–60; "Discrimination by Labor Union Bargaining Representatives Against Racial Minorities," Note in *Yale Law Journal*, Vol. 56 (1947), pp. 731–37.

[14] See the proposal unanimously presented by the tripartite committee appointed by the Governor of Massachusetts, March 18, 1947. The proposal for protection from arbitrary discharge under a union-shop clause was adopted by the Commonwealth.

[15] The union is required to file other information with the Secretary of Labor (See Section 9 f), but only these financial reports must be "furnished to all of the members."

on "excessive or discriminatory" initiation fees as an unfair labor practice on the part of the union. (d) The act makes it an unfair labor practice on the part of the *employer* to discriminate against an employee for non-membership in a labor organization for other grounds than non-payment of dues.

The first and third of these provisions are not excessive or uncommon by the standards of other countries. In Australia, for example, any labor organization must have rules and by-laws which conform to standards set by law before it can appear before the Commonwealth Court of Conciliation and Arbitration.[16] (All unions with federal jurisdiction do.) Moreover, the court can deny or remove registration on grounds that civil liberties have been denied to members. The actions of the court have involved sweeping and extensive review of the internal government of unions, by American standards. "It disapproves of a rule, drawn in wide terms, prohibiting, under pain of expulsion, the divulging of union business that covers harmless and innocent statements by a member about a trifling routine matter of the union's affair. It admits, nevertheless, the desirability and the propriety of some rule to protect the legitimate interests of an organization from injury by publicity." [17] The Australian labor movement has not found such regulation unbearable nor has it sought to escape these safeguards of individual rights.[18]

While the principle of the public guarantee of civil rights within labor organizations established in the Taft-Hartley Act is an essential feature of a national labor policy, the provision for limitation on discharge under a union shop to the condition of non-payment of dues is objectionable. Other grounds for separation from employment should be recognized, as in cases of extreme disloyalty to the union. Moreover, the obligation for compliance with essential civil liberties should be placed directly on the union rather than upon the employer. The distinction between expulsion from the union and discharge from employment is not satisfactory.

[16] See, Orwell de R. Foenander, *Industrial Regulation in Australia* (Melbourne, 1947), pp. 176–201.

[17] *Ibid.*, p. 184.

[18] The union shop as known in America is precluded by the court in Australia.

The Taft-Hartley Act reflects a false picture of the relation between the union and its members. The union member is pictured as coerced into membership and continually trying to escape. The view which would identify on all occasions the union and its members is equally a caricature of the facts.[19] The simple fact is that our unions are among the most democratic institutions in our society. The legal status of collective bargaining, however, requires the public guarantee of a minimum of civil liberties in labor organizations.

One of the primary tenets of a national labor policy should be a code providing for the public protection of basic civil liberties of union members in labor organizations. The obligation should be placed directly on the union for compliance with the prescribed standards.[20] The union could be denied status before the NLRB for failure to abide by these minimum standards.

Dispute Settlement   Public policy on dispute settlement may be divided into two parts. First there are problems of machinery for the resolution of those few disputes in areas so affecting the national health, welfare, and safety that no Administration could avoid direct governmental intervention. Threatened work stoppages on a national scale on the railroads, in the steel industry, and in local electric utilities are examples of this type of situation. At the present time, the Taft-Hartley Act provides elaborate, but inconclusive, procedures which may be invoked in an emergency dispute situation. All other disputes would fall in the second category. They are to be handled, so far as public policy is concerned, by voluntary negotiations and mediation.

1. One simple fact needs to be clear about the emergency dispute. No government can allow the parties to collective bargaining in these vital spots the time required for a genuine test of strength. The public interest cannot tolerate work stoppages to force one side to change the position of the other and reach agreement. No government has stood idly by in such cases, and none would and remain long in office. Con-

[19] For a penetrating analysis of the internal government of labor organizations, see Will Herberg, "Bureaucracy and Democracy in Labor Unions," *Antioch Review*, III (1943), pp. 405–17.

[20] For the Australian standards, see *ibid.*, pp. 178–79.

sequently, the right to strike or lock out exists only so long as it is not generally used. This is not to deny that even in such cases the right to strike may be an important aspect of the bargaining relationship.

The significant issue, then, in emergency disputes is whether a clear-cut machinery be established in advance. The case for such machinery is that the parties know their obligations ahead of time; the machinery may be made essentially non-political. The case against any definite machinery is that governmental action can be more flexible and better adapted to the case; there is less danger of the parties avoiding their obligations and relying on machinery to make unpopular decisions; there is less danger of governmental policy in a few key situations coming to determine the whole structure of wage rates and industrial-relation practices by the precedents of a governmental decision.

The Taft-Hartley Act adopts the course of explicit machinery. After involved procedures a dispute may be left in the inconclusive form of referral to the Congress. Simplified procedures modeled after the Railway Labor Act would have been preferable if explicit machinery was to be established.

2. The great mass of disputes fall into the second category where present policy calls for voluntary mediation. It is in this area that most needs to be done. Relative to other countries in the world, collective bargaining in the United States is in its infancy with respect to machinery for settlement of disputes.

A long-range policy should contemplate the development in each industry or locality, depending on the real locus of decision making, committees of spokesmen for unions and employers. These joint committees should assume primary responsibility for maintaining industrial peace. They could intervene in local disputes to offer mediation services; they could formulate in advance national panels of arbitrators to be offered in the event of a dispute.

The most significant barrier to the development of joint machinery for settlement of disputes in the United States is the lack of adequate organization of employers in most industries. In this respect the contrast with the situation in other countries is striking. The traditional individualism of American business leaders, the fear of anti-trust action, the fear of revealing data on prices, costs, even wages to an association including competitors, and the hope of driving better individual bargains to suit special problems have all been factors hindering the growth of effective employers' associations. Yet no adequate voluntary system of dispute settlement can be evolved without considerable organization of employers. There are some signs of development in this direction in such industries as local transit, building construction, and public utilities,[21] in addition to the well-known cases of association bargaining [22] in such industries as glass bottles, flat glass, pottery, railroads, etc. Some localities,[23] notably San Francisco and Toledo, have also developed this type of employer organization.

For the purposes of dispute settlement, the employer organization may have been established primarily for bargaining purposes or for the sole purpose of intervention in disputes. Public policy should not be indifferent to employer organization. Much can be done to stimulate the growth of private dispute-settling agencies, industry by industry. The anti-trust laws can be clarified to make certain that joint employer action is not precluded on labor matters, so long as no price-fixing agreements are involved. Government leadership could be provided for a program to encourage—slowly and gradually—the appropriate committees and agencies in various localities and industries. No mass approach will work. Public policy for the settlement of most disputes should involve the active encouragement of joint agreements to provide private machinery by area and industry.[24]

[21] See Joint Statement issued by Labor-Management Representatives in the Utility Industry, December 9, 1936.

[22] Richard A. Lester and Edward A. Robie, *Wages Under National and Regional Collective Bargaining* (Princeton, N. J., 1946).

[23] Arthur W. Hepner, "Local and Unofficial Arrangements for Labor Dispute Settlement," *Law and Contemporary Problems*, XII (1947), pp. 220–31.

[24] No mention has been made of improving machinery in the local plant and company. Considerable progress has been made in this area, and more is possible. See *The President's National Labor-Management Conference* (November, 1945), Bulletin 77, Division of Labor Standards, Department of Labor (1946), pp. 42–47.

Wage Policy   The impact of collective bargaining on wages is not well understood. Wage rates rose significantly in this country even before unions were an important factor in the local market. A few observations may be risked to provide a tentative judgment concerning the effects of collective bargaining on wages.

(1) The process of organizing a firm, or changing a company wage policy from non-union to union, in itself tends to raise the money wage. Some firms may try to "buy off" organization; if the attempt is successful, wages are increased even if the organization fails. And, if organization is to succeed, the union must have an increase to prove its worth to its new members. A period of widespread and rapid organization in itself would make for a rise in the general wage level.

(2) Collective bargaining results in an explicit wage scale in the plant. The management is forced to defend variations in wages among different groups of workers in the bargaining unit.

(3) Differentials in the wage structure among occupations, firms, and regions tend to be reduced with the expansion of collective bargaining.

(4) The effect of collective bargaining in industries with permanent and mature labor relations is particularly difficult to indicate. It is probable that in these circumstances the separate effects of collective bargaining become secondary to such factors as the secular growth of the industry, profits, prices, and productivity. Unionization in itself ceases to be a significant factor except as it affects such basic determinants of wages.

A national wage policy awaits instrumentalities to formulate and administer it. At the present time collective bargaining is organized only to establish particularistic wage policies —not a national wage policy.[25] Logically, the bodies essential to a national wage policy could be developed in one of two ways. First, the scope of collective-bargaining organizations could expand to the extent that a group of top union leaders and employers would negotiate a national wage pattern and

[25] See Sumner H. Slichter, *The Challenge of Industrial Relations* (Ithaca, 1947), pp. 71–98.

policy. In so far as certain key bargains come to be recognized as leaders by the rest of the economy, these key negotiations would set a national wage policy without resort to any more formal association. Second, one side or the other could secure political power and use governmental authority to formulate a wage policy.

In this connection the interest and concern shown by labor governments in developing a wage policy is instructive. The judgment would probably be widely accepted that the labor governments of Europe in recent years have kept wages more stable than other political parties could have done. While trade unionists speaking for particular unions may have difficulty in formulating a coherent national wage policy, particularly under conditions of high employment, they seem to have achieved this objective when operating as a labor government.

In this country, it may be senseless to speak of a national wage policy for many years to come—except in time of economic emergency. However, even in acting on wage issues in emergency disputes the government is certain to influence wage levels one way or the other. Requisite to the beginnings of a national wage policy should be the revival of a permanent advisory body to the president composed of the top leaders of American agriculture, industry, and labor. The discussions and interchange in such a body would be effective in helping to formulate a national policy. The body would provide a forum in which the Administration could use its informal influence to affect wages, prices, and other decisions by the principal economic groups in the society.

Summary: A National Policy   The country stands at a fork in the road on labor policy. One road would determine most matters of industrial relations by resort to political processes; the other road would confine political processes to the fairly narrow area of fixing a few matters of framework. These rules would be fairly generally accepted by the diverse groups within the community and would be changed only slowly after careful impartial study. The basic difficulty with the Taft-Hartley Act is that it leads down the political road while professing to follow the other.

Starting from the cornerstone of collective bargaining, a national labor policy should have these three elements: [26]

(1) A system for guaranteeing essential civil liberties within labor unions. These guarantees could have been provided by the unions themselves or by contract with the employers. As in most countries they will no doubt have to be established by statute here. These minimum guarantees should be clearly stated obligations upon the unions.

(2) While the government will always need to intervene directly in emergency disputes, there is need to develop a national system of dispute settlement in which labor and industry assume more responsibility on an industry and locality basis. The first requisite for this expansion in the scope of collective bargaining, to include procedures for settling new contracts, is expansion in employers organizations. The government should take informal leadership in this process of setting up joint machinery.

(3) A national wage policy is needed. A first step can be taken by the re-establishment of an advisory group representative of the top leaders of American agriculture, industry, and labor.

[26] Many difficult and impossible features of the Taft-Hartley Act would need to be modified.

CHAPTER XXVI

Social Security

by Edwin E. Witte

Social security is not something that can be devised once and for all. What is a sound program for social security depends upon the conditions prevailing in a given nation at a given time. To be taken into account are both economic and political considerations. What is practical and attainable is at least as important as a guide to policy as is what is theoretically most desirable.

It is probable that the Congress within the next few years will materially revise the social-security program of the United States. Extensive changes in their social-security programs to fit postwar conditions have been made in all other English-speaking nations as well as in many other countries. In the United States, hearings on several proposals for far-reaching changes were conducted in both houses in the 1946 and 1947 sessions. In December 1947, a Citizens' Advisory Committee, named pursuant to Senate action and headed by former Secretary of State E. Stettinius, Jr., and Sumner H. Slichter of Harvard, held meetings to consider the recommendations for a thoroughgoing revision of the Social Security Act. It is the author's opinion that such a revision, while possible, is not likely in a presidential election year. But the present program is so out of line with conditions now existing or likely to develop in the not distant future that extensive changes seem inevitable before long.

An Ideal Program Theoretically most desirable is a unified social-security program which would assure a minimum income to all American families and self-supporting individuals in all contingencies of life. Such a program would provide "cradle to grave" security, but in amounts not so large as to discourage industry and initiative, providing only a floor below which Americans would not fall whatever catastrophe might strike them. Such an ideal program, while recognizing that social-security institutions are necessary even under conditions of full employment, would integrate them with other economic policies designed to insure full employment and itself contribute to this major objective. To that end, the contributions (earmarked taxes) to support the program would be varied with the level of employment, while benefits would be increased, regardless of the state of social-security funds, when necessary to sustain purchasing power. Such a program would, at least, have to be federally controlled, if not federally administered.

Such an ideal program has never been worked out by anyone and in its entirety exists nowhere in the world. Bills approximating cradle-to-grave security for all Americans, without the feature of contributions and benefits varying with over-all business conditions, have been before Congress and have received considerable support. These bills, popularly known as "the Wagner-Murray-Dingell bill," however, have never won even a favorable committee report. At present, they have no prospects of passage. Their advocacy, to the neglect of less comprehensive changes, may well result in letting people who have little use for social security "write the ticket" when Congress in the near future revises the Social Security Act.

Counter-Proposals from the Right   This danger arises not only because there are large conservative majorities in both houses of Congress but because the groups interested in extending social security are disorganized and at this time much more concerned about other matters. On the other hand, the opponents from the Right, for the first time, have developed comprehensive counter-proposals, which have considerable popular appeal. It is unlikely that even a conservative Congress will go so far as to adopt the proposal of Lewis Meriam in his Brookings Institution study, *Relief and*

Social Security (1946). This is a proposal that social security be made over into nothing more than a relief program, with benefits being paid only to people in need but with all workers required to meet a major part of the costs through a tax on wages and salaries, levied without exemptions. But the program of the Chamber of Commerce of the United States must be taken much more seriously, if for no other reason than that the people who wrote it are strongly represented on the Citizens' Advisory Committee. This is a program which, while proposing some desirable changes, also includes others the net effect of which would be to weaken what we now have and to block progress for quite a few years to come.

Opinions will differ about what people who believe in cradle-to-grave security should do in this situation. To the author, it seems sound to recognize that this country is not ready for any Beveridge Plan. This plan proposed a social security program for Britain which would cover virtually all contingencies, would be well integrated, and would provide generous benefits, in no small part at the expense of the taxpayer. We must take account of our stage of development and must build upon what we have rather than to imitate what any other country may have done. The United States has a federal, not a unitary, government, and any social-security program which fails to take account of this basic fact is doomed. While near full employment continues, or until some crisis develops, the most that can be hoped for is piecemeal progress. Such premises underlie the rest of this chapter, which is devoted to practical suggestions for improving the social security protection of the American people, although combined the suggestions fall far short of an ideal program and of what other countries have accomplished.

Old-Age and Survivors' Insurance In such a practical approach, major attention at this time should be given to old-age and survivors' (that is, retirement) insurance. This need arises because this is the part of the Social Security Act most likely to be materially changed before long and also because it is at present the least adequate of all existing social-security programs. Benefits to workers receiving retirement benefits under the present system average only a little more than $25 per month, contrasted with averages over $36 per month to the recipients of old-age assistance, over $40 to the general-relief recipients, and $78 per month to workers receiving unemployment insurance under state laws and $85 to unemployed veterans. An even more serious weakness is the fact that less than 10 per cent of the people over 65 years of age are receiving any benefits under the system. This fortunate minority, moreover, does not include any large percentage of those who have the greatest need for retirement allowances.

This situation results in part from the newness of the system. In large part, however, it is due to changes in the conditions of eligibility for benefits made in the Social Security Act Amendments of 1939. Under the original Social Security Act of 1935, nearly all those who paid old-age (retirement) insurance taxes could look forward to becoming eligible to retirement benefits on retirement at age 65 or later. In 1939 the conditions of eligibility were changed to deny benefits to all who are not "fully insured" at the time of retirement. This is a term applied only to those who have paid taxes on at least $50 of earnings in covered employment in half of the quarters which have elapsed since January 1, 1937, or since they became 21, if later, or in 40 quarters altogether. The effect of this provision is to deny benefits to most of those who shift between covered and uncovered employment and also to most of the women workers. Of nearly 80,000,000 living Americans who have paid old-age insurance taxes, less than one-half are now fully insured. It is optimistically estimated that in course of time, if employment conditions continue good, 60 per cent of the workers who will have to pay taxes will also acquire eligibility to benefits by the time they get to be 65 years of age. Broadening the coverage for tax purposes would operate to increase this percentage, but would still leave ineligible most of the women workers who leave employment to become married.

There are many other needed changes in the old-age and survivors' insurance system. Coverage should be extended, as the Social Security Administration recommends, to include nearly all employed and self-employed persons. Persons per-

manently and totally disabled should be entitled to benefits
even if not yet 65. For women employees also, a younger retirement age than 65 is in line with actual conditions, and
both the minimum and maximum benefits should be increased
to correspond with the lessened value of the dollar. Clearly
also the veterans of World War II should be credited in the
old-age and survivors' insurance system with at least the
average earnings of stay-at-homes for the period of their
service, instead of having the time they spent with the colors
count against them as it does under the present law. With these
changes go fairer methods of computing average earnings for
purposes of determining benefits than the 1939 plan of divid-
ing the lifetime taxable earnings by the total number of quarters since 1937, including all those in which the worker was
not in covered private employment.

In a sound old-age and survivors' insurance system, the
author believes, the costs should be more nearly met by current taxes than they are under the present system. The slogan
"pay as you go," which carried the 1939 amendments, was
spurious, as it amounts to disregarding all accruing liabilities.
It is a very bad practice not only to fail to meet current liabilities but to keep from the public the fact of an ever growing
debt additional to the acknowledged debt of the United
States. It was most unfortunate that the social-security taxes
were reduced just as World War II was beginning and remained frozen throughout the war boom and the present
inflationary period. But there is no prospect that Congress
will now increase the tax rates, and probably not even that
it will require disclosure of the accruing liabilities. So the
author believes that it is wisest to concentrate upon the extension of coverage and the improvement of the benefit
provisions, with special emphasis upon the elimination of the
extremely restrictive eligibility conditions and the accompanying unfair method of computing average earnings.

Unemployment Insurance   Organized labor is strongly
in favor of the federalization of unemployment insurance,
which is now largely under state control as well as administered by the states. But it is clear that Congress and the country in its present mood do not want such a basic change. Ac-

cordingly, if progress toward more adequate unemployment insurance is to continue, it must at this time be made on the state level.

Unemployment compensation benefits are not nearly as low as those of the old-age and survivors' insurance system. The benefit scales, however, were established before the great postwar price increases. Increases in these benefits to at least the extent of the increases in the cost of living are imperative.

The coverage of the unemployment insurance laws is much less broad than that of the old-age and survivors' insurance system. That system is a demonstration that it is administratively feasible to eliminate the exemption of small employers which still prevails in unemployment insurance.

Cash sickness insurance is now a supplement to unemployment insurance in Rhode Island and California, as well as in the federal railroad unemployment insurance law. This represents one of the most promising present opportunities for the improvement of the social-security protection enjoyed by American workers.

A final suggestion of a negative character is appropriate. Supporters of unemployment insurance should resist all efforts further to reduce unemployment insurance taxes, whether this be done through experience rating or across-the-board tax reductions. While present tax collections greatly exceed the benefit payments, it needs to be remembered that the federal government has been meeting the costs of unemployment among the veterans from the United States Treasury but will not continue to do so much longer. In 1946, the total of the benefit payments under state laws and the unemployment allowances paid veterans was twice as great as the total unemployment insurance tax collections. And 1946 was not a year of depression; in fact, ever since unemployment compensation payments first began business has either been on the up grade or at a very high level.

Workmen's Compensation   The third social-insurance institution, workmen's compensation, is entirely state controlled. It has generally been neglected by academic advocates of social security, but is our oldest form of social insurance and, probably, also the most popular.

The greatest need in workmen's compensation is an increase in benefits to bring them into line with the existing price levels. Even before the price increases, workmen's compensation, on the average, made up only 50 per cent of the wage loss of the workers suffering industrial accidents. Today, that percentage is much less. Great also is the need for the extension of the coverage of the workmen's compensation laws.

Social Assistance and Social Services   Social assistance, a term applied to non-contributory types of public aid to people in need and in varying amounts measured by their needs, is very important in this country. Total payments under the social-assistance programs exceed those under any type of social insurance other than unemployment insurance.

Under the Social Security Act, federal aid is extended to the states for three of the social-assistance programs—old-age assistance, aid to dependent children, and aid to the blind. The administration of these programs, however, is within control of the states, as are all major conditions governing the aid to be given except that it may be granted only on the basis of need. The fourth major program, general public assistance or relief, as it is more commonly called, is not only under exclusive state and local control but also is financed without any federal aid.

The organized social workers have long proposed that federal aid be given to the states for general public assistance. This is logical and desirable. While making such a forward-looking proposal, attention needs also to be given to the counter-proposal of the Chamber of Commerce of the United States, which is that the federal aid for the three federally recognized programs of social assistance be gradually tapered off and ultimately totally discontinued. In the present drive for federal tax reduction, this proposal seems more likely to be adopted than any extension of federal aid. Cutting off or reducing the federal aid, however, will not solve the problem but only shift the part of the costs of supporting the needy now falling upon federal corporation and individual income taxes to the property and sales taxes, which are the main sources of state and local revenues.

In addition to social assistance, there is great need for the development of many types of social services designed to prevent dependency or to provide better care for dependents than is afforded through cash grants. A good illustration of such services is vocational rehabilitation, which is restoring many seriously injured and handicapped people to self-support. Foremost among additionally needed social services are medical and hospital services for people unable to pay the total costs of needed care. There is much need also for recognition that many of the old people require care in addition to financial support. This calls for improved homes for the aged and public nursing homes or closely supervised private homes, partially publicly supported.

Health Insurance and Public Medical Services   It is in health insurance and public medical services that the frontier in social security now lies in the United States, with new fertile territory within near reach, which should be developed for the benefit of the American people.

Health insurance is the oldest form of social insurance and except for old-age insurance now the most widely prevalent the world over. In the United States, it has been discussed for more than thirty years, but so far not even a single state has enacted a compulsory health insurance law. The proposal, however, has shown remarkable vitality and probably has more support today than ever before. This is attributable primarily to the fact that a large percentage of all Americans are not getting adequate medical care because they are unable to pay for it. Until fairly recently this fact was disputed by organized medicine, but it is today conceded even by the American Medical Association. This great medical organization has now reversed its earlier position and is supporting voluntary forms of health insurance. Some progress has been made with voluntary medical-care insurance, and voluntary hospital insurance has attained large proportions, now covering approximately one-fifth of all Americans. There is little prospect, however, that voluntary health insurance will ever reach anywhere near all Americans who do not get adequate medical care for economic reasons. Even compulsory health insurance will not alone meet this need. It will have to be supplemented by expanded public health services, particularly preventive services and medical care at public expense for the more expensive diseases, which require long continued treatment.

The alternatives before the American people are pretty well illustrated by the position on this issue taken by leading candidates for the presidency. Senator Taft is the author of a bill in Congress to give aid to the states, in the amount of 200 million dollars per year, for medical and hospital care for indigents or for payments by the states to voluntary health insurance plans on behalf of such indigents. Governor Stassen has come out for compulsory health insurance, limited to the payment of medical bills in excess of $250. Governor Warren put before the California legislature, both in 1945 and 1947, a complete compulsory health insurance program. President Truman has recommended a national health program, which includes compulsory health insurance and expanded public health services.

If any legislation in this field is passed by the present Congress, it probably will be some version of the Taft bill. This would be in line with the trend toward more medical care at public expense, which has been very pronounced in this country in recent years. While this is socialized medicine, it is much less opposed by organized medicine than is compulsory health insurance, which, at least to some extent, is a substitute for state-financed medical care. Passage of the Taft bill would represent progress toward more adequate medical care for all Americans. A more complete program which seems within possibility of attainment in the not-distant future includes both compulsory health insurance and expanded public health services of the types previously mentioned.

CHAPTER XXVII

Some Aspects of Social Security, Education, and Labor Policy

by Seymour E. Harris

Witte's essay deals in a realistic manner with the problem of social security; for he proposes a program which stands a reasonable chance of enactment. It is well to distinguish between the targets of many liberals, for example, an American Beveridge Plan, and what is possible of enactment. What I have to say on social security is merely by way of amplification and implementation, not in any sense criticism of Witte's judicious remarks. In this chapter, I shall also deal with the important problem of education.

Inadequacy of the Social-Security Program　It is clear from Witte's essay that our social-security program is deficient, the main weaknesses being inadequacy of coverage both of population and contingencies, inadequacy of benefits, and mistaken methods of financing. A program devised in 1934–35, in the midst of a great depression, and modified in 1939, in the midst of a recession, would be insufficient after seven years of unprecedented prosperity, even if the original program had been ample. It was not; and in the meanwhile incomes have increased by two times, and prices by two-thirds. Although both old-age and unemployment insurance, the main programs in this country, provide to some extent for relating benefits to wage scales, nevertheless ceilings on unemployment benefits and on old-age insurance preclude the payment of adequate benefits even to those eligible. In 1945, benefits in force for an aged couple under the old-age and survivors' insurance system averaged $37.60 a month. In no case can the beneficiary, including his family and dependents, receive more than $85 a month, or 80 per cent of the wage earner's average monthly wage. It is well to put these figures against a per capita national income in 1945 of $1,300, and of $1,500 in the latter part of 1947. In 1945, the maximum benefit payments under unemployment insurance were $15 a week in 10 states, $18 in 14 other states, while 27 states (with four-fifths of the covered population) had a maximum weekly benefit rate of $20 or more; and only one worker in ten was in a state where the maximum was $25, including provision for dependent benefits. Minimum and average benefits by states are, of course, much smaller. Average payment for a week of total unemployment ranged from $9.22 in North Carolina to $19.39 in Michigan. At the same time, average weekly wages in manufacturing were close to $50. The provisions for duration of benefits, the waiting period, and conditions of disqualification could also be greatly improved.

Strengthening the Program   Government could greatly strengthen the system of social security. The present total reserves of around 10 billion dollars for unemployment insurance should be put against the potential losses of *annual* wages of 30 billion dollars following a depression much smaller than that of 1929–32; and even benefits for 26 weeks at $20 per week—a large improvement over what is now generally available—would cover but 20 per cent of the yearly wage, and failing new credits, rights would then be exhausted. This country should provide a system (a) which does not allow whittling down of contributions, reserves and benefits merely because the employer shows a good employment record, which for the most part is not his doing, (b) which yields benefits averaging $30 weekly for 26 weeks (the benefits should not, however, exceed two-thirds of the weekly wage), and—most important—(c) a system which responds to rising incomes and prices. In order to achieve adequate benefits, it will be necessary to unify the program beyond state lines: reinsurance with the federal government or, better, a *federal* program should be enacted. A social-security program cannot meet all the contingencies of modern life; but it can make a much greater contribution than does the program in force in 1948.

A serious gap in social security is health insurance which enactment of the Wagner-Murray-Dingell bill would fill. Estimates by the Social Security Board suggest that a payment of 3 per cent of payrolls now and 4 to 5 per cent later will yield the resources required to provide adequate health service to all, with a general improvement for the nation and a greatly improved distribution.

Past Errors of Financing   Finally, we should examine the mistakes of financing made in the past. In 1935, too much reliance was put upon the accumulation of reserves, a policy inspired by fear of putting an excessive burden on the taxpayer in 1980. By 1939, the reserve principle had largely been abandoned, a result of the effort of those who feared the deflationary effects of reserve accumulation (that is, taking in more than was paid out), of labor, which opposed high payroll taxes to accumulate reserves, and of Senator Taft, John Flynn, and others who were confused by the theory of reserves and saw in them an attempt to despoil the insured. Actually, the influence of the anti-reserve forces was toward increasing the public debt; for under the 1939 program those who were then, or were soon to be, eligible for old-age benefits were to be given annuities way beyond what they had earned, and the government was to go into debt to the present young for billions of dollars. Curiously enough, the opponents of deficit financing had supported a financing program for social security which has already added many billions to the public debt.

This reversal of policy in 1939 was in many ways a disaster. There followed nine years of prosperity, of inflationary pressures during which the collection of 15 to 20 billion dollars of additional payroll taxes would have eased the pressure, strengthened the system, and made possible a more vigorous general tax program. This is another demonstration of the danger of committing the nation to a fiscal policy for many years irrespective of the developing economic situation.

Social Security and Labor Policy It is well to keep in mind the fact that a formal social-security program can solve only part of the problem of economic distress, and can only partly satisfy those who are prepared to seek security even if it is obtained to some extent at the expense of progress. In a dynamic world punctured by frequent spells of depression, social security gains increasing importance. But attainment of a modicum of security depends even more on labor and wage policy than on social security narrowly considered. Minimum-wage legislation and especially the state of collective bargaining are of vital importance. Dunlop's essay on a National Labor Policy is a well-balanced discussion of the major labor problems. It is clear that the Taft-Hartley Act has corrected some excesses on the part of labor. But it is clear also that in many respects the act goes too far, for example, in offering legal support to employers who would obstruct the advance of collective bargaining; in protecting the worker excessively in his rights against those of the union; in extending the prohibition against the closed shop where it is not justified. Dunlop also shows that the Taft-Hartley Act was in fact political action by employers, and that it may prove to be a boomerang; even now adequate machinery is still not available for settlement of disputes by negotiation, in no small part because of the absence of employer cooperation and association.

Expenditures on Education [1] Expenditures on education and social security influence the total pattern of spending: they may make important contributions towards keeping consumption at a sufficiently high level and stabilizing the economy, and they should raise the general level of productivity.

This country devotes a surprisingly small proportion of its income to education and social security. An outside figure in 1948 would be 4 per cent of the national income. Americans would do well to compare the 25 per cent of the wage bill allotted for these purposes in the last Soviet Five-Year Plan; and they should consider also that from the early thirties to

[1] Cf., S. E. Harris, *How Shall We Pay for Education?* (New York, 1948).

1947, a period during which national income rose by 165 billion dollars and consumption by 115 billion, private expenditures for education, and public expenditures other than temporary aid to veterans rose by less than a billion dollars. Our educational deficiencies do not originate in the unavailability of resources. The fact is that private citizens refuse to assume a responsibility which they certainly could meet, and in the present distribution of responsibilities government is unable to spend enough on education.

Shifting the Burden to the Federal Government   Education is a national responsibility, and the federal government should pay a large part of its cost. At present, local governments contribute about 85 per cent of the cost of the public schools, and 90 per cent of tax receipts of local government come from the general property tax, a tax less equitable, less flexible, and more depressing than any other important tax. In the fifteen years ending in 1946, during which national income rose by more than three times and prices and costs by two-thirds, the yield of the general property tax scarcely changed. A historical accident which has put the burden of education almost exclusively on local government and on the general property tax is the main cause of our perennial educational crisis.

If adequate funds are to be provided for education it will be necessary to shift part of the burden to state governments, and especially to the federal government, where tax capacity primarily resides. The Aiken bill providing for federal aid to education is therefore a much more courageous and realistic bill than that sponsored by Senator Taft. Only thus shall we be able to equalize educational opportunities and obtain adequate resources for education. In an expanding and inflationary economy, the inflation termite consumes the educational dollar; in a depressed economy, the property tax crushes industry, and the pressure to pinch the schools becomes irresistible. Only federal aid can raise standards in poor states which rear a disproportionately large number of the nation's children and which, despite expenditures per classroom as low as $100 (the median figure is $1,560, the maximum $6,000), are not failing for lack of trying. Educational expenditures as a percentage of tax resources available to the state were 25 in New York and 38 per cent for all state governments; but 78 per cent for Mississippi, 77 per cent for South Carolina, 61 per cent for Alabama, and 56 per cent for North Carolina. Chart 9 suggests differences in expenditures and in resources available for education.

The Problem of Higher Education   Furthermore, educational opportunity is unequal in institutions of higher learning. Inflation, falling rates of interest, the pressure of increased numbers—these and other factors have greatly weakened the long-run financial position of these institutions, buttressed temporarily by the G. I. Bill of Rights. Even more

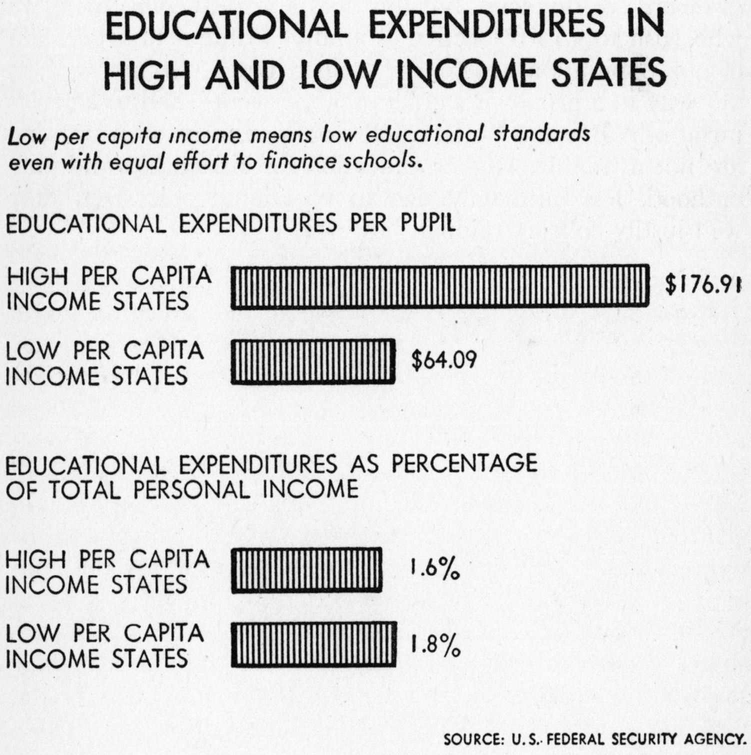

EDUCATIONAL EXPENDITURES IN HIGH AND LOW INCOME STATES

Low per capita income means low educational standards even with equal effort to finance schools.

EDUCATIONAL EXPENDITURES PER PUPIL

HIGH PER CAPITA
INCOME STATES $176.91

LOW PER CAPITA
INCOME STATES $64.09

EDUCATIONAL EXPENDITURES AS PERCENTAGE
OF TOTAL PERSONAL INCOME

HIGH PER CAPITA
INCOME STATES   1.6%

LOW PER CAPITA
INCOME STATES   1.8%

SOURCE: U.S. FEDERAL SECURITY AGENCY.

CHART 9

important is the fact that economic status and proximity of residence to a college are altogether too important in determining entry. Recent studies show that a student from a family with an income of $10,000 has three times as good a chance of getting to college as one from a family with the median income of $2,500; and those within 20 miles of a college are 2 to 3 times as likely to go as those living beyond 20 miles. For every able student who goes to college, an equally able one cannot.

It is the government's responsibility to provide the resources which will make possible a sound education for all those who are capable of profiting from it. Democracy in education means equal opportunity for all, irrespective of the accident of income or domicile. But this does not mean subsidizing all who wish to go irrespective of ability. While 4 to 5 per cent of our population are college trained today, we are well on our way to a proportion of 25 to 30 per cent—and to a proletariat of A.B.'s and Ph.D.'s; jobs commensurate with training are not available. Higher education for citizenship and parenthood, less intimately tied to vocational objectives, may well justify college training, however.

PART EIGHT

Democracy, Literature, and Science

Introduction

by Seymour E. Harris

In this, the last part of the book, we grouped three essays not closely related, but each dealing with a significant problem which is intimately associated with the liberal economic program. The reader will find in these papers by Taylor on Democracy, Jones on Literature, and Newman on Science significant contributions, well written and touching upon fundamental problems concerning our economic order.

    Taylor on the Evolution of Liberalism   Earlier in this volume, Berle commented on the liberal creed, emphasizing that it springs from faith in a moral order of the universe; that its ultimate objective is the fullest development of each individual, for which freedom is the *sine qua non;* that it does not countenance oppression of the many by the few; and that it is committed to no politico-economic system. It insists upon the practical test of efficiency in the determination of the distribution of responsibility between government and private enterprise.

In his substantial essay, Taylor sketches the history of liberalism from the eighteenth century, when it was the rallying cry of those who would throw off the shackles of mercantilism, to the end of the nineteenth century when it had become a system designed to oppress the many on behalf of the few; and then until the 1930's, when the view begins to prevail that the fullest development of the masses will not be achieved unless the government intervenes on their behalf. In the first half of the nineteenth century, particularly in

England, businessmen and labor united in seeking a liberal program against the monopolistic propensies of the landed classes and the privileged merchants, and in favor of larger markets and competitive enterprise. Unfortunately, businessmen soon abandoned their liberal tradition and sought and received favors from government, which enabled them to oppress labor and exploit consumers. As Taylor well shows, the growing opposition of the conservatives against a strong government prepared to intervene on behalf of labor and consumers, and in favor of a do-nothing government, is indeed paradoxical; for the laissez faire they profess means freedom from governmental interference with monopoly and with privileges granted and protected by government itself. This is not the liberal system fought for in England in the first decades of the nineteenth century. These critics of New Dealism and Keynesianism or any other system which would tolerate interference on behalf of the masses, seek or pretend to demand an old-fashioned liberal program, unmindful of the absence of competition and the favors bestowed on business.

Literature and Economic Problems   Men and women who write are faced with the economic problem of finding a publisher and a market; and though authors may shut their eyes to these problems, they are real nevertheless. Jones elaborates this theme fully and well. It is significant that unless a novel promises a market of 10,000 buyers, the publisher will not be interested. For technical books, a potential sale of 5,000 volumes is required. With the current wasteful manner of selling books, and at present high costs of publishing, the writer with ideas and particularly the scientist, both natural and social, is frequently unable to disseminate his views. The more original or technical his book and the more select his audience, the greater the obstacles confronting him. To assure the advance of science, it may be necessary to find new economies in publishing and selling books, or else to obtain government subsidies for publishing outstanding books with small markets.

Writers in the humanities may make important contributions to the solution of economic problems by paying attention to these problems. American writers, as Jones says, have not "characteristically concerned themselves with what is timeless and unlocalized." They deal with human beings who have problems; and the problems are often economic. Some authors, as Jones points out, have enlisted under the Jeffersonian banner. Economists could write learned volumes, one after another, on the issue of migration; but their influence would be infinitesimal compared with that of John Steinbeck's *Grapes of Wrath*. Through the medium of the brush, the pen, or the voice, artists bring home to the people the great economic issues of the day: malnutrition, poverty, exploitation, unemployment, class struggle. They prepare the voter and the Congressman for the revelations and proposals of the technical expert. Jones himself is an excellent example of the scholar in the humanities who assumes the responsibility of tying literature to the everyday problems of a troubled world, and of seeking solutions consistent with liberal traditions.

Science in a Liberal Program   Finally, there is the problem of science. We all realize that the future of this country depends upon science, not only to protect us against aggressors but also to yield the high standard of living and the wide distribution of goods required for a stable and happy society. Hiroshima dramatized the arrival of the age of science, but advances in non-military areas should not go unnoticed. Over the last 30 years, this country, using an unchanged amount of land, increased its agricultural output by 60 per cent. Profiting from the Mendelian theory of eugenics, farmers developed hybrid corn to a point that made possible over 5 to 10 years a rise in output of 25 per cent. Advances which made possible the support of 27 times as many people at a standard of living at least 10 times as high as 150 years ago would have been impossible without the developments in pure science. We might remember that these developments were largely the contributions of foreigners.

Newman effectively points out that our expenditures on science and particularly on pure science are scandalously small (less than one-half of 1 per cent of our income even in 1941–45); that the major part goes to the military; that large improvements in integration and planning of science expenditures are required; that serious lacunae prevail in medical research; and that a man-power famine threatens our programs. He is careful to shun a view frequently expressed that science should not serve the military. In this insecure world, the United States has to move ahead in military science as well as on other fronts. Our problem is not only that of making the advances which will raise standards of living here and elsewhere, but also to improve our institutions in a manner to exclude war and provide fair and equitable distribution at home, without strife. Science advances rapidly, but adaptation of our institutions proceeds at a snail's pace. We are confronted, as Newman suggests, with the absurdity of a Science Foundation bill without provision for the social sciences.

CHAPTER XXVIII

Free Enterprise and Democracy

by O. H. Taylor

Other parts of this volume are economic studies of various particular problems of national policy. This essay, in contrast, is concerned with general ideas about an over-all problem, and owing to the nature of its theme is a discourse more in the domain of political thought than in that of economics. My hope is that it may throw light on, and help readers to appraise, the current American liberal and conservative attitudes to public authority and private liberties in our economy. My own position on this question places me—along with the other contributors to this volume—in the liberal group. But that in itself cannot become a very informative statement until some clarifying "light" has at least diminished the "dark" confusions today pervading most American thought, as to what we liberals and our conservative opponents, respectively, stand for. To do what I can here to dispel those confusions is my purpose.

History of the Word "Liberal" As is indicated by the word "liberal" itself, and demonstrated by the entire history of "liberalism," we liberals—apart from extremists who misuse and are not entitled to the name—are friends of liberty and loyal heirs of the main American tradition, aiming at the nearest feasible approach to a society of (in the main) voluntarily co-operating, free individuals. But by an accident in the history of American political terminology, the word "liberal" has come into general use here only in the quite recent period, which has been marked by some new enlargements

331

of the sphere of activity of the people's government. And in this period the expansion of our government—while occurring chiefly under the pressure of prevailing conditions and the resulting insistent needs and demands of the popular majority—has been brought about through a movement led precisely by those (the liberals) most anxious to see the full blessings of liberty extended to *all* Americans. Not the group's liberal purpose, however, but merely its support (in seeming conflict with that purpose) of new governmental economic controls has been most clearly evident to the public. Thus it has come about that, ignoring both the literal and the older historic meaning of the word, our national usage means by "liberals" persons advocating a degree and kind of humanitarian "big government"; a thing which the conservative opposition can all too easily represent as, and which if misdirected can degenerate into, a general, dangerous curtailment of traditional and still desirable private liberties.

Birth of the Liberal Creed   Now I think a glance over the long history of liberal and conservative thought and controversy in the democratic-capitalist world as a whole, on the question of governmental controls and private liberties in the business economy, may help us to see in the right perspective, and appraise, the present-day American phase of this controversy. The old gospel of entirely or very "free enterprise" and very limited government is today identified in our politics with conservatism, and even in that quarter is not much more than a wistful memory. But in the epoch of its birth—the late eighteenth and early nineteenth centuries, the epoch of the American and French Revolutions and England's first steps toward democracy—the same gospel (with a subtle difference) was a vital part of the *liberal* creed. Along with the ideal and theory of political democracy, it was then the first philosophy of the liberal-democratic movement to emancipate the common people from oppression by the privileged few. For in that age, this movement was directed against the regimes established in the preceding epoch—regimes of despotic monarchy, oligarchy (actual rule, under the reigning monarchs, by small groups of aristocratic landowners and rich merchants), and "mercantilism," the economic policy of those governments. The character of mercantilism, above all, is the key to the original, liberal meaning of the gospel of free enterprise. Mercantilism was a system of governmental promotion and friendly control of high "capitalist" enterprise and wide control of economic affairs for the benefit of the ruling, privileged, rich minorities and to bolster up the military power of each great imperial nation-state, and not for the sake of improving the economic welfare of the common people. In short, the liberal movement in its earliest phase was a revolt against the alliance of "big government" and what was then "big business."

Liberalism versus Mercantilism   It was in opposition to mercantilism that the first liberal economists—Adam Smith and others—developed the ideal and theory of an economic system of universal free enterprise, free competition, and free trade. Governments were to function only as "impartial umpires." Central in mercantilist policy were lavish grants of legal monopolies to associations of established, wealthy businessmen, and a mass of restrictive regulations of the normal, gain-seeking activities of "little" businessmen and of farmers, working men, and the people as consumers. And so, by opposition, it became the central idea of the liberal economists that a regime of minimal government and maximal economic freedom for all individuals would subject the former monopolies and all businesses to competitive pressures beneficial to the public; distribute opportunities impartially to all the people, and elicit from all the people their best productive efforts and contributions to the common welfare; and in general, harmonize the self-interest of each individual with the collective interest of mankind. With its strong individualism, that economic-liberal philosophy combined, inseparably, a no less strong internationalism. All individuals everywhere were to have large, equal, and sacred freedoms to pursue their interests anywhere, across as well as within the national frontiers; and the national governments were to be made to stop "interfering" in the economic world in those ways which had favored the already rich and oppressed the common people, as well as served the spirit of aggressive nationalism, to the detriment of international trade, prosperity, and peace.

Economic Liberalism and Political Democracy   Now that ideal and theory of the free world economy attained a fairly full development and some influence a few decades before the ideal and theory of political democracy—the other half of the complete philosophy of nineteenth-century liberalism—became of equal, practical importance. In other words, the main body of the liberal reformers first tried for a while only to make the old, pre-democratic kind of government as little harmful as possible by curtailing its powers and sphere of activity, before they went on to the further effort to replace it with a new kind of government, so organized as to be responsive and responsible to all the people. But then in the second, more complete, phase of the liberal movement, most leading advocates of fully democratic, popular government long remained also advocates of minimal government and the economic system of free, unregulated, individual enterprise, competition, and trade. The utmost freedom for all individuals at all consistent with their common welfare was still the first concern. Fear of "big government" as likely to be oppressive misgovernment, perverted to the ends of a rich, powerful, and selfish few, was still the dominant fear. Generations of experience of the old type of government had produced in the people a deep distrust of government in general, which could die out only with the gradual, full development of, and new generations of experience under, political democracy. Political democracy at first was usually thought of, not as enabling the popular majority to control and use a widely active, strong government to attain their ends by positive action, but rather as enabling the people to protect themselves from too much government, by using the vote as a veto on ambitious governmental plans.

Moreover, the theory of the ideal "free market" economy still impressed most democratic leaders as a "democratic" conception in its own sphere and the logical counterpart of political democracy. Free competition of all enterprises for the patronage of the people would oblige them to serve all the people as amply, well, and cheaply as possible, just as political "free competition" of parties, candidates, ideas, and programs for the votes of the people would force *them* into line with prevailing, popular desires. Thus, through the early decades of the nineteenth century, free enterprise and democracy were as a rule supported together in pro-popular, progressive, liberal, and democratic quarters, and opposed together in well-to-do and conservative quarters. For example, in this country then it was the Jeffersonian and, later, the Jacksonian Democrats who preached free enterprise and limited government along with full political democracy. The Hamiltonian Federalists and, later, the Whigs—representatives of the northern, larger business interests and forerunners of the present-day Republican Party—were not supporters either of free enterprise or of full democracy. Instead, those early parties of the "well born," well-to-do, and conservative families in our land still more or less openly favored a regime of oligarchy or rule, in effect, by themselves; a strong and active federal government, responsive mainly to their interests and ideas; and an economic policy on the part of that government akin to the traditions of European mercantilism.

The English Experience   Not only here but in every country of what was to be the democratic-capitalist world, conversion of business leaders to the creed of free enterprise and democracy was a more or less late development. But this development occurred earliest—in the early-to-middle decades of the nineteenth century—and most completely, in England, the first country to go through the Industrial Revolution or enter the industrial machine age. For the rise of the new industrialism, in England then and later elsewhere, transferred the controlling voice in the business community to a new set of men with new attitudes. In the place of the former class of "merchant princes," whose hopes of large profits lay in monopolistic or/and state-aided control of markets, there arose the new class of manufacturing capitalists, whose hopes lay at first in a wholly free competition of ever improving methods of production. Having as their best route to profits free exertion of their own individual enterprise and ingenuity, the new industrialists in general tended to be

more independent, "rugged individualists," asking the state
only to give them a wide, free, unobstructed field for their
endeavors. Moreover, in the special case of the early British
industrialists, their whole situation—never fully, in all aspects,
repeated elsewhere—gave them inducements to become especially complete supporters of democracy and humane reforms as well as of free enterprise, and of free trade abroad as
well as free enterprise at home. As it bears on other points yet
to come in my narrative and argument, let me now spell
out this last point briefly.

In Britain's old-world social hierarchy of a century and
more ago, not her businessmen but her landowning aristocrats and "gentlemen" were and had been the ruling class.
No matter how rich they were the businessmen in general
ranked only as members of the middle class, and had much
tendency to be, in feeling, a part of the common people. And
this now became more significantly true than it had been
earlier; the earlier "merchant princes" had been accepted
into the governing-class circles and could feel identified with
the old, traditional, social and political system of the country.
But the new industrialists in most cases rose from humbler
social origins and long retained "democratic" feelings. And
those feelings were often accentuated by the tendency of their
social superiors—the aristocrats and "gentlemen"—to dislike
their "pushing" ways and so to snub them. Again, being the
chief "backers" of and first gainers from the technological
progress in industry which was transforming society, the industrialists tended to aspire to be leaders of social progress
in general—leading supporters of new, progressive ideas in
all fields, including politics. Also, industrialism required a
mass market, enlargement of the market for all commodities
to include all the people, or progressive elevation of mass living standards. This requirement aligned the interests of the
businessmen with democratic progress. They could well support political democracy, for it enlarged their own political
influence as well as that of the working people, and as yet any
fears that the latter would use the new political system against
them were lulled by the fact that the gospel of free enterprise
was still a part of the democratic creed. In the higher, non-

business circles of the aristocracy and gentry, or patrician landlords, there was in that half-century just after the French Revolution much reactionary fear of democracy, of the new cult of liberty or individualism, and of all progressivism. There was a vigorous growth of a new conservative or Tory philosophy of authoritarian, "paternal" government over all the people and the economy by the ancient, limited, hereditary ruling class. But in the main the British industrial capitalists opposed that reaction and joined the liberal, democratic, progressive movement. And finally, the resulting political alignment of labor and capital together against the "Tory Landlords" became crystallized around the special issue of the corn laws, or agricultural protectionism, versus the complete freedom of foreign trade which the British industrialists, in their special situation in that epoch, desired as in both their own and the national interest. They saw free trade as the way to cheapen food and thus lower money wages without injuring labor, and as a means of facilitating expansion of industrial exports in exchange for imported food and raw material.

Self-Interest and the Common Welfare   Such were the backgrounds of the first and fullest adoption, by any national business community, of the entire philosophy of the now old, obsolescent, early, special form of "liberalism" which included the gospel of very free enterprise and very limited government. Nor did its adoption by business at once transform the old liberalism into the new conservatism it has since become; that transformation was to be another, still later, development, and is yet to be explained here. The mid-nineteenth-century British liberal businessmen had, I think— in a measure not often excelled by normal, not saintly, human beings—the true liberal, generous, humane, idealistic, democratic, and progressive spirit. At the same time it is true, as I have indicated, that a shrewd perception of where their own interests lay in the special circumstances they confronted in their time and country had very much to do with making them adherents of the liberal outlook. They should not on that account be singled out for special censure. The tendency to be much influenced by self-interest in arriving at political

opinions—which even so are usually honest and sometimes
valid beliefs as to what public policies are morally right and
best for the welfare of the entire community—is a tendency
not at all peculiar to businessmen or to any class, in any epoch
or society. It is an all but universal human weakness; and I
do not share either attitude of those among my fellow American
liberals of today who apparently, on the one hand, see
only nobility in the devotion, say, of union labor to any cause
of its own, and yet on the other hand, see only immoral selfishness
and hypocrisy in the exactly similar devotion of business
to ideals in harmony with business interests. The point is,
there was a time, especially in England, when conditions
were such that a genuine liberalism, in the form then current,
harmonized with the interests and so had the support
of business, together with the common people.

The American Experience   There was never at any
time in this country, however, or indeed elsewhere outside
of England, any complete parallel to that situation in mid-
nineteenth-century England. American business, for example,
never as a whole accepted the old economic-liberal views on
the question of the tariff, or on that of the trusts—free trade
abroad, or free competition at home. Conditions here, during
and after our industrial revolution, which came later by a
few decades than England's, did not so generally align the
interests of our industrialists with those policies. We have had,
in great numbers, our own ruggedly individualistic captains
of industry; but by and large our business leaders in the past
have sought and won much active, governmental help—
interference for their benefit in the economy—and governmental
tolerance of their own collusive endeavors to build up
monopolies and to handicap their competitors. Since we
never had a European-model aristocracy, the top layer of
the American business community has always constituted our
topmost social class, wielding from the outset a very great
influence over all American life. Through all generations and
changes in our country, and despite steady growth of the
reality and vigor of our political democracy, this group has
continued to seek to retain its early control over government,
and insure a mixed set of policies: protection of the business

freedoms desired by big interests, and active furtherance of their designs entailing restrictions of the free enterprise of other people. Until very recently, American progressivism had to concentrate its efforts mainly on the task of ending business control and misuse of government, or in other words perfecting our real, political democracy. And despite some appearances to the contrary at times, I think it is true that until very recently American individualism—the ideal of great freedom for all individuals and very limited government—remained more a popular than a business ideal. Precisely that fact is what now gives our business defenders of free enterprise, the opponents of present-day liberal, democratic, governmental controls over business, an unfair advantage in political debate.

Expansion of Democracy and the Rift with Business Meanwhile, there began long ago in the democratic-capitalist world as a whole and even in mid-nineteenth-century England, a rift in the early harmony—which was never complete even there—of business, democracy, and free enterprise. Democracy began to go beyond removal of the pre-democratic, governmental controls over individual enterprise which had suited the "big business" of an earlier day, and impose new and different controls of its own on the new industrialists. For while the Industrial Revolution and its consequence, the new industrial capitalism, brought great benefits to all the people, they also brought new evils into being; and as governments became more democratic and responsive to popular needs, they were obliged even while professing the free-enterprise creed in general, to begin to take on new functions and evolve new organs in the effort to alleviate the new evils. Thus, for example, the English Factory Acts came into being in the very heyday of the country's devotion to extreme individualistic liberalism. And a steady, gradual expansion of government and social legislation of many kinds followed, there and elsewhere, right on down to the present.

Also, in the meantime, in a minority quarter far to the left of and unconnected with that main trend but adding still more to the distress of business, socialist movements got under way. The grain of truth in their gospel was and is the fact that under industrial capitalism a measure of conflict does exist between the interests of the class of owners (and their agents, managers), and those of the class of wage-earning workers. The two "classes" have a common interest in high production, but a clash of interests over the division of the proceeds. The old economic-liberal theory of the potential, perfect harmony of all interests in the ideal free-market economy evaded recognition of the fact of "classes" and the partial conflict of their interests. On the other hand the socialist view falsely depicts that conflict as an absolute one, denies the actual bond of common interests between the "masses" and the "capitalists," and holds that democracy must in the end become incompatible with and abolish private capitalism. The socialist body of doctrine is, I believe, in definite error, and a threat to all individual liberties including those most vital to the working people. But its spread has been stimulated by the labor-capital conflict, the slowness of democracy in developing controls over business for the general welfare, and the resistance of business to the moderate controls and reforms which alone can preserve a viable union of the democratic, liberal state and the business economy.

Conservative Redefinition of Free Enterprise, and Today's Liberalism Now it was in the reaction of business and its friends against the menace of socialism and the expanding activities of democratic governments, that, in the late nineteenth and early twentieth centuries, the old, originally liberal, economic ideal and theory of the free-enterprise economy became, by a subtle change, the gospel of conservatism. The reorientation involved little apparent change in economic theory. The neo-classical economists and the pro-business popularizers of their teachings appeared to be only further elaborating and refining the scheme of thought of Adam Smith and his immediate successors, the old classical economists. But what had been the vision of a group of liberal reformers, of a possible, ideal economy, now became an unreal, alleged account of the mode of operation of a later, actual system which was *not* a realization of the original ideal. And above all, the utopia now confused with reality, now was defended or exalted in contrast not with the original alternatives—despotism, oligarchy, mercantilism, all business monopolies, and the remains of feudalism—but with the new, advancing, and dreaded alternatives —mild democratic control over capitalism and, as the frightful specter seen as looming beyond that, socialism.

Finally, when the old economic-liberal theory had thus been refitted to the uses of, and taken over by, conservatism, liberal thought began its new, recent and current, still confused gropings toward a new vision, of a really possible and sound "middle way" between the extremes of entirely free enterprise, and socialism. Thus far, this latest development has attained great importance only in this country. In Europe, socialism has become the creed of the discontented "many" and their sympathetic leaders; the main conservative forces there have turned back to ancient anti-democratic, authoritarian ideas; and the term "liberalism" there still means as a rule the old creed of extreme individualism, now supported only by tiny, ineffective groups of essentially conservative although anti-authoritarian intellectuals. But the current new or latter-day American liberalism, despite its measure of conflict with that older creed, is the true continuation of the old, authentic, liberal movement, in the new conditions of today. As such it has yet to achieve, however, an adequately clear and coherent vision, analysis, and program. One initial source of a serious fault in much liberal thinking of the new variety, a short time ago, was its reaction against economic theory or analysis as represented then by the reigning neoclassical economics. In their scorn for the obvious unrealism and conservative bias of that particular body of economic theory, too many of the "new" liberals became unwisely averse to all economic theory, that is, to serious analytical study of the market mechanisms, processes, and requirements of the business economy; and prone to support all reforms humanitarian in purpose without careful study of their to-be-expected, actual consequences. But this is now being remedied, because economists recently have produced much new, improved work in economic theory, of a kind fruitful in suggestions of effective and sound means to liberal ends.

Today's Liberalism and Individual Freedoms　Two questions remain now to be touched on here—of necessity, too briefly. What are the main things which our democracy now can and should do, through its government, to make our business economy work better for the general welfare of all the people? And what, in the doing of these things, may be the dangers of undue curtailment of individual freedoms, and the proper safeguards against those dangers? General answers to the first question—elaborated elsewhere in this volume—are easily enumerated. In the first place, the worst single failure of the business economy in the past to serve the general welfare as it should, has been its failure to avoid the rhythmic sequence of "booms and busts," entailing recurrent periods of depression, wasteful idleness of machines and men, and demoralizing hardships for millions. Governmental action on the lines suggested by Keynesian economics, to abolish or control and greatly mitigate the booms and busts, is now possible and can be effective, and need entail only a very minimal degree of interference with private business. In the second place, the automatic mechanisms of the market system cannot today adequately bring about in all fields of enterprise or at all times the proper adjustments of the relative prices of different goods and services and the proper, non-wasteful allocation of the nation's productive efforts and resources among different activities. Monopolies and other obstructions of the market processes at many points, in many cases irremovable, make them only incompletely effective for this purpose. We must work toward a combination of controls by the markets, and by government, of relative prices and the allocation of resources—making full use of the market mechanisms where they can be effective, and supplementing them with governmental action in special fields and at crucial times.

In the third place, a moderate change from the historic pattern of the distribution of incomes, in the direction of reducing the net, disposable incomes of the rich and raising those of the low-income classes, must be sought, through adjustments of governmental policies with respect to taxation and public spending, and policies affecting wages and prices. Care must be taken in this connection to avoid undue discouragement of private saving, investment, and enterprise;

but with care this line of action can be so developed as actually to aid, not hamper, private, real capital formation and economic progress through private enterprise, by helping the consuming power of the great mass of the people to grow in step with the economy's producing power. And finally, the often excessive and useless hardships and hazards of unaided, private adjustments by workers, farmers, "little" businessmen, and others, to incessant technological and economic change—getting from vanished jobs into new jobs, or out of declining and into expanding fields of activity—can be mitigated by government in many ways; through employment exchanges, public diffusion of authentic knowledge of changing conditions and opportunities, social-security measures, and temporary subsidies. Care must be taken not to go too far in removing pressures and incentives for the voluntary adjustments to new conditions, which must go on in a free, progressive society; but the old "rugged" ideal of requiring everyone to make all needed readjustments by his own unaided efforts, or perish, cannot be defended or maintained in a modern, humane or fraternal democracy.

And now finally, how are individual freedoms likely to fare under such a program? Conservative alarmists about this generally have, I think, distorted perspectives on the total problem. Among all the freedoms to be considered they see mainly (a) the business freedoms prized by the owners and managers of large enterprises, more than the freedoms prized or sought by most other people; (b) in general, economic freedoms, more than the civil liberties directly essential to democracy; and (c) freedoms from government, not freedoms from other sorts of compulsions or pressures having private sources. Not hostility nor indifference to, but a better balanced concern for, the freedoms of Americans marks today's liberals. Not only are they constant crusaders for the civil liberties, for all Americans; they also, in advocating new public controls over business, are seeking to enlarge the economic freedoms of the many from compulsions privately imposed by the great enterprises on their masses of employees, small suppliers, would-be competitors, and customers. Of course it is true at the same time that in some respects the new governmental economic controls are bound to impinge on the people generally, and not only on Big Business; but the dangers to the peoples' freedoms from government are of several kinds, needing separate evaluations. Some are indeed real and unavoidable, but unimportant; as they did under wartime rationing and price control, many people will suffer partial losses of minor freedoms familiar in the past, and resent this bitterly—as a rule from petty, selfish motives. One's idea of freedom may be a true moral ideal—freedom for all men, not mainly for oneself, in matters important for human dignity and free development; or it may be a mere expression of petty selfishness, or selfish pettiness—lack of the feeling of responsibility to and for others and the common welfare, and refusal to accept gracefully even merely inconvenient restrictions on oneself, for public ends however important. The love of liberty of too many Americans is too largely of this character. Some restrictions distasteful to such people are bound to be entailed in any substantial measure of positive government for the general welfare; but the loss of freedom which comes under this head will be no great loss.

In a different category are imaginary dangers to our vital freedoms—the alleged dangers of a growth, through lust for power in our public officials, of a really tyrannical, despotic government. In this country, in view of the character of its well-established political system and traditions, the notion of a sheer lust for power in our elected and appointed officials as a serious danger to the freedoms of the governed is a ridiculous myth. The prevailing fault of our officials is the opposite: excessive fear of offending voters; a timid desire to please everybody; great proneness to only follow, not lead, trends of public opinion, and to wait for clear evidence of overwhelming majority demands before acting; and the greatest reluctance to accept and exercise any new bit of power if it means having to contend with strong opposition in any quarter. The real dangers to American freedoms have their sources not within our existing government—in any power-lust in our officials—but in the precarious balance of external pressures upon the government, from private blocs; and the chance that if the struggle among these leads to anarchy, or deadlock, or excessive gains by some blocs at the expense of others, aggrieved millions and those willing to exploit their frustrations may build up a frenzy against the disorder of democracy, and for dictatorship.

That brings me to the only real, potential dangers to our vital freedoms which *may* arise in or from a mismanaged "new liberal" program. Expansion of the government's sphere of action, power, and importance does intensify and multiply the pressures or demands upon it. The conflict of pressures makes it more difficult to maintain internal harmony, efficiency, wisdom, and vigor in the operation of the government. And so if the government too largely fails to overcome these difficulties, takes on too much and mishandles it and becomes "a mess," creates and disappoints diverse high hopes, and through its own disorders aggravates instead of mitigating those in the working of our economy—then indeed, in reaction to its failures, Fascism may happen here. But I think this danger can be avoided only by making our democratic government more equal to its tasks, and performing them well— not by refusing to undertake them. If it leaves the needs of the many unmet, the extreme Left will gain, and in alarm over that result the extreme Right will grow even more, and grow reckless, and Fascism will arrive by this route. Only by making a success of the "new" liberalism—the middle way between old-fashioned free enterprise and socialism—can we hope to make freedom secure.

CHAPTER XXIX

"Literature" and the Economic Order

by Howard Mumford Jones

To speak of literature in relation to a liberal program of economic and social development seems at first glance to represent that kind of wishful thinking propagandists mistake for action. They believe that literature must be on "our side." But in the first place, literary men are notoriously poor economists either in the original Greek sense of the word or in its modern professional meaning. In the second place, there seems to be no real connection between economics and imaginative writing. In the third place, great literature has flourished in times and places quite opposite to the utopian ideal of a liberal social program. Most of the great periods of Asiatic literature, for example, are associated with the name of a despot, benevolent or otherwise; and the Augustan age of Rome, the cultural glories of Medici Florence, and the development of French neo-classicism under Louis XIV are three familiar European examples of splendid literature and undemocratic economy.

Moreover, one of the elementary errors a literary critic does not wish to commit is to confound political and economic righteousness with literary merit. It is to the credit of William Hazlitt that, detesting the ideas of Edmund Burke, he lavished admiration upon the Irishman's prose style, just as it is to the discredit of Marxian critics a little while ago that any novel "on their side," no matter how ephemeral it might be, was given a favorable hearing, and literary work opposing their program was slighted or attacked not merely as political iniquity but also as bad art. Perhaps no one can surely draw the line where propaganda ends and literature begins, since superb propaganda sometimes rises into literature and mediocre literature often sinks into propaganda. Yet for ordinary purposes we can distinguish the two spheres well enough; and to connect the literary defence of a liberal program with the art of writing seems at the outset to confound this distinction and to violate the first caution of criticism.

But the age of Truman is not the age of Pericles. Of course, to use the word "literature" implies a lofty frame of reference, discussion soaring above such transient problems as royalties and movie rights into that serene abode where the classics are; but as soon as one speaks only of the writer, of the publishing business, of literary agents, of advertising contracts, of book reviewing, one sinks back to the rough and practical ground. However high the pretensions of literature may be, if even the poet is to succeed, he must be heard, which means in modern times that a machine must turn him into print in sufficient quantities to be read by a sufficient number of pairs of eyes to bring back to an entrepreneur at least his original investment and preferably something more. Of course, if the poet has his private Maecenas, economic responsibility shifts.

What literary history principally ignores, however, is that manuscripts are objects of bargain and sale; that literary brains are bought in that strange market where hucksters and agents contend, and book clubs hope to find something that will sell astronomical numbers of copies. Literary historians imperfectly apprehend the truth that the basis of a writing career in 1947 has almost no economic relation to what it was in the fifth century B.C. or the sixteenth century A.D. or, for that matter, 1847 when Macaulay, the publisher's delight, was settling down to finish the first volume of *The History of England from the Accession of James II*. At no previous period in literary history have economic and social pressures upon the writer been as tremendous as they are now; and the process of literary production, from the first thought in the author's mind to the final sale of the plates when his book falls out of fashion, constitutes the most elaborate economic behavior pattern the literary world has known. Even if he wanted to, one would think, the author cannot avoid the economic issue. That practicing writers do not avoid that issue is evidenced by the creation of those guilds and unions which protect, or try to protect, the novelist, the song-writer, the dramatist, the radio man and the Hollywood gag man, not to speak of the newspaper reporter.

Although this is true, what is probably the most influential single force shaping "literature" in the Republic will not admit that there is any connection between merit and merchandising. I refer to the schools and colleges. The more we investigate literary careers, the more decisive we find the school years of a writer to be. Hence the supreme importance of what is taught as orthodoxy in the schools or of the discerning teacher who discovers young talent in formative years. Instances will occur to everyone, from Milton's years at Cambridge to the decisive influence upon Frank Norris of Lewis E. Gates at Harvard. Indeed, the flourishing writers' conferences which make glad the summer from Middlebury to Puget Sound are but the latest tribute to the academic years. The influence of English departments upon literary values is therefore often decisive.

When we ask whether the professional training writers receive from English departments prepares them in any way for economic responsibility, whether one means their private careers as income-earning citizens or their public responsibility as men of letters in a republic, the answer is not satisfactory. English departments recognize literature as an art; they have not yet awakened to the fact that writing and publishing are also an industry. And in two particulars I think their influence is bad.

Literary opinion at high and therefore persuasive levels— the kind of opinion that builds up the repute of a James Joyce, a Franz Kafka, or a T.S. Eliot—is usually shaped in the early stage by quarterly reviews established at various college and university centers; by courses in contemporary literature taught on so pure a plane that the publisher of the books taught is never mentioned; and by the increasing give and take between the classroom and the lecture platform, the radio ("Invitation to Learning" is an example), and other forms of public persuasion only slightly tainted with pecuniary returns. In this world of discussion all is "art"; nothing is economics.

There should of course be places where the enduring values of art are maintained and defended without reference to bargain and sale. Certainly the light thrown upon Shakespeare's plays by scholarly investigation into the conditions of Elizabethan printing is so dim and uncertain as scarcely to increase illumination. Imperial Rome had its publishing centers, but the art of Horace is not improved by our knowing this historic truth.

Nevertheless, we are not living under Augustus nor under Good Queen Bess, and the tiny original audience for the *Aeneid* or even for *Romeo and Juliet* is to the public reached by *Strange Fruit* or *Forever Amber* as a rowboat to an ocean liner. Nothing therefore is gained by refusing to recognize the patent fact that book and magazine publishing is as much a branch of big business in the modern world as is the manufacture of airplanes or cosmetics. Indeed, not only is nothing gained, but damage is done the liberal state by this refusal—by, in sum, the advanced academic attitude towards "literature." In the first place, the divorce in the classroom of literary evaluation from any consideration that literature must be put into print and sold in a fiercely competitive market is but a symptom of a deeper critical malady. The ingenious essays with which advanced academic critics assail writers and each other turn upon intricate problems of interpretation so esoteric as to be comprehended only by an initiated few, and are in fact written in a sociological vacuum for what is, in terms of modern life, an essentially irresponsible audience. We inherit this condition from the Bohemia of the nineteenth century, which also desired to shock the bourgeoisie. That the tradition is still active is evident from a recent bit of advertising sent out by an *avant-garde* publisher who stated that the reading tastes of the multitude were of no concern to him—he and a few choice spirits would continue to cherish the fine art of literature in limited editions as Prometheus concealed the sacred flame in a hollow reed. And the criticism for which this publisher produces books is Alexandrian criticism—that of a generation of English professors who write a secret language for each other. The multitude, happily ignoring this cult, goes its way imbibing opiate from magazines whose circulations run into millions, whose fiction is slick, whose pictures bleed smartly to the margin, whose advertising is essentially corrupt, and whose owners are publishing tycoons. Never in American history has the gulf been deeper between the aesthetic few and the entertainment-seeking many.

The academic few seem from time to time uneasily aware of their cultural and moral isolation, and offer a simple cure —join us. Taste consists not in what you like, but in what I like. Taste being by this admission anything the academic few write, the multitude is wrong if it does not like the esoteric. This is as if Shakespeare, in place of pleasing the groundlings with *Richard III*, should have desired them to read that sound academic pedant, Gabriel Harvey. Yet rich men, cultural foundations, university presses, and snob printers are expected to support poetry and prose too refined for the vulgar; and in the circle of the hierophants one acquires virtue by being popularly ignored. The result is that the fugitive and cloistered virtue of the English department, though it shapes poets, does not shape publishing except remotely; and neither the poet nor the professor is willing to express interest in or accept responsibility for the economic system which furnishes royalties to the one and righteousness to the other. Like the unction of doctors committed to the sacred obligation of service in healing but unable to reconcile themselves to socialized medicine, this attitude would be merely annoying, were it not that young writers are really forced into a refusal of direct civic responsibility. The irresponsibles brilliantly defined by Archibald MacLeish are therefore continually being recruited from the ranks of the aesthetic. Rationalization consists in the defence that it is proper to rise above transient politics and the ephemerae of the market place and to consider only tragic values (or philosophy or religious absolutism or the eternal form of the Platonic commonwealth). Would that readers could also thus be freed from the economic prison of individual lives!

But if the *littérateur* is a characteristic product of academic activity, he is not its sole offspring. The "creative" work of English departments, particularly in large service universities, together with correspondence courses and other forms of commercial instruction, may also produce writers trained, not to soar above the economic order, but to exploit and be exploited by it. The familiar advertisement: "How do you know you can't write?" is the simple symbol of this aspect of literary technology. Fiction is reduced to formulae, verse is taught by mail, directions are given for analyzing the wants of prospective customers—greeting-card makers, Hollywood magazines, detective fiction, religious weeklies, adventure stories, or periodicals dealing with science. The writer is conditioned like a greyhound to race after a mechanical goal, and if he succeeds, succeeds in terms of speed. Writing is not art, but manufacture; and the writer is the economic man of the nineteenth century pitted against the corporation of the twentieth. The successful product is he who shops around among employers until his diligence is noted and his trade skill regimented to the proper machine. For such a "writer," it is clear, the economic order—any economic order—is absolute; his sole duty is cunningly to analyze the entrepreneur of manuscripts and to outsmart him if he can. The height of attainment in this metallic world is to write on commission and by and by to employ an agent as a marketing device insuring continuous consumption of endless wordage. No question of responsibility for the ordering of the state has any meaning in a world purely given over to brute demand and supply.

The professional training of young writers seems to be faulty, then, in that it ignores the economics of the profession and thence, as it were, the economic and political responsibility of the art of literature. Fortunately, not all young writers confine themselves to a transcendental aesthetics; fortunately, an important section of mature writers accepts responsibility for *res publica*. Publication is a public act, which carries with it a notification of public responsibility. And though the work of novelist, dramatist, or poet is not necessarily improved by being tied up with a particular program of action (indeed, is often injured by too close an alliance with reform), it is nevertheless in the American tradition for the overwhelming number of writers in a given decade to be concerned for the health of the republic. Few have been merely Tory. Most have enlisted, both as writers and as citizens, under Jeffersonian banners. American empiricism has in fact shaped writing in this country in this special sense: that writers have not characteristically concerned themselves with what is timeless and unlocalized (as Goethe's *Elective Affinities* is timeless and unlocalized), but have rather concerned themselves with American morale, less in the sense of mere patriotism than in the sense of civism it is the highest duty of literature to show.

If we pass beyond the obvious cases of Tom Paine, Emerson, Thoreau, Henry George, and the like advocates of this or that reform, we note how intimate the interrelation of American poetry with public event has been and how close is the connection (and responsibility) of American fiction with the general health of the republic. The grave reflective poetry of Bryant not only presents the austere morality most people find in it, but springs also from a cyclical theory of history that leads directly to Bryant's work as a newspaper editor. The important poems of Lowell denounce an outrageous war and celebrate the heroes of the great American conflict, North and South. One of the best-known poems of Longfellow is a metaphor of the ship-of-state—a poem modern secretaries of state might meditate with profit. The post-Civil-War poets, forgotten nowadays, of whom Edmund C. Stedman, Bayard Taylor, and R. W. Gilder are representative, were deeply concerned about decay in civic morality and addressed themselves to the ideal republic. The best poems of William Vaughn Moody are civic odes denouncing imperialism. One can find plenty of interest in public event in the writings of E. A. Robinson, Carl Sandburg, Vachel Lindsay, and others of the so-called Poetic Renaissance. Benét's *John Brown's Body*, besides being an epic, is a plea for the liberal republic. It is only in our own time that sensitive poets, with some exceptions, seem embarrassed by large political issues and disinclined to regard themselves as servants of the civic muse.

An enormous library of fiction originates from the impact of economic and political issues upon the lives of private men. One of our earliest novels, Brackenridge's *Modern Chivalry*, a satire on demagoguery, nevertheless measures failure in terms of civic responsibility. The interest of Cooper in problems of political, economic, and cultural life (sometimes confined to Whig solutions) is known to students, however the general reader may dismiss him as an adventure writer for boys; and in direct comment like *Notions of the Americans* or oblique references as in the *Satanstoe* series, he illumines public issues— queerly anticipating in some books the strictures of Hamlin Garland. We are beginning to be aware of the amount of social criticism in Hawthorne, too long dismissed as lost in a dim Puritan past. *Uncle Tom's Cabin* came at once to mind when Steinbeck's *The Grapes of Wrath* swept the bookstores. Innumerable novels after the Civil War, some of them propaganda, some of them ephemeral, some of them utopian, but some of them rising to the dignity and power of Howells' *A Hazard of New Fortunes* and Norris's *The Octopus*, attacked monopoly and corruption and prepared the public imagination for the Progressive Movement, the New Freedom, and the New Deal. As for twentieth-century fiction, its roll-call would include a list of notables from Dos Passos to Steinbeck, from Fitzgerald to Dreiser, from Ernest Poole to James T. Farrell.

In truth, the American writer, though he admire Henry James and study Gertrude Stein, can scarcely avoid commitment to the liberal cause. Since most men lead lives of quiet desperation, the writer is bound to inquire into the causes of the dis-ease the books reflect; and though these causes may be private and psychological, they are also economic and political. The honest craftsman cannot avoid the problem. He need not be a professional economist, he need not be an expert in government to be profoundly concerned for the incidence of big business on private lives, the dissatisfactions arising from finance capitalism. He need not commit himself to a particular party, a particular program. But he must register what he sees; and what he sees is that the contemporary equivalent of *panem et circenses*—the movies and professional football—does not long content the American soul. The hucksters are poor successors to the founding fathers, who, if they looked after their own interests, were nevertheless men capable of great programs and immense vision. What the novelist must record is the failure of nerve and the absence of vision in politics and economic life. He notes, because he cannot help noting, the uncertainties about employment, family life, health, old age, religious faith, and war and peace, which haunt our social system.

What is true of fiction is equally true in the theater, where notable plays have been written out of a liberal philosophy of values.

We have had, of course, conservatives of the type of John Hay, John Jay Chapman, and Henry Adams, who have despaired of the republic or of labor or of education. But they at least came to grips with public questions, they were not guilty of the sin of indifferentism, of that fascination with one's private psyche which makes so much contemporary poetry merely solipsistic. The majority of American men of letters have not been of this persuasion. Most of them have contributed to the liberal faith by sympathetic observation and interpretation of American needs. It is not necessary to sit on committees or to speak from platforms (though some must do so) to be a good soldier in the war of liberation; and so long as writers both believe in the dignity of the individual and actively resent infringements upon that dignity, they will contribute imaginative power to the liberal cause.

CHAPTER XXX

Research Policies of the
Federal Government

by James R. Newman

In the United States today science is in a strange state of disequilibrium. On one hand, it is honored, lavishly supported, and seated in high councils. On the other, it is distorted in emphasis, beset by severe shortages of man-power, and gravely uncertain of its future. Science, like many another activity, is both the victim and beneficiary of our mercurial traits.

To understand the opportunities open to science and the difficulties besetting it, one must realize that the place science now occupies, the prestige it enjoys, were only recently won. Not more than 25 or 30 years have elapsed since industry began paying financial tribute to research; only in the last five years has the federal government begun its full-scale support of science, at least of those portions which are considered of military value. The bomb which fell on Hiroshima made science the cry of the public at large.

Place of Science in the Nineteenth Century   Throughout the nineteenth century and the first two decades of the twentieth, even as the United States grew rich and industrially pre-eminent, science was a conspicuous victim of indifference and neglect. Particularly was this true of basic research wherein our dependence on the contributions of the laboratories of Europe was complete—and almost fatal. In a nation worshipping at the shrine of James's bitch goddess, it is not

355

surprising that "pure science" found little support. It is not a pursuit that brings profits, and it has not the appeal, to patrons and philanthropists, of music, art, or literature, though it is as rich an expression of the human spirit as any of these. Successful inventors might become national heroes but men who did research as a full-time profession and, after a decent interval, had no engine or compound to show for their efforts were, if not cranks, certainly no better than philosophers. Science, wrote Oliver Wendell Holmes, is a "first rate piece of furniture for a man's upper chamber, if he has common sense on the ground floor." Condescending, perhaps, but considerably more enlightened than the prevailing view.

Place of Science Today   Fashions have changed, however. Our reverence for science now extends beyond the successful inventor. To be sure, the mere mention of Edison's name still throws the average listener, as Percy Bridgman once remarked, into a "coma of veneration"; but the mention of Einstein's name achieves almost the same result and everyone is eager to assert that science is the thing. What thing?—well, no matter. It is sufficient to know that America is a leader in science and few would grudge the expenditure needed to keep her so. Even the academic scientist is today an estimable man; if it is even vaguely suspected that he knows a secret or two he is as well guarded as Fort Knox.

The war is the main reason for the transformation. Other factors contributed to the tremendous expansion in research spending; but in enhancing the prestige of science and in making its achievements known, the war outstripped all other factors combined. It gave wider currency to a truth long known to philosophers, that knowledge is power and that science and scientific method are indispensable for gaining knowledge. It afforded public enlightenment on the relationship (uniquely appreciated by scientists) which obtains between basic and applied research: the development of science is organic; like a tree, it grows upward and outward only as its roots go deeper; only as they provide nourishment will the fruit of the tree appear. It demonstrated that science requires steady financial support, careful planning, and a wide ambit of freedom within the general framework of co-ordination. Above all, the experience of the war made it clear that science could be made to furnish weapons in the fight against poverty and disease as brilliantly effective as those which assured our soldiers supremacy in combat.

It would be an exaggeration to say that the lessons of the war even in the narrow sense of according research its rightful place have been fully learned. Yet it is undeniable that the need for federal leadership and support in the field of research now compels the attention of many once wholly ignorant of the meaning and value of science, and a growing number of those who direct the affairs of government, who make and lead opinion, who determine policies in education and elsewhere, are today persuaded that the welfare of the United States depends in large measure on a sound national policy for scientific research and development.

National Expenditures for Science To what extent science has become the mode may be seen in the record of national expenditures. The figures deserve scrutiny because they reveal not only the extent of participation of the federal government in current programs, but also the shift which has taken place in the proportional distribution of research expenditures as between government, industry, and university.

TABLE 4

COMPARISON OF NATIONAL RESEARCH AND DEVELOPMENT EXPENDITURES, 1930-45

(Excluding Atomic Energy)

	Millions of Dollars Expended				Percentage of Total Expenditures			
Year	Total	Fed. Gov.	Indus-try	Uni-ver-sities	Other*	Fed. Gov.	Indus-try	Uni-ver-sities	Other*
1930	166	23	116	20	7	14	70	12	4
1932	191	39	120	25	7	20	63	13	4
1934	172	21	124	19	8	12	73	11	4
1936	218	33	152	25	8	15	70	11	4
1938	264	48	177	28	11	18	67	11	4
1940	345	67	234	31	13	19	68	9	4
1941–45 average	600	500	80	10	10	83	13	2	2

* State governments, private foundations and research institutes, including non-profit industrial institutes.

Source: *Report of the President's Scientific Research Board*, Vol. I, Table I.

TABLE 5

THE NATIONAL RESEARCH AND DEVELOPMENT BUDGET, 1947
(Excluding Atomic Energy)

*Expenditures in 1947
(in Millions)*

Agency	Total	Basic Research	Applied Research and Development
Total	$1,160	$110	$1,050
Federal Government	625	55	570
War and Navy Departments	500	35	465
Other Departments	125	20	105
Industry	450	10	440
University	45	35	10
Other	40	10	30

Distribution of Federal Funds

	Total	War and Navy	Other
Total	$625	$500	$125
Government Laboratories	200	100	100
Industrial and University Laboratories on Contracts	425	400	25

Source: *Report of the President's Scientific Research Board*, Vol. I, Table II.

In 1938 the country spent 264 million dollars on research, industry's share being 177 million, that of the federal government 48 million, that of the universities 28 million. In 1940 the amount increased to 345 million dollars, of which 234 million was spent by industry, 67 million by the government, and 31 million by universities. With the war came further expansion, and a radical change in the spending pattern. The total jumped suddenly to 600 million dollars, the government furnishing 500 million, industry 80 million and universities 10 million.

In the second year of the Cold War (1947), we spent 1,160 million dollars on research (a large sum, but considerably less than the annual expenditure on, say, tobacco), of which industry accounted for 450 million (two and a half times the prewar total), universities 45 million (less than twice the prewar amount) and the federal government 625 million (almost 13 times its prewar total). Note carefully that of the federal science budget, just about 75 per cent was allocated to the military establishment for weapon research and that the figures quoted exclude immense amounts for research, again mostly military, in atomic energy.

Shortage of Scientists   Despite its good fortune in having found so generous a patron in the federal government, contemporary science faces problems and dangers which jeopardize not merely the leadership in research that America has so recently won, but the maintenance of even that minimum level of scientific competence without which no modern nation can hope to survive.

Among the more serious problems resulting directly from the great expansion of research is a desperate shortage of scientific man-power. This is the inevitable consequence of our wartime man-power policies, especially as carried out by Selective Service in cutting a reckless swath through the nation's campuses without taking thought to the future needs of the nation. Existing shortages are further aggravated by the incessant levies of the military departments on the fresh crop of research workers and technicians, who are either recruited for federal employ or pre-empted for federally financed projects.[1]

According to the Report of the Presidential Research Board: [2] "Between 1940 and 1947 the national research and development budget increased 335% while the supply of trained manpower was expanding only 35%." The result, so far as universities are concerned, is that, today, at least 15,000 university instructors are needed merely to restore the prewar student-teacher ratio—a ratio even then regarded as wholly unsatisfactory. Industry and the government departments themselves, other than the military, are almost as badly off.

Inadequate Support to Basic Research   The point was made earlier that the U. S. has in the past lagged seriously in its contributions to fundamental scientific discoveries. Yet the proportion of our large science budget allotted to basic

[1] The newly enacted Selective Service Act threatens further to aggravate the existing critical manpower shortage in all areas of scientific endeavor.

[2] Established in October of 1946 to study federal and non-federal scientific research and development activities and to prepare recommendations based on such studies. See *Report of the President's Scientific Research Board*. 5 volumes (Washington, D. C., 1947).

research, compared with the amount devoted to applied research and development, remains shockingly small. The report of the President's Scientific Research Board throws a clear light on the lack of balance in the nation's research program. In 1947 less than 10 per cent of the total of national research expenditures went to basic research. The federal government itself devoted little more than 5 per cent of its huge outlay for science to fundamental investigations.

"The drying up of European scientific sources, the disruption of normal international exchange of scientific knowledge, and the virtual exhaustion of our stockpile of basic knowledge in important areas alter every premise upon which our thinking about scientific research and development has been based." This warning by the Presidential Board underlies its recommendation that federal spending for basic research be tripled, at least, by 1957.

The neglect of basic research is concomitant, of course, with the heavy emphasis on developmental work and the overwhelming priority extended to weapon research. Whatever the reasonable requirements for military research, we are faced with this dilemma: high policy has decided on the present military program and the likelihood is that the effort devoted to it will be increased rather than diminished while the tense international situation continues. On the other hand, even in the field of military development further advances in a number of crucial sectors, notably military aviation, wait upon the extension of fundamental knowledge. Thus the support of basic research is just as essential to the common defense as the procurement of weapons, the training of manpower, and the stockpiling of strategic materials. The need for basic research to assure the advance of science in non-military activities on which the common welfare depends augments the force of this conclusion.

Lack of Co-ordination and Planning The rapid expansion of federal research activities has been attended by an inevitable but serious failure in co-ordination and planning. During the war the existence of the Office of Scientific Research and Development assured a measure of central direction to all military research projects. The OSRD has now ceased to function and nothing has taken its place. This is the more unfortunate since the peacetime research program is not only larger but more varied and complex than the single-purpose program of the nation at war. Federal research activities besides the vast weapon program of the national military establishment include functions of the Department of Commerce (Bureau of Standards, Civil Aeronautics Administration, Weather Bureau), Department of Agriculture, Department of Interior (Land Reclamation, Geological Survey, Bureau of Mines), TVA, Atomic Energy Commission, Federal Communications Commission, Federal Power Commission, National Advisory Committee on Aeronautics, U. S. Maritime Commission, Federal Security Agency (U. S. Public Health Service, National Institute of Health, National Cancer Institute, Office of Surgeon General, Bureaus of Medical and State Services, Food and Drug Administration, Children's Bureau).

Within the military establishment itself research is poorly integrated; there is waste, overlapping, interdepartmental jealousy, and a tendency to believe that if only enough money is wangled out of Congress and promptly spent, science will steadily get bigger and better. On balance it is fair to say that military research is in a state comparable to that of war production in the first years of the war, when the procurement program, despite immense but not unlimited resources, approached a state of collapse because of the failure to plan and co-ordinate; a stubborn indifference to civilian needs; and a firm conviction among military procurement officials that the way to get supplies in overwhelming quantities was to place overwhelming orders. The establishment of a Research and Development Board in the military establishment promises to improve matters, but this can be little more than a beginning. The newly acquired love of the military for science is no doubt commendable; it is also for the moment so ardent that science is in some danger of being overwhelmed by it. The research programs of other governmental agencies are less extravagant and the lack of co-ordination among them therefore less striking. But here too the lack of a federal plan and of central direction reduces the effectiveness of the total effort and creates difficulties.

The need for co-ordination of federal research programs raises problems other than those of administration. For to speak of "planning" and "co-ordination" by government, especially where the exercise of such functions may touch upon private activities is, in our time, to court charges of endorsing political philosophies held to be altogether repugnant to American concepts of democracy and freedom. I have discussed these matters at length elsewhere and I cannot pause over them now.[3] But it is well to remind ourselves that complete freedom in any activity deemed essential to the welfare and safety of the state is an illusion. There are some, of course, who profit politically by pretending that any form of federal support, other than an untrammeled donation of funds, will enslave science. We need not concern ourselves with such nonsense. Properly understood, freedom of science is not a slogan but a practical necessity. There is no science unless science is free, just as there can be no literature, no social expression or political life unless speech and thought are free. Freedom of science can be destroyed if the military monopolizes science; freedom of science wholly vanishes in a military state. But if our social and political democracy is preserved, state support for science no more endangers its freedom than state support of agriculture, let us say, menaces the freedom of the farmer. Unsupported, science is a weak thing dependent upon favors and sporadic benefactions. Unorganized and unplanned, science is incapable of mustering more than a small part of its strength in the service of man.

Proposals for Federal Action   Let me conclude with a syllabus for federal action in science, one I regard as compatible with the principles of a democratic America.

(1) We depend increasingly upon science for our safety and welfare. Realization of this truth demands that science be assured of adequate, uninterrupted financial support, the major portion of which must be supplied by the federal gov-

[3] *The Control of Atomic Energy* (New York, 1948). See especially the chapter on Research.

ernment in the form of grants to federal agencies, universities, and industry.

(2) The present pattern of expenditures for scientific research and development is dangerously distorted. It is perhaps inevitable that some parts of science have donned a uniform; this merely re-emphasizes the need for restoring balance. Since scientific applications in every field, military and non-military, rest upon foundations of fundamental knowledge, these must be broadened and strengthened systematically and unceasingly. Basic research is best performed in universities and for such programs they must be assured of adequate federal support.

(3) The principal limitation on the expansion of scientific programs is the shortage of man-power. The federal government through direct subventions to educational institutions, creation of new facilities and equipment, establishment of training and aid programs for graduate and undergraduate students, enlightened Selective Service policies, extension of veterans' programs, and similar help must overcome this deficiency.

(4) In medical research the national effort, federal and non-federal, is grossly inadequate. Judging by expenditures, the physical well-being of Americans is of less concern to their government than guided missiles, atomic bombs, or submarines. The total expended by the OSRD on medical research during the war (25 million dollars) was less than 10 per cent of the amount expended on war activities in a single day during 1945. A heavy increase in national expenditures on medical research (at least a three-fold increase, from 100 to 300 million dollars, is the recommendation of the Presidential Research Board) is imperative to preserve the nation's health.

(5) Unorganized science is disorganized science. Planning and co-ordination of research are indispensable to scientific advance. Neither of these is incompatible with scientific freedom. An integral part of the co-ordinating function is the frequent examination and evaluation of all federal research and development programs, military and non-military. The assessment cannot be left to any single agency or any

limited interdepartmental board. Final decisions of policy must be made by the president himself based upon the recommendations of competent, objective observers.

(6)   The legislature must establish a federal agency for the support of basic research. Two successive Congresses have considered bills for setting up a National Science Foundation. The measure finally adopted by the last Congress was an administrative monstrosity and was therefore properly vetoed by the President. The criteria for an effective agency are these: the foundation should be directed by full-time government officials; it should support basic research in universities, give scholarships, grants in aid and otherwise promote programs for enlarging our resources of scientific manpower; and it should be empowered to co-ordinate the patent policies of the federal government in line with the recommendations of the Attorney General.[4]

(7)   No science program which omits the social sciences can even remotely fulfill its responsibilities. The distortion of emphasis in federal science activities is nowhere more evident than in the neglect of those disciplines which attempt to describe and explain the mysterious and fateful working of the human mind, of social, political, and economic forces, of society as a whole. To say that the social sciences lag behind the physical sciences is a commonplace, usually uttered with a portentous air as if to say: "This is the nature of things and nothing can be done about it." We cannot, of course, lastingly tolerate this disingenuous counsel of despair. To say that the social sciences are far more difficult (and clearly more important) than mathematical physics or astronomy is merely to say that they merit extraordinary effort. In the program of a National Science Foundation, the social sciences must be on an equal footing with the other sciences. This is the first step towards the solution of a series of problems of utmost urgency.

I may end with the reminder that in a world "forever on the brink of war," it is idle to believe that science can flourish. Science is not a thing set apart; it shares the climate and vicis-

---

[4] *Investigation of Government Patent Practices and Policies. Report and Recommendations of the Attorney General to the President* (Washington, D. C., 1947).

situdes of the time. The clamp of secrecy imposed on science in the name of security already has diminished the flow of ideas essential to scientific life. The President's Committee on Civil Rights has warned us that the United States is not so strong that it can ignore the opinion of the world. We are not so strong in science that we can live alone. We cannot prepare endlessly for war and expect peace.

PART NINE

Conclusion

CHAPTER XXXI

A Liberal Economic Program

by Seymour E. Harris

1. No contributor to this volume is disposed to dispense with a system of free private enterprise. They want a system, however, which operates efficiently and without periodic collapse or long-run stagnation. They are aware that the system which prevailed before 1929 will not do, and they are hopeful that a modified capitalism, with limited responsibilities for government, will produce an economic machine operating steadily on all cylinders. They are prepared to accept the modern liberal creed which not only requires government to intervene against monopolistic and restrictive policies, but also encourages it to intervene with positive programs on behalf of the majority of people—thus assuring the fullest development of all individuals, and not merely a minority. Under this type of hybrid system, the essentials of capitalism—consumer's sovereignty of choice, freedom to invest, and liberty to choose occupations—can be preserved.

2. Our economy is no longer predominantly one of millions of workers, farmers, and small enterprises operating in a competitive manner; rather, each monopolistic group is organized in large agglomerations, struggling for the maximum share of the national output. Each monopolistic group has tremendous political as well as economic power, and is in a position to paralyze our economy. Although still disposed to restrain monopolies, the government's practical policy, in the light of present institutional arrangements, has to be to recognize their existence and make the strongest efforts to get them

to achieve fair and workable arrangements in their wage, price, and output policies. These arrangements should assure above all the maximum output and a distribution of purchasing power consistent with the sale of this output at reasonable prices. The more nearly the groups work out their own salvation, the less dependent they will be upon government intervention.

3. It is not clear to most of us that we can count on these arrangements always being made in the public interest. Even when they are, the government's responsibility will be important; at the very least, it will have to apply the Keynesian medicine. Americans who are determined to preserve capitalism should welcome this way out because it does not interfere with the individual's choice of goods, his freedom to invest as and when he pleases, and his prerogative to choose his occupation; it merely proposes to keep the economy at a high and stable level by appropriate monetary and fiscal policy. The less satisfactory from the national viewpoint the achievements of labor, capital, and agriculture on their own, the larger the part that will have to be played by monetary and fiscal policy. Increased loan expenditures and reduced taxes in periods of depression, and curtailed monetary supplies and public expenditures with increased taxes in periods of buoyancy— these are the appropriate policies.

Use of the monetary and fiscal policies in the New Deal period was sporadic and inadequate; but a good beginning was made. Their effective application in the future requires improved timing and forecasting, and especially a willingness by Congress to delegate authority to the executive to adjust spending and tax rates to the changing prospects of business. Above all, the policy is not one of incessantly rising debt and taxes: the Keynesian policy calls for adding to purchasing power in periods of depression and reducing it, in part through debt reduction, in periods of exuberance.

4. In so far as government has to spend, expenditures should be productive; and for this purpose, plans should be made far ahead. In the thirties, when government was caught unprepared by the greatest depression in modern history, it had to improvise. Despite the failure of Congress in recent

years to stimulate planning for anti-depression measures, the country is now in a much better position than it was in the thirties to spend wisely. Improved housing, urban redevelopment, river and regional development, education, health—all of these offer outlets for government funds which are not a threat to private enterprise, and which in part offer the promise not only of keeping demand at a sufficiently high level, but of contributing to a more productive economy. Not only will the nation's income rise with these expenditures—adapted as far as possible to lace with private spending—but they should raise income sufficiently to make the investments profitable from a narrow Treasury viewpoint. Most of us would not, however, go so far as to limit public expenditures to those which show a profit in this narrow sense.

5. Mature policies by private groups working together, courageous and judicious monetary, fiscal, and (related) resource policies by the government should make the continuance of our present system of enterprise possible. Under special conditions, it may be necessary to implement these policies by the use of controls. For example, in the economy of 1947–48, the inflationary threat has been serious indeed. Had farmers, labor, and capital been more restrained in their price, wage, and profit policies, respectively, the danger of inflation would have been considerably less. Had the government not reduced taxes, and had it restrained credit much more effectively, the rise of prices would have been less serious. But even the most effective use of monetary and fiscal policies and the pursuit of moderate wage and price policies probably would not have sufficed to contain the inflationary pressures adequately. With serious shortages following an all-out war, with Europe in dire need, with a vast accumulation of purchasing power, and large back-logs of demand, it would have been sound policy to rely also on controls—allocations to ease demand on insufficiently provisioned markets, export control to assure the best use of the limited supplies available for export; and limited price control and rationing in areas where demand was intense and shortages were likely to persist for a considerable time.

6. Acceptance of the policies suggested up to this point

would probably solve most of our economic problems; but more could be done. We need a wage policy which will assure workers wages that correspond to the rise of productivity and that assure the sale of goods currently produced. From 1944 to the first half of 1947, for example, employees' compensation rose by but 3 per cent, although the cost of living rose by 24 per cent, corporate profits after taxes by 96 per cent, and property and rental income by 36 per cent. This maldistribution promises an ultimate excess of supply over demand in a peaceful world. Again, an adequate social-security program is a means not only of relieving distress but also of putting a floor under spending. What we seek is maximum output: prosperity depends on both supply and demand. Featherbedding, restriction of output by business, and despoiling or failing to make effective use of resources all prevent the attainment of this objective. Positively, we need more spending for research, both pure and applied, and even better management; and we want an incentive system which will assure the maximum output and the correction of structural maladjustments. Such an incentive system does not, however, exclude measures for improved distribution.

7. This, then, is the liberal economic creed for the years to come. The world does not stand still. There are many conservatives in Congress and business who, believing the interests of business enterprise to be identical with those of society, would try to bring back the days of an alliance between government and business, restricting government to a do-nothing policy for the vast majority of our citizens. Surely no more certain way of destroying the capitalist system is to be found than the obtuse policy of relying *exclusively* on business enterprise for the fullest development of our resources, for the provision of adequate demand, for decisions concerning the distribution of the national output, and for the allocation of economic resources.

8. The contributors to this volume have as their goal courageous and adequate use of our resources, better and more housing, adequate social security, and an improved time distribution of taxes and public expenditures. This is a program which we believe will be as germane in 1960 as in 1950, though

we hope that by 1960 our goals can be raised even higher. Ours is not a static world.

We are all aware that there is need for integration of the numerous planks of our platform for economic and political liberals; and that the growing importance of foreign aid and rearmament may make it necessary to adapt our proposals to changing conditions. We are, however, restrained in our proposals. We do not ask for the impossible—for example, 25 million houses in 10 years and a guarantee of $3000 for each farm family—as did one political party in 1948; for we realize that in the milieu of the late forties, all proposals to spend may deserve the charge of "inflationary." Our program can, however, be fashioned to the times. We may, for instance, now have to be satisfied with a million houses a year should the military threat continue to prevail. Yet we are convinced that if the government and the people yield on some of their lesser liberties—to accept the limited controls required to assure sound distribution of scarce resources—our people can obtain a large measure of benefits as suggested in this volume, and retain their larger liberties. For example, extravagances in transportation and expenditures for luxury housing and commercial building should yield to the demands of ERP, low cost housing, slum clearance, resource development, conservation, and education.

Index

i

A Note on the Type

The text of this book has been set on the Monotype in a type-face called "Baskerville." The face is a facsimile reproduction of types cast from molds made for John Baskerville (1706–75) from his designs. The original face was the forerunner of the "modern" group of type faces.

John Baskerville, of Birmingham, England, a writing-master, with a special renown for cutting inscriptions in stone, began experimenting about 1750 with punch-cutting and making typographical material. It was not until 1757 that he published his first work, a Virgil in royal quarto, with great-primer letters. This was followed by his famous editions of Milton, the Bible, the Book of Common Prayer, and several Latin classic authors. His types, at first criticized as unnecessarily slender, delicate, and feminine, in time were recognized as both distinct and elegant, and his types as well as his printing were greatly admired.

COMPOSED, PRINTED, AND BOUND BY
KINGSPORT PRESS, INC., KINGSPORT, TENN.